SAXON

Algebra 1, Geometry, Algebra 2

Prerequisite Skills Intervention

SAXON™

An Imprint of HMH
Supplemental Publishers

www.SaxonPublishers.com
1-800-531-5015

ISBN 13: 978-1-6027-7507-7

ISBN 10:   1-6027-7507-9

Printed in the United States of America

1 2 3 4 5 6 7 8   170 15 14 13 12 11 10 09 08

Contents

Saxon Algebra 1

Contents continued

 Saxon Algebra 1

Teaching Skill 1

Objective Write the multiples of a number.

Direct students to read the definition at the top of the page and to read the example. Ask: **What number is missing from the list of numbers?** (0) Explain that zero should not be used when finding multiples of numbers.

Ask: **What do the three dots at the end of the list of numbers mean?** (The list goes on to include all numbers from 1 to infinity.)

Ask: **If you multiply a number times 1000, will you get a multiple of the number?** (Yes)

Ask: **For what number is the example finding multiples?** (6)

PRACTICE ON YOUR OWN

Review the example.

In exercises 1–5, students find the first five multiples of numbers using a multiplication table as a guide.

In exercises 6–13, students apply what they have learned to find the next three multiples of the numbers given without a multiplication table.

CHECK

Determine that students know how to find multiples of numbers.

Students who successfully complete the **Practice on Your Own** and **Check** are ready to move on to the next skill.

COMMON ERRORS

Students may list incorrect multiples due to lack of proficiency of multiplication facts.

Students who made more than 3 errors in the **Practice on Your Own**, or who were not successful in the **Check** section, may benefit from the **Alternative Teaching Strategy**.

Alternative Teaching Strategy

Objective Write the multiples of a number.

Some students remember "counting by numbers" better than remembering multiplication facts.

Ask students to count by 2s beginning with 2. Direct them to write the numbers down as they count.

Point out that the numbers the students wrote down are multiples of 2.

Ask: **How do you get from one number to the next?** (You add 2 each time.)

Have students count by 10s beginning with 10 and write down the numbers as they count.

Ask: **The numbers you just wrote down are multiples of what number?** (10)

Write: 10, 20, 30, 40, 50, 60, …

Guide students in understanding that each term in the sequence they wrote down, is the product of 10 and another whole number.

Ask: **Ten times what number is 10?** (1)

Ask: **Ten times what number is 20?** (2)

Ask: **Ten times what number is 30?** (3)

Point out that "counting by numbers" results in the same multiples as multiplying 10 by the numbers 1, 2, 3, … .

Remind students that just like they can count forever, they can also multiply forever. That means there are an infinite number of multiples for every number.

Have students count by 3s, then by 4s, then by 5s, and write the numbers as they count. Remind them that they are writing some of the multiples of those numbers.

When students show an understanding of finding multiples by counting, have them find the first five multiples of several numbers using multiplication only.

Saxon Algebra 1

Name _____ Date _____ Class _____

Prerequisite Skills Intervention

Multiples

The multiple of a number is the product of the number and a whole number.

Example:
$6 \times 1 = 6$
$6 \times 2 = 12$
$6 \times 3 = 18$ ⟶ The multiples of 6 are {6, 12, 18, 24, 30, ...}.
$6 \times 4 = 24$
$6 \times 5 = 30$

Practice on Your Own
List the first five multiples of the numbers.

1. $3 \cdot 1 =$ _____ 2. $7 \cdot 1 =$ _____ 3. $12 \cdot 1 =$ _____ 4. $16 \cdot 1 =$ _____ 5. $25 \cdot 1 =$ _____

$3 \cdot 2 =$ _____ $7 \cdot 2 =$ _____ $12 \cdot 2 =$ _____ $16 \cdot 2 =$ _____ $25 \cdot 2 =$ _____

$3 \cdot 3 =$ _____ $7 \cdot 3 =$ _____ $12 \cdot 3 =$ _____ $16 \cdot 3 =$ _____ $25 \cdot 3 =$ _____

$3 \cdot 4 =$ _____ $7 \cdot 4 =$ _____ $12 \cdot 4 =$ _____ $16 \cdot 4 =$ _____ $25 \cdot 4 =$ _____

$3 \cdot 5 =$ _____ $7 \cdot 5 =$ _____ $12 \cdot 5 =$ _____ $16 \cdot 5 =$ _____ $25 \cdot 5 =$ _____

List the next three multiples of the number.

6. 5, 10, 15, ____, ____, ____   7. 6, 12, 18, ____, ____, ____   8. 1, 2, 3, ____, ____, ____

9. 11, 22, 33, ____, ____, ____   10. 8, 16, 24, ____, ____, ____   11. 2, 4, 6, ____, ____, ____

12. 100, 200, 300, _____, _____, _____   13. 500, 1000, 1500, _____, _____, _____

Check
List the next four multiples of the number.

14. 4, 8, 12, ____, ____, ____, ____   15. 9, 18, 27, ____, ____, ____, ____

16. 10, 20, 30, ____, ____, ____, ____   17. 15, 30, 45, ____, ____, ____, ____

18. 45, 90, 135, ____, ____, ____, ____   19. 250, 500, 750, ____, ____, ____, ____

20. 2000, 4000, 6000, _____, _____, _____, _____

Saxon Algebra 1

Teaching Skill 2

Objective Find the least common multiple.

Direct students to read the definition at the top of the page. Ask: **Can two numbers have more than one multiple in common?** (Yes)

Direct students' attention to the example. Ask: **According to the lists, what two multiples do 6 and 8 have in common?** (24 and 48) Ask: **Which of these is the smallest?** (24)

Have students read the definition of least common multiple. Ask: **What is the least common multiple of 6 and 8?** (24)

Point out that since every number has an infinite number of multiples, every pair of numbers has an infinite number of common multiples. Ask: **Will there always be a least common multiple?** (Yes) Ask: **Is there ever a greatest common multiple?** (No)

PRACTICE ON YOUR OWN

Review the example at the top of the page.

In exercises 1–12, students find the least common multiples for each pair of numbers.

CHECK

Determine that students know how to find the least common multiple of two numbers.

Students who successfully complete the **Practice on Your Own** and **Check** are ready to move on to the next skill.

COMMON ERRORS

Students may choose a common multiple that is not the smallest number, particularly when the LCM is one of the numbers.

Students who made more than 3 errors in the **Practice on Your Own**, or who were not successful in the **Check** section, may benefit from the **Alternative Teaching Strategy**.

Alternative Teaching Strategy

Objective Find the least common multiple using number lines.

Provide students with number lines 0 to 40, drawn in pairs. The lines in each pair should be lined up directly beneath each other. Refer to the sample below, but lines should be numbered 0 to 40.

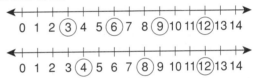

On the first pair of number lines, have students circle the multiples of 3 on the top number line and multiples of 4 on the bottom number line.

Ask: **Which numbers are circled on both number lines?** (12, 24, and 36 on students' number lines) Explain that these numbers are the common multiples of 3 and 4.

Ask: **Which of the common multiples is the smallest?** (12) Explain that 12 is called the least common multiple, or LCM, of 3 and 4.

Repeat the activity for multiples of 6 and 8. Students should arrive at an LCM of 24.

Repeat the activity for multiples of 4 and 12. Students should arrive at an LCM of 12. Draw attention to the fact that sometimes the LCM of two numbers is one of the numbers.

Ask: **When is the LCM one of the two numbers for which you are finding the multiples?** (If the larger number is a multiple of the smaller number, then the LCM of the two numbers is the larger number.)

Continue using number lines until you feel comfortable that students understand the concept of how to identify a least common multiple. Then have them find LCMs using lists of multiples instead of number lines.

Saxon Algebra 1

Prerequisite Skills Intervention

Least Common Multiples

Multiples that are common to two or more numbers are called common multiples of those numbers.

Example:

Multiples of 6	**Multiples of 8**
$6 \times 1 = 6$	$8 \times 1 = 8$
$6 \times 2 = 12$	$8 \times 2 = 16$
$6 \times 3 = 18$	$8 \times 3 = \mathbf{24}$
$6 \times 4 = \mathbf{24}$	$8 \times 4 = 32$
$6 \times 5 = 30$	$8 \times 5 = 40$
$6 \times 6 = 36$	$8 \times 6 = \mathbf{48}$
$6 \times 7 = 42$	$8 \times 7 = 56$
$6 \times 8 = \mathbf{48}$	$8 \times 8 = 64$

The common multiples of 6 and 8 are 24, 48, ...

The least common multiple, or LCM, of two or more numbers is the smallest multiple the numbers have in common.

→ The LCM of 6 and 8 is 24.

Practice on Your Own

Find the least common multiple, or LCM, for each pair of numbers.

1. 8, 12

2. 20, 8

3. 20, 5

4. 5, 12

5. 7, 15

6. 16, 96

7. 4, 15

8. 30, 18

9. 16, 48

10. 40, 15

11. 16, 6

12. 10, 36

Check

Find the least common multiple, or LCM, for the pair of numbers.

13. 9, 6

14. 5, 6

15. 18, 10

16. 15, 50

17. 7, 12

18. 9, 12

19. 24, 64

20. 28, 42

Saxon Algebra 1

Teaching Skill 3
Objective Write the factors of a number.

Direct students to read the definition of factors at the top of the page and to review the example.

Ask: **How many factors does a number have?** (The number of factors depends on how many different ways whole numbers can be multiplied together to arrive at the number.)

Direct students to Step 1: Ask: **What is the least number of factors a number has?** (2; 1 and the number itself)

For Step 2: **How do you know if 2 is one of the factors?** (All even numbers have a factor of 2.)

For Step 4, instructs students to write each factor only once (i.e. do not repeat factors).

PRACTICE ON YOUR OWN
In exercises 1–4, students determine whether the second number is a factor of the first.

In exercises 5–12, students list all the factors of the numbers.

CHECK
Determine that students know how to find factors of numbers.

Students who successfully complete the **Practice on Your Own** and **Check** are ready to move on to the next skill.

COMMON ERRORS
Students may leave out factors when writing the list of factors.

Students may list multiples instead of factors.

Students who made more than 3 errors in the **Practice on Your Own**, or who were not successful in the **Check** section, may benefit from the **Alternative Teaching Strategy**.

Alternative Teaching Strategy
Objective Find the factors of a number by dividing.

Provide students with a different definition of a factor: a factor is a whole number that divides without a remainder into a larger whole number.

For example, since $20 \div 2 = 10$, 2 is a factor of 20. Remind students that 1 and the number itself are both factors of the number since they divide without a remainder into the number.

Have students set up a table to find the other factors of 20.

Number to Test	Division	Quotient
2	$20 \div 2$	10
3	$20 \div 3$	6 r 2
4	$20 \div 4$	5
5	$20 \div 5$	4

Instruct students to stop testing factors when they begin to repeat. In this example, 4×5 and 5×4 are the same factors repeated.

Point out that the quotients (where there are no remainders) are also factors of the number.

Instruct students to circle those numbers in the table for which there is no remainder when divided into 20. Also circle the quotient.

Ask: **Based on the definition of a factor, which of the numbers tested are factors of 20?** (2, 4, 5, and 10)

Ask: **What other two numbers are also factors of 20?** (1 and 20) Stress that students should be careful to always include 1 and the number itself when listing factors.

Ask: **Why isn't 3 a factor of 20?** (There is a remainder of 2 when 3 is divided into 20.)

Continue with other examples, using numbers less than 30. When you feel comfortable that students understand how to find factors, have them list factors without using a table.

***Saxon** Algebra 1*

Name _____ Date _____ Class _____

Prerequisite Skills Intervention
Factors

Factors are whole numbers that are multiplied together to obtain another whole number.

Example: Since $2 \times 7 = 14$, both 2 and 7 are factors of 14.

To find all the factors of a number:

- Step 1: Begin with 1 and the number itself. These will be the smallest and the largest factors of the number.

  Example: List the factors of 36.
  $1 \times 36 = 36$

- Step 2: Test other factor pairs.

  $2 \times 18 = 36, 3 \times 12 = 36, 4 \times 9 = 36$
  $6 \times 6 = 36$

- Step 3: Continue until factors repeat.

  $9 \times 4 = 36$

- Step 4: List all the factors.

  {1, 2, 3, 4, 6, 9, 12, 18, 36}

Practice on Your Own
Determine whether the second number is a factor of the first.

1. 20, 6   **2.** 8, 2   **3.** 35, 35   **4.** 48, 12

_____   _____   _____   _____

List all the factors of the numbers.

5. 24 _____

6. 56 _____

7. 23 _____

8. 120 _____

9. 19 _____

10. 20 _____

11. 35 _____

12. 100 _____

Check
Determine whether the second number is a factor of the first.

13. 32, 7   **14.** 60, 15   **15.** 144, 24   **16.** 40, 6

_____   _____   _____   _____

List all the factors of the numbers.

17. 17

_____

18. 45

_____

19. 160

_____

20. 28

_____

Saxon Algebra 1

Teaching Skill 4

Objective Find the greatest common factor of two expressions.

Explain to students that the greatest common factor, or GCF, of two expressions is the largest of the common factors that the expressions share.

Direct students to Steps 1–3.

Ask: **What are variables?** (Variables are the letters in an expression.)

Ask: **What is a coefficient?** (A coefficient is the number that precedes one or more variables in an expression.)

Direct students to the example. Ask: **What are the coefficients of the two expressions?** (18 and 30)

Ask: **What is the smallest exponent of the variable x in the two expressions?** (1) **What is the smallest exponent of the variable y in the two expressions?** (2)

PRACTICE ON YOUR OWN

Review each step in the example.

In exercises 1–9, students find the greatest common factor for each pair of numbers or expressions.

CHECK

Determine that students know how to find the greatest common factor for a pair of expressions.

Students who successfully complete the **Practice on Your Own** and **Check** are ready to move on to the next skill.

COMMON ERRORS

When the expressions include variables, students choose the largest exponent of the variable, rather than the smallest exponent.

Students who made more than 2 errors in the **Practice on Your Own**, or who were not successful in the **Check** section, may benefit from the **Alternative Teaching Strategy**.

Alternative Teaching Strategy

Objective Find the greatest common factor using prime factorization.

Explain to students that monomial expressions include a coefficient (number), one or more variables (letters), or both.

Provide the following examples of monomial expressions: $24x^3y$ and $80x^2y^2$.

Ask: **What are the coefficients of these two expressions?** (24 and 80) Ask: **What are the variables in the expressions?** (x and y)

Remind students that they can use prime factorization to find the greatest common factor, or GCF, of the coefficients. Work through the process using 24 and 80.

$$
\begin{array}{ll}
2\,|\,24 & 2\,|\,80 \\
\ \ \ 2\,|\,12 & \ \ \ 2\,|\,40 \\
\ \ \ \ \ \ 2\,|\,6 & \ \ \ \ \ \ 2\,|\,20 \\
\ \ \ \ \ \ \ \ \ 3 & \ \ \ \ \ \ \ \ \ 2\,|\,10 \\
& \ \ \ \ \ \ \ \ \ \ \ \ 5
\end{array}
$$

Have students write the prime factorization of the two numbers.

$24 = 2 \times 2 \times 2 \times 3$
$80 = 2 \times 2 \times 2 \times 2 \times 5$

Next have students line up matching factors according to occurrence and circle complete pairs.

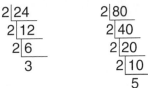

$24 = \circled{2} \times \circled{2} \times \circled{2} \times \quad 3$
$80 = \circled{2} \times \circled{2} \times \circled{2} \times 2 \times \quad 5$

Explain that the GCF of the two numbers is the product of the matched pairs only.

Ask: **What is the GCF of 24 and 80?** ($2 \times 2 \times 2 = 8$)

Explain that finding the GCF of the variables is much easier–simply choose the smallest power of each variable.

Ask: **What is the GCF of the variables in the two expressions and why?** (x^2y since 2 is the smallest exponent of x and 1 is the smallest exponent of y)

The GCF of $24x^3y$ and $80x^2y^2$ is $8x^2y$.

Saxon Algebra 1

Name _____ Date _____ Class _____

Prerequisite Skills Intervention

Greatest Common Factors

To find the greatest common factor, or GCF, in algebraic expressions:

- Step 1: Find the GCF of the coefficients of the expressions.
- Step 2: Find the GCF of each variable by choosing the one with the smallest exponent.
- Step 3: Write the GCF of the two expressions as a product of the GCFs found in Steps 1 and 2.

Example: Find the GCF of $18xy^4$ and $30x^2y^2$.

Step 1	Step 2	Step 3
coefficients: 18 and 30	variables: xy^4 and x^2y^2	GCF of coefficients: 6
factors of 18: {1, 2, 3, **6**, 9, 18}	smallest exponent of x: x	GCF of variables: xy^2
factors of 30: {1, 2, 3, 5, **6**, 10, 15, 30}	smallest exponent of y: y^2	product: 6 times xy^2
GCF = 6	GCF = xy^2	GCF = $6xy^2$

Practice on Your Own

Find the greatest common factor of each pair of numbers or expressions.

1. 8 and 20

2. 14 and 28

3. $32a$ and $60a^3$

4. x^3y and x^2y^4

5. $18a^2$ and $42a^5$

6. $4x^2y$ and $6x^2y^3$

7. $16e^2f$ and $64ef^3$

8. $28r^2st$ and $70rs^3$

9. $10xyz$ and $5x^3z$

Check

Find the greatest common factor of each pair of expressions.

10. 24 and 60

11. $60e^4f$ and $24e^2f$

12. $12a^5$ and $28a^3$

13. $15gh$ and $8g^2h$

14. $12a^3b^2$ and $30a^3d$

15. $50x^5$ and $40x^3$

Saxon Algebra 1

Teaching Skill 5

Objective Determine whether a number is a prime or composite number.

Review the definition and the example of a prime number. Ask: **What is the smallest prime number?** (2)

Explain that the number 1 is neither prime nor composite because it has exactly one factor, itself.

Ask: **What is the next smallest prime number?** (3)

Next, review the definition and the example of a composite number. Ask: **What is the smallest composite number?** (4)

Review the steps for determining whether a number is prime or composite. Ask: **What kinds of numbers are always composite?** (even numbers and multiples of numbers)

PRACTICE ON YOUR OWN

In exercises 1–4, students practice listing factors of numbers.

In exercises 5–12, students determine whether a number is prime or composite, and write composite numbers as products.

CHECK

Determine that students know how to determine whether a number is prime or composite.

Students who successfully complete the **Practice on Your Own** and **Check** are ready to move on to the next skill.

COMMON ERRORS

Students may miss factors of numbers and incorrectly identify the number as being prime.

Students who made more than 3 errors in the **Practice on Your Own**, or who were not successful in the **Check** section, may benefit from the **Alternative Teaching Strategy**.

Alternative Teaching Strategy

Objective Determine whether a number is a prime or composite number.

Materials needed: graph paper

Tell students that they can use graph paper to help them determine whether a number is prime or composite.

Instruct students to shade three unit squares on the graph paper in the shape of a rectangle. Have them arrange the shading in different ways if possible.

Discuss with students how the shading is arranged. Point out that in order to arrange three squares in the shape of a rectangle, you must either use 1 column by 3 rows or 3 rows by 1 column. Equate this to factors of 1×3 or 3×1, which are the same factors.

Tell students that a prime number, such as 3, can only be arranged as one set of factors.

Next, have students shade 6 unit squares, in as many ways as possible, keeping them in the shape of a rectangle.

Ask: **What arrangements were you able to make with six squares?** (1×6, 6×1, 2×3, and 3×2). Tell students that a composite number, such as 6, can be arranged in multiple ways.

Have students shade unit squares representing the numbers 2, 4, 5, 7, 8, and 9. Ask: **Which of the numbers are prime?** (2, 5, and 7) **Which of the numbers are composite?** (4, 8, and 9)

Saxon Algebra 1

Prerequisite Skills Intervention

Prime and Composite Numbers

Prime Numbers	Composite Numbers
A prime number is a whole number, greater than 1, that has exactly two factors, 1 and the number itself.	A composite number is a whole number, greater than 1, that has more than two factors.
Example 1: Prime Number	**Example 2: Composite Number**
Factors of 17: {1, 17} ⟶ 17 is a prime number.	Factors of 18: {1, 2, 3, 6, 9, 18} ⟶ 18 is a composite number.

To determine whether a number is prime or composite:

• Step 1: List all the factors of the number.

• Step 2: If there are exactly two factors, then the number is prime; if there are more than two factors, the number is composite.

Practice on Your Own
List all the factors of the numbers.

1. 33

2. 23

3. 90

4. 20

Tell whether each number is prime or composite. If the number is composite, write it as the product of two numbers.

5. 25

6. 46

7. 7

8. 12

9. 137

10. 43

11. 121

12. 19

Check
Tell whether each number is prime or composite. If the number is composite, write it as the product of two numbers.

13. 27

14. 13

15. 81

16. 28

17. 31

18. 18

19. 21

20. 83

Saxon Algebra 1

Teaching Skill 6

Objective Find the square or square root of a number.

Review the definition and the example of square of numbers. Stress that squaring a number is NOT the same as doubling a number. Ask: **What is the square of 3?** (9)

Review the definition and the example of perfect squares. Ask: **What are the first three perfect square numbers?** (1, 4, 9)

Review the definition and the example of square roots. Ask: **What is the square root of 9?** (3)

Point out that squaring a number and taking the square root of a number "undo" each other: $3^2 = 9$, $\sqrt{9} = 3$

PRACTICE ON YOUR OWN

In exercises 1–4, students find the squares of numbers.

In exercises 5–8, students find the square roots of numbers.

In exercises 9–16, students determine if a number is a perfect square, and if so, find its positive square root.

CHECK

Determine that students know how to identify perfect square numbers and how to take square roots.

Students who successfully complete the **Practice on Your Own** and **Check** are ready to move on to the next skill.

COMMON ERRORS

Students may double a number instead of squaring it when raising the number to the second power.

Students who made more than 3 errors in the **Practice on Your Own**, or who were not successful in the Check section, may benefit from the **Alternative Teaching Strategy**.

Alternative Teaching Strategy

Objective Find the square of a number.

Materials needed: graph paper

Tell students they can use graph paper to help determine what the square of a number is and whether a number is a perfect square.

Instruct students to form a larger shaded square by shading 3 rows and 3 columns on the graph paper.

Point out that this is the geometric representation of "3 squared" because it forms a square of length 3 and width 3.

Have students count the number of small squares inside the larger square. There are a total of 9. Ask: **Aside from counting, how would you find the area of the larger square?** (Multiply the length times the width, 3 · 3.) Equate this to the fact that 3 squared, or 3^2, is equal to 3 · 3 or 9.

Have students repeat this exercise with the numbers 5 and 6. Ask: **What is 5^2?** (25) **What is 6^2?** (36)

Remind students that "squared" is the same thing as raised to the second power.

Next, have students try to shade 12 small squares in the shape of a larger square. Ask? **Is it possible to form a large square using 12 small squares?** (No)

Tell students that a number is not a perfect square if they are not able to form a large square.

Have students try to form a large square with the numbers 4, 8, 9, and 10. Ask: **Which of the numbers are perfect squares?** (4 and 9)

Saxon Algebra 1

Prerequisite Skills Intervention

Squares and Square Roots

SKILL
6

Square of Numbers	Perfect Squares	Square Roots
The square of a number is the product of the number and itself.	A number is a perfect square if it is of the form n^2, where n is any whole number.	If a number is a perfect square, with two identical factors, then either factor is the square root of the number.
Example 1	**Example 2**	**Example 3**
The square of 5, or 5^2, is $5 \cdot 5 = 25$.	The number 49 is a perfect square because it can be written as $7 \cdot 7$ or 7^2.	The square root of 100, or $\sqrt{100}$, is 10 since $10 \cdot 10 = 100$.

Practice on Your Own

Find the square of each number.

1. 3^2 _____ 2. 8^2 _____ 3. 16^2 _____ 4. 25^2 _____

Find each square root.

5. $\sqrt{16}$ _____ 6. $\sqrt{144}$ _____ 7. $\sqrt{400}$ _____ 8. $\sqrt{81}$ _____

Tell whether each number is a perfect square. If so, identify its positive square root.

9. 24   10. 1   11. 225   12. 48

_____   _____   _____   _____

13. 169   14. 196   15. 50   16. 1000

_____   _____   _____   _____

Check

Find the square or square root of each number.

17. 7^2 18. $\sqrt{25}$ 19. 12^2 20. $\sqrt{100}$

_____   _____   _____   _____

Tell whether each number is a perfect square. If so, identify its positive square root.

21. 36   22. 75   23. 121   24. 65

_____   _____   _____   _____

Saxon Algebra 1

Teaching Skill 7
Objective Read, write, and understand exponents.

Explain to students that using exponents is nothing more than writing multiplication in a form of shorthand.

Write on the board: 4^3. Identify the 4 as the base of the expression and the 3 as the exponent. Write: 6^3 and ask: **Which number is the base?** (6) **Which number is the exponent?** (3)

Point out that the base is a regular sized number and the exponent is a superscript (a small raised number).

Return to the expression 4^3. Explain that 4 is to be multiplied times itself three times. Write: $4 \cdot 4 \cdot 4$

Review the examples of Writing Exponents. Ask: **How many times would you multiply a number that is raised to the tenth power?** (10)

PRACTICE ON YOUR OWN
In exercises 1–6, students write expressions as a multiplication of factors.

In exercises 7–12, students write expressions using a base and an exponent.

CHECK
Determine that students understand how to read and write exponents.

Students who successfully complete the **Practice on Your Own** and **Check** are ready to move on to the next skill.

COMMON ERRORS
Students may confuse the base and the exponent.

Students who made more than 3 errors in the **Practice on Your Own**, or who were not successful in the **Check** section, may benefit from the **Alternative Teaching Strategy**.

Alternative Teaching Strategy
Objective Write a number using exponents.

Materials needed: number cards shown below. Index cards work nicely.

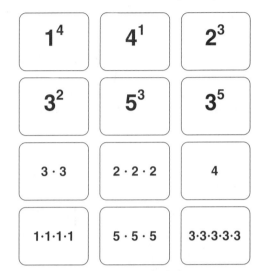

Tell students that they are going to play a memory game.

Before the game begins, remind students that an exponent tells how many times a base number is used as a factor.

Provide them with the following examples:

$6^2 = 6 \cdot 6$

$4^5 = 4 \cdot 4 \cdot 4 \cdot 4 \cdot 4$

Mix the cards up and place them in rows, face down. Each student will flip over two cards. If the values of the expressions on the two cards are the same, the student keeps the cards. If the values are different, the student flips the cards back over and another student takes a turn. The winner is the student who has the most cards at the end of the game.

As an extension of this exercise, have the students make their own number cards and play again. Instruct them to create 12 new cards. The cards should be created in pairs – one with an expression that contains an exponent and one that uses only multiplication.

Saxon Algebra 1

Name _____ Date _____ Class _____

Prerequisite Skills Intervention

Exponents

Using an exponent is a shorthand way of writing out the multiplication of the same number one or more times.

Understanding Exponents	Writing Exponents	Reading Exponents
An exponent tells how many times a base number (or variable) is used as a factor.	The base is written as a standard number (or variable). The exponent is written as a superscript.	The product of repeated factors is called a power. Read 6^5 as "6 raised to the fifth power" or the "fifth power of 6."
Example: In the expression 4^3, the base, 4, is a factor 3 times or $4 \cdot 4 \cdot 4$.	Examples: $6 \cdot 6 \cdot 6 \cdot 6 \cdot 6 = 6^5$ $g \cdot g \cdot g \cdot g = g^4$ $(-5) \cdot (-5) \cdot (-5) = (-5)^3$	Special cases: The second and third powers of numbers have special names: 7^2 can be read as "7 squared" and 9^3 can be read as "9 cubed."

Practice on Your Own

Write each expression as a multiplication of factors.

1. 9^4 _____

2. 1^5 _____

3. x^3 _____

4. 8^2 _____

5. $(-2)^3$ _____

6. p^6 _____

Write each expression using a base and an exponent.

7. $10 \cdot 10 \cdot 10 \cdot 10 \cdot 10 \cdot 10$ _____

8. $12 \cdot 12 \cdot 12 \cdot 12$ _____

9. $m \cdot m \cdot m \cdot m \cdot m$ _____

10. five raised to the sixth power _____

11. nine squared _____

12. p cubed _____

Check

Write each expression as a multiplication of factors.

13. 2^4 _____

14. $(-4)^2$ _____

15. h^5 _____

Write each expression using a base and an exponent.

16. $25 \cdot 25 \cdot 25$ _____

17. $s \cdot s \cdot s \cdot s$ _____

18. eight cubed _____

19. four raised to the first power _____

Teaching Skill 8

Objective Evaluate powers of a number.

Review the definition of a power. Ask: **What does 3 raised to the fourth power mean?** ($3 \cdot 3 \cdot 3 \cdot 3$) Stress to students that raising a number to a power is NOT the same as multiplying the number by that power.

Review the example. Emphasize that it is a good idea to multiply the expression out one product at a time, rather than trying to calculate the entire product mentally.

Explain how to evaluate a number raised to the first power, and to the zero power.

Ask: **When you are evaluating powers of negative numbers, when will the result be negative and when will it be positive?** (The result will be negative when the exponent is an odd number and it will be positive when the exponent is an even number.) Give a few examples to demonstrate why this is true.

Review the example explaining how to add expressions that contain powers.

PRACTICE ON YOUR OWN

In exercises 1–9, students evaluate powers of numbers and perform operations that include powers of numbers.

CHECK

Determine that students know how to evaluate powers of numbers.

Students who successfully complete the **Practice on Your Own** and **Check** are ready to move on to the next skill.

COMMON ERRORS

Students may multiply the base by the exponent instead of raising it to a power.

Students who made more than 2 errors in the **Practice on Your Own**, or who were not successful in the **Check** section, may benefit from the **Alternative Teaching Strategy**.

Alternative Teaching Strategy

Objective Evaluate powers of a number.

Materials needed: number cards shown below. Index cards work nicely.

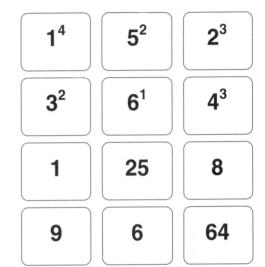

Tell students that they are going to play a memory game.

Before the game begins, remind students that an exponent tells how many times a base number is used as a factor. To evaluate an expression that contains an exponent, multiply the factors out to arrive at the product. For example,

$5^3 = 5 \cdot 5 \cdot 5 = 125$

Shuffle the cards and place them in rows, face down. Each student will flip over two cards. If the values of the expressions on the two cards are the same, the student keeps the cards. If the values are different, the student flips the cards back over and another student takes a turn. The winner is the student who has the most cards at the end of the game.

As an extension of this exercise, have the students make their own number cards and play again. Instruct them to create 12 new cards. The cards should be created in pairs – one with an expression that contains an exponent and one that has an equivalent number value.

Saxon Algebra 1

Name _____ Date _____ Class _____

Prerequisite Skills Intervention

Evaluate Powers

The product of a repeated factor is called a power. To evaluate the power of a number, multiply the factor the correct number of times to arrive at the product.

Example: the 4th power of 3, or 3^4:

$3 \cdot 3 \cdot 3 \cdot 3 =$

$9 \cdot 3 \cdot 3 =$

$27 \cdot 3 = 81$

Special powers:

• Any nonzero number raised to a power of one is the number itself: $5^1 = 5$.

• Any nonzero number raised to a power of zero is 1: $13^0 = 1$.

To add, subtract, multiply, or divide powers of numbers, evaluate each expression and then perform the indicated operation:

$(-4)^3 + 6^2 = (-4 \cdot -4 \cdot -4) + (6 \cdot 6) = -64 + 36 = -28$

Practice on Your Own
Find the value of each expression.

1. 2^5

2. 4^2

3. 113^0

4. 15 raised to the second power

5. −10 cubed

6. $5^0 + 8^0$

7. $(-2)^4 + 3^2$

8. $6^2 \cdot 2^2$

9. $8^2 \div 2^4$

Check
Find the value of each expression.

10. 4^3

11. $(-1)^8$

12. 9 squared

13. $10^2 - 20^0$

14. $(-2)^3 + 3^3$

15. $(-1)^3 \cdot 2^5$

16. $5^2 \cdot 10$

17. $10^3 \div 5^3$

18. $\dfrac{3^4}{6^0}$

Saxon Algebra 1

Teaching Skill 9

Objective Round or estimate a number.

Point out to students that rounding is a way of approximating a number. Ask: **Do real life situations always require exact numbers?** (No) Discuss some examples where you would not need exact measurements, numbers, etc.

Work through the example to demonstrate how to round a decimal number, following the steps provided.

Explain that estimating is a way of using rounded numbers to simplify calculations and arrive at an approximate answer.

Ask: **If a problem involved adding 297 and 412, how would you round each number to make the calculations simpler?** (Round 297 to 300 and 412 to 400.) **Why?** (It is easier to work with numbers that only have one nonzero digit.)

Work a similar example with multiplication.

PRACTICE ON YOUR OWN

In exercises 1–6, students round numbers to the indicated place values.

In exercises 7–12, students estimate sums and products using rounding techniques.

CHECK

Determine that students know how to round numbers and estimate quantities.

Students who successfully complete the Practice on Your Own and Check are ready to move on to the next skill.

COMMON ERRORS

Students may look at the last digit in a number to decide whether to round up or down, rather than looking at the digit to the immediate right of the rounding place.

Students who made more than 3 errors in the **Practice on Your Own,** or who were not successful in the **Check** section, may benefit from the **Alternative Teaching Strategy.**

Alternative Teaching Strategy

Objective Round a number using a number line.

It may benefit some students to see a visual representation of how to round. Provide students with copies of the number lines shown below.

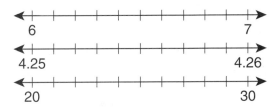

Tell students they are going to use the first number line to round the number 6.7 to the nearest whole number. Ask: **What do the tick marks between the numbers 6 and 7 represent?** (Since there are 10 parts, they represent 10ths.)

Have students label 6.5 on the number line. Next, have students place a dot on the number line where 6.7 would be.

Ask: **Is 6.7 closer to 6 or to 7?** (7) **What is 6.7 rounded to the nearest whole number?** (7)

Tell students they are going to use the second number line to round the number 4.254 to the nearest hundredth. Repeat the process above—identify what the tick marks represent; label 4.255; place a dot on 4.254; and use the information to round 4.254 to 4.25.

Repeat the process using the third number line to round the number 25 to the nearest tens place. (30)

Practice this method with students until you feel that they have mastered the technique of rounding numbers using a number line. Choose numbers for them to round and have them create their own number lines.

When you feel comfortable that students understand how to round using a visual representation, have them round numbers without using the number lines.

Saxon Algebra 1

Prerequisite Skills Intervention
Rounding and Estimation

Rounding a number provides an approximate value of the number. Estimation is often used when the final result does not need to be an exact number.

To round a number:

Step 1: Find the place to which you are rounding.

Step 2: Look at the digit immediately to the right of that place.

Step 3: If this digit is greater than or equal to 5, round the digit in the rounding place up 1. If the digit is less than 5, the digit in the rounding place is unchanged.

Step 4: If you are rounding to a decimal place or to the nearest whole number, drop the digits to the right of the rounding place. If you are rounding to tens, hundreds, or any larger place value, fill in zeros as needed.

Example: Round 14.638 to the nearest tenth.

Step 1: The digit to be rounded is 6.
Step 2: 3 is to the right of 6.
Step 3: $3 < 5$, so 6 is unchanged.
Step 4: Drop the digits 3 and 8.
Answer: 14.6

Practice on Your Own
Round each number to the indicated place value.

1. 146.3892; hundredth

2. 235.7; whole number

3. 47; tens

4. 15.275; tenth

5. 0.0048; thousandth

6. 3.99; tenth

Estimate the sum or product by rounding each number to the indicated place value.

7. $76 + 148$; tens

8. 9.46×18; tens

9. $10.2 \div 1.975$; ones

10. $412 + 709 + 99$; hundreds

11. 6.62×1.89; tens

12. $780.5 \div 7.88$; tens

Check
Estimate each number by rounding it to the indicated place value.

13. 0.0748; hundredth

14. 1324.8; whole number

15. 18.996; tenth

Estimate the sum or product by rounding each number to the indicated place value.

16. 11.8×47; tens

17. $862 + 59.4$; hundreds

18. $9.2 \div 2.866$; ones

Saxon Algebra 1

Teaching Skill 10

Objective Write a fraction in simplest form.

Review the definition of simplest form with students.

Ask: **Is $\frac{3}{7}$ written in simplest form? Why or why not?** (Yes, because 3 and 7 do not share any factors other than 1.)

Is $\frac{6}{8}$ written in simplest form? Why or why not? (No, because 6 and 8 share a factor of 2.)

Point out that finding the GCF of two numbers is the same thing as asking "what is the biggest number that will divide without a remainder into the numerator and the denominator." If students choose a common factor that is not the GCF, they may have to simplify the fraction again to find the simplest form.

Review the example.

PRACTICE ON YOUR OWN

In exercises 1 and 2, students practice finding the GCF of two numbers.

In exercises 3–8, students apply what they have learned to simplify fractions.

CHECK

Determine that students know how to write a fraction in simplest form.

Students who successfully complete the **Practice on Your Own** and **Check** are ready to move on to the next skill.

COMMON ERRORS

Students may choose a common factor that is not the greatest common factor. Their answer will be a simplified fraction, but not the simplest form of the fraction.

Students who made more than 2 errors in the **Practice on Your Own,** or who were not successful in the **Check** section, may benefit from the **Alternative Teaching Strategy.**

Alternative Teaching Strategy

Objective Write a fraction in simplest form.

Some students may benefit from a visual method for identifying a GCF. Provide students with a 10 by 10 multiplication table as shown below (no shading included).

	1	2	3	4	5	6	7	8	9	10
1	1	2	3	4	5	6	7	8	9	10
2	2	4	6	8	10	12	14	16	18	20
3	3	6	9	12	15	18	21	24	27	30
4	4	8	12	16	20	24	28	32	36	40
5	5	10	15	20	25	30	35	40	45	50
6	6	12	18	24	30	36	42	48	54	60
7	7	14	21	27	35	42	49	56	63	70
8	8	16	24	32	40	48	56	64	72	80
9	9	18	27	36	45	54	63	72	81	90
10	10	20	30	40	50	60	70	80	90	100

Tell students they are going to use the table to help them simplify $\frac{35}{63}$.

Instruct students to search for the horizontal row in which they see both the numerator and the denominator of the fraction. Start at the bottom of the table to begin the search. (Row 7)

Explain that since this is a multiplication table, all the numbers in that row are divisible by 7. Instruct students to divide the numerator and the denominator of the fraction by 7: $\frac{35 \div 7}{63 \div 7} = \frac{5}{9}$.

Point out that the only row that contains both 5 and 9 is row 1, which means 5 and 9 do not have any factors in common except 1. Ask:

What is $\frac{35}{63}$ written in simplest form? $\left(\frac{5}{9}\right)$

Repeat the exercise to simplify $\frac{28}{48}$. $\left(\frac{7}{12}\right)$

Point out that sometimes multiple simplifications may be needed. Work through the process to simplify $\frac{54}{81}$. $\left(\frac{6}{9} \text{ then } \frac{2}{3}\right)$

Saxon Algebra 1

Name ______________________ Date __________ Class __________

Prerequisite Skills Intervention

Simplify Fractions

LESSON 10

Definition: a fraction is in simplest form when the numerator and the denominator do not share any common factors, other than the factor of 1. An improper fraction should be written as a mixed number.

> To write a fraction in simplest form:
>
> **Step 1:** List all the factors of the numerator and the denominator.
>
> **Step 2:** Identify the greatest common factor (GCF).
>
> **Step 3:** Divide both the numerator and the denominator by the GCF.

Example: Write $\frac{18}{45}$ in simplest form.

Factors of 18: {1, 2, 3, 6, 9, 18}

Factors of 45: {1, 3, 5, 9, 15, 45}

GCF: 9

$\frac{18 \div 9}{45 \div 9} = \frac{2}{5}$ $\quad \frac{18}{45}$ written in simplest form is $\frac{2}{5}$.

Practice on Your Own

Identify the greatest common factor of the numerator and denominator of the fractions given.

1. $\frac{16}{24}$ Factors of 16: ______________

   Factors of 24: ______________

   GCF: ________

2. $\frac{36}{63}$ Factors of 36: ______________

   Factors of 63: ______________

   GCF: ________

Write each fraction in simplest form.

3. $\frac{6 \div \square}{20 \div \square} = \frac{\square}{\square}$

4. $\frac{60 \div \square}{72 \div \square} = \frac{\square}{\square}$

5. $\frac{45 \div \square}{54 \div \square} = \frac{\square}{\square}$

6. $\frac{121}{66}$ ________

7. $\frac{49}{56}$ ________

8. $\frac{24}{26}$ ________

Check

Identify the greatest common factor of the numerator and denominator of the fractions given.

9. $\frac{4}{12}$ GCF = ____

10. $\frac{4}{9}$ GCF = ____

11. $\frac{15}{35}$ GCF = ____

12. $\frac{24}{180}$ GCF = ____

Write each fraction in simplest form.

13. $\frac{15 \div \square}{21 \div \square} = \frac{\square}{\square}$

14. $\frac{5 \div \square}{18 \div \square} = \frac{\square}{\square}$

15. $\frac{14 \div \square}{49 \div \square} = \frac{\square}{\square}$

16. $\frac{32}{40}$ ________

17. $\frac{20}{16}$ ________

18. $\frac{72}{81}$ ________

© Saxon. All rights reserved.

Teaching Skill 11

Objective Write a fraction as a decimal.

Review with students the different ways to indicate division. Ask: **How would you read $\frac{6}{8}$ as a division problem?** (6 divided by 8)

Review the names of terms in a division problem. Stress that the numerator is <u>always</u> the dividend, regardless of whether it is smaller or greater than the denominator.

Review the example. Point out that only one zero was needed in the dividend in this example to complete the division, but more than one may be required for other fractions.

Ask: **What happens if the numerator is greater than the denominator?** (The first digit of the quotient will not be 0.)

Ask: **What do you do with the whole number in a mixed number?** (Ignore it, divide out the fraction part of the number, and attach the whole back to the final answer.)

PRACTICE ON YOUR OWN

In exercises 1–8, students write fractions as decimals using division.

CHECK

Determine that students know how to write a fraction as a decimal.

Students who successfully complete the **Practice on Your Own** and **Check** are ready to move on to the next skill.

COMMON ERRORS

Students may use the denominator as the dividend, rather than the numerator, particularly if the denominator is the greater number.

Students who made more than 2 errors in the **Practice on Your Own,** or who were not successful in the **Check section,** may benefit from the **Alternative Teaching Strategy.**

Alternative Teaching Strategy

Objective Use equivalent fractions to write fractions as decimals.

Point out to students that fractions with certain denominators can be easily written as decimals.

Review the following equivalencies:

$\frac{1}{10} = 0.1; \frac{6}{10} = 0.6; \frac{1}{100} = 0.01; \frac{15}{100} = 0.15$

Ask: **Will it make it easier to write a fraction as a decimal if you can find an equivalent fraction with a denominator of 10, 100, etc.?** (Yes)

Review with students how to find an equivalent fraction. Begin with $\frac{3}{5}$. Ask: **If you want to change fifths to tenths, what do you need to multiply by?** (2) **What do you multiply by 2?** (You must multiply both the numerator and the denominator by 2.)

$\frac{3 \times 2}{5 \times 2} = \frac{6}{10}$. Ask: **What is the decimal form of $\frac{6}{10}$?** (0.6)

Repeat the exercise with the fraction $\frac{9}{25}$. Ask: **Can this fraction be written as tenths?** (No) **What will the new denominator be instead?** (100)

Work through the problem using the same questioning as before: $\frac{9 \times 4}{25 \times 4} = \frac{36}{100} = 0.36$.

Point out that this technique only works for fractions that have denominators which are factors of 10, 100, 1000, etc.

Repeat the activity using the fractions $\frac{11}{20} \left(\frac{55}{100} = 0.5 \right) 5$, $\frac{3}{4} \left(\frac{75}{100} = 0.7 \right) 5$ and $\frac{5}{8} \left(\frac{625}{1000} = 0.62 \right) 5$.

Saxon Algebra 1

Name _____ Date _____ Class _____

Prerequisite Skills Intervention

Fractions and Decimals

Division Notation: $2 \div 3$ $3\overline{)2}$ $\dfrac{2}{3}$

Vocabulary: $\dfrac{2}{3}$ $\longrightarrow$ Numerator $\dfrac{\text{Quotient}}{\text{Divisor}\overline{)\text{Dividend}}}$
$\phantom{\dfrac{2}{3}}$ $\longrightarrow$ Denominator

Example: Write $\dfrac{4}{5}$ as a decimal.

Step 1: Write the fraction as a division problem. The numerator $\longrightarrow$ is the dividend and the denominator is the divisor.	$5\overline{)4}$
Step 2: Add a decimal point followed by a 0 in the dividend $\longrightarrow$ and another decimal point in the quotient.	$5\overline{)4.0}$
Step 3: Follow whole number division rules until you have a $\longrightarrow$ remainder of 0 or until you have the number of decimal places you need. Adding additional zeros may be necessary.	$\begin{array}{r} 0.8 \\ 5\overline{)4.0} \\ \underline{4\,0} \\ 0 \end{array}$ So, $\dfrac{4}{5} = 0.8$

Note: If the number is a mixed number, ignore the whole number portion until you are ready to write your answer.

$$3\tfrac{4}{5} = 3.8$$

Practice on Your Own
Write each fraction or mixed number as a decimal.

1. $\dfrac{3}{5}$ 2. $\dfrac{5}{8}$ 3. $2\tfrac{1}{4}$ 4. $\dfrac{12}{15}$

_____   _____   _____   _____

5. $-\dfrac{9}{10}$ 6. $\dfrac{12}{8}$ 7. $\dfrac{23}{10}$ 8. $-3\tfrac{1}{5}$

_____   _____   _____   _____

Check
Write each fraction or mixed number as a decimal.

9. $\dfrac{7}{10}$ 10. $-\dfrac{11}{8}$ 11. $6\tfrac{3}{20}$ 12. $\dfrac{2}{25}$

_____   _____   _____   _____

13. $\dfrac{7}{8}$ 14. $\dfrac{11}{2}$ 15. $-\dfrac{4}{5}$ 16. $\dfrac{24}{100}$

_____   _____   _____   _____

22   **Saxon** Algebra 1

Teaching Skill 12
Objective Write ratios.

Review with students the definition of a ratio. Explain that a ratio can be used to compare anything that can be assigned a number value.

Provide the following examples: number of boys in the class to number of girls; number of students taking Algebra 2 to number of students taking Geometry; and height of one particular student to that of another.

Ask each student to describe one ratio that they can think of to write.

Review each of the different ways in which a ratio may be written: word form, ratio form, and fraction form.

Ask: **Is it possible to simplify a ratio and if so, when?** (Yes, if the terms of the ratio share any factors other than 1, then the ratio can be simplified, just like simplifying a fraction.)

Review the example. Point out that units are not included in a ratio.

PRACTICE ON YOUR OWN
In exercises 1–8, students use a triangle and a table to write a variety of ratios.

CHECK
Determine that students know how to write ratios.

Students who successfully complete the **Practice on Your Own** and **Check** are ready to move on to the next skill.

COMMON ERRORS
Students write the terms of the ratio in the wrong order. To avoid this, encourage students to write the words first, then the numbers.

Students who made more than 2 errors in the **Practice on Your Own,** or who were not successful in the **Check** section, may benefit from the **Alternative Teaching Strategy.**

Alternative Teaching Strategy
Objective Write ratios using a deck of cards.

Have students work in pairs. Give each pair of students a standard deck of cards.

Have each pair of students do the following:

- Mix the decks of cards.

- Cut the deck so that each student has roughly half the deck. The deck does not need to be divided exactly in half.

- Have each student create the following table on a piece of paper.

Distribution of Cards	
Hearts	
Diamonds	
Spades	
Clubs	
Total	

- Have students count the number of cards they have for each suit and record the results in the table.

Review each of the different ways in which a ratio may be written: word form, ratio form, and fraction form.

Have each student use the information they recorded in the table to write the following ratios in three different ways:

1. Number of hearts to diamonds

2. Number of spades to clubs

3. Number of red cards to black cards

4. Number of hearts to total number of cards

(Students' answers will vary depending on the cards that are in their half of the deck.)

When all the students have written their ratios, instruct them to exchange their half of the deck with their partner. Partners should check each other's answers by counting their cards and writing the correct ratios.

Saxon Algebra 1

Name _____ Date _____ Class _____

Prerequisite Skills Intervention

Ratios

Definition: A ratio is a comparison of two or more numbers, called the terms of the ratio.

Ways to Write Ratios		
Words	Ratio	Fraction
2 to 3	2:3	$\frac{2}{3}$

Example: Write the ratio of the measures of angle *A* to angle *B* in triangle *ABC* below.

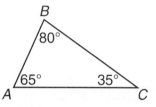

Step 1: What are the terms of the ratio? angle *A* and angle *B*
Step 2: What is the measure of angle *A*? 65°
What is the measure of angle *B*? 80°

Step 3: Write the ratio in the order requested: 65 to 80 or 65:80 or $\frac{65}{80}$

Step 4: Simplify if possible: 13 to 16 or 13:16 or $\frac{13}{60}$

Practice on Your Own

Use △*ABC* to write each ratio three different ways. Write your answers in simplest form.

1. *AB* to *AC* _____ _____ _____

2. *AC* to *AB* _____ _____ _____

3. length of shortest leg to hypotenuse _____ _____ _____

4. perimeter of △*ABC* to area _____ _____ _____

Use the table to write each ratio in simplest fraction form.

5. red cars to black cars _____

6. red cars to white cars _____

7. red cars to not red cars _____

8. red cars to total cars _____

Cars in the Parking Lot	
Red	20
Black	43
White	10

Check

Use △*DEF* to write each ratio three different ways. Write your answers in simplest form.

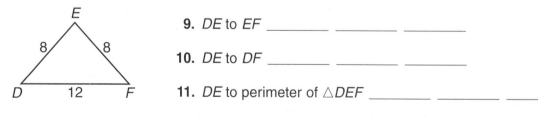

9. *DE* to *EF* _____ _____ _____

10. *DE* to *DF* _____ _____ _____

11. *DE* to perimeter of △*DEF* _____ _____ _____

Saxon Algebra 1

Prerequisite Skills Intervention

Teaching Skill 13
Objective Find a unit rate.

Review with students the definition of a rate and a unit rate.

Give the following common examples: miles per hour and miles per gallon. Ask students to come up with other common rates.

Ask: **It takes a typist 4 minutes to type 320 words. How would you write this as a rate?** (320 words in 4 minutes)

Review how to find a unit rate and the example.

Ask: **In the typing example presented earlier, what kind of unit rate would you write?** (words per minute) **What is the unit rate?** (80 words per minute)

Emphasize that it is not always the greatest number divided by the smallest number—it depends on the "per item" or "per unit of time" for which you are looking.

Ask: **If you can paint 2 fences in 8 hours, and you are trying to find the unit rate, what is the correct division?** (2 ÷ 8) **What is the unit rate?** (0.25 fences per hour)

PRACTICE ON YOUR OWN
In exercises 1–9, students find a variety of unit rates.

CHECK
Determine that students know how to find unit rates.

Students who successfully complete the **Practice on Your Own** and **Check** are ready to move on to the next skill.

COMMON ERRORS
Students divide incorrectly, or in the wrong order, and arrive at the wrong unit rate.

Students who made more than 2 errors in the **Practice on Your Own,** or who were not successful in the **Check** section, may benefit from the **Alternative Teaching Strategy.**

Alternative Teaching Strategy
Objective Find a unit rate.

Materials needed: a juice box, a bag of pretzels, and a bag of almonds

Give students a copy of the following:

Nutrition Facts
Serving Size 5 crackers (20 g)

Amount Per Serving

Calories	80
Total Fat	4.5 g
Sodium	150 mg
Carbohydrates	9 g
Protein	1 g

Explain that these are the primary nutrition facts provided on the back of a box of crackers.

Point out that all of the amounts are given per serving. Ask: **What other kinds of unit rates can you find using the information provided in the nutrition facts?** (per cracker and per gram)

Review how to find unit rates.

Ask: **To find per cracker unit rates, what will you divide by each time?** (5) **To find per gram unit rates, what will you divide by each time?** (20)

Instruct students to find each of the following unit rates: calories per cracker (16); calories per gram (4); total fat per cracker (0.9); total fat per gram (0.225); sodium per cracker (30); sodium per gram (7.5); carbohydrates per cracker (1.8); carbohydrates per gram (0.45); protein per cracker (0.20); and protein per gram (0.05).

Pass the juice box around and have students copy down the primary nutrition facts. (You don't have to use all of the facts if you don't wish to.) Repeat the exercise above finding similar unit rates. Then use the bag of pretzels and the bag of almonds in a similar fashion.

Name _____ Date _____ Class _____

Prerequisite Skills Intervention

Rates and Unit Rates

Rate	Unit Rate
Definition: A rate is a ratio that compares two quantities that have different units of measure.	Definition: A unit rate is a rate in which the second term is 1.
Example 1: $3.60 per dozen oranges Example 2: traveling 100 miles in 2 hours	Example 1: 30¢ per orange Example 2: traveling 50 miles per hour

How to write a rate as a unit rate:
Step 1: Divide the first term of the rate by the second term of the rate.
Step 2: Rewrite the rate as a quantity per unit of time or per item.

Example: Write "120 students for every 4 buses" as a unit rate.
Step 1: 120 ÷ 4 = 30
Step 2: Rewrite the rate as "30 students per bus" or 30 students/bus.

Note: When unit rates involve money, they are also referred to as unit prices.

Practice on Your Own
Find each unit rate.

1. 348 miles in 6 hours

2. 520 calories in 2 servings

3. $10 for 4 hours

4. 200 homes in 4 subdivisions

5. 80 miles for 8 gallons of gas

6. $3.75 for 5 pens

7. 18 grams of fat in 4 ounces

8. 150 francs in 25 dollars

9. $5.75 for 100 copies

Check
Find each unit rate.

10. 6000 trees in 20 acres

11. $180 for 4 credit hours

12. 5 km in 20 minutes

13. 960 miles in 12 hours

14. 96 books on 6 shelves

15. $4.00 for 5 rides

Teaching Skill 14

Objective Write equivalent fractions, decimals, and percents.

Explain to students that fractions, decimals, and percents are all different ways to write "parts" of numbers.

Ask: **If I eat half a pizza, what percent of the pizza did I eat?** (50%)

Review the steps for finding equivalent fractions, decimals, and percents. Go over each example.

Point out that "cent" means hundred. Discuss words like century, dollars and cents, etc. Ask: **What does percent mean?** (per hundred)

Explain to students that moving a decimal point 2 places is the same as writing per hundred since each decimal place represents a multiple of tenths.

Ask: **Which fractions are the easiest to write as decimals and percents?** (fractions with a denominator of 100)

PRACTICE ON YOUR OWN

In exercises 1–8, students write fractions and percents as decimals.

In exercises 9–16, students write fractions and decimals as percents.

CHECK

Determine that students know how to write equivalent fractions, decimals, and percents.

Students who successfully complete the **Practice on Your Own** and **Check** are ready to move on to the next skill.

COMMON ERRORS

Students may move the decimal point in the wrong direction when writing a decimal as a percent.

Students who made more than 4 errors in the **Practice on Your Own,** or who were not successful in the **Check** section, may benefit from the **Alternative Teaching Strategy.**

Alternative Teaching Strategy

Objective Write fractions as decimals using proportions.

Explain to students that percent means per hundred or a ratio of a number to 100.

Remind students that a proportion is a statement that two ratios are equal. Give the following example: $\frac{4}{5} = \frac{80}{100}$. Point out that $\frac{80}{100}$ can be read as "80 per 100" or in other words, 80 percent.

Ask: **What proportion would you set up to write $\frac{12}{25}$ as a percent?** $\left(\frac{12}{25} = \frac{?}{100}\right)$

To solve the proportion, set up the following statement: $\frac{12 \times \square}{25 \times \square} = \frac{\square}{100}$. Ask: **What do you need to multiply 25 by to get 100?** (4) **If you multiply the bottom of the fraction by 4, what must you multiply the top of the fraction by?** (4)

Since $12 \times 4 = 48$, the per hundred fraction is $\frac{48}{100}$. Remind students that another way to say per hundred is percent. Ask: **What is $\frac{12}{25}$ as a percent?** (48%)

Repeat this process using the following examples: $\frac{2}{5}, \frac{7}{10}, \frac{22}{50}$. (40%, 70%, 44%)

Students should set up a per hundred proportion for each example and solve using the process above.

When you feel comfortable that students can write fractions as percents using this process, practice writing the percent as a decimal by moving the decimal point two places to the left. Use the examples you have already worked.

(48% = 0.48; 40% = 0.40; 70% = 0.70; and 44% = 0.44)

Saxon Algebra 1

Prerequisite Skills Intervention

Fractions, Decimals, and Percents

SKILL
14

Writing Decimal Form		
From a fraction	Divide the numerator by the denominator.	Example: $\frac{1}{4} = 1 \div 4 = 0.25$
From a percent	Drop the % symbol and place a decimal after the last digit. Move the decimal 2 places to the left.	Example: $25\% = 25. = 0.25$

Writing Percent Form		
From a decimal	Move the decimal 2 places to the right and add the % symbol.	Example: $0.225 = 0.225 = 22.5\%$
From a fraction	First write as a decimal by dividing. Then move the decimal 2 places to the right and add the % symbol.	Example: $\frac{1}{5} = 1 \div 5 = 0.20 = 20\%$

Practice on Your Own
Write the equivalent decimal.

1. $\frac{1}{2}$ _____

2. 28% _____

3. $\frac{7}{10}$ _____

4. 84% _____

5. $\frac{17}{20}$ _____

6. 6% _____

7. $\frac{3}{8}$ _____

8. 150% _____

Write the equivalent percent.

9. $\frac{3}{4}$ _____

10. 0.6 _____

11. $\frac{3}{10}$ _____

12. 0.09 _____

13. $\frac{5}{8}$ _____

14. 0.45 _____

15. $\frac{6}{5}$ _____

16. 1.25 _____

Check
Write the equivalent decimal.

17. 97% _____

18. $\frac{4}{5}$ _____

19. 2.5% _____

20. $\frac{11}{100}$ _____

Write the equivalent percent.

21. 0.8 _____

22. $\frac{2}{5}$ _____

23. 0.055 _____

24. $\frac{31}{50}$ _____

Saxon Algebra 1

Teaching Skill 15

Objective Write numbers in scientific notation and in standard form.

Explain that scientific notation is a shorthand way to write very large and very small numbers.

Discuss with students the following examples: temperature at the sun's core (1,550,000 K); distance light travels in a year (5,880,000,000,000 miles); mass of an ant (0.000073 grams)

Point out that numbers with lots of zeros are sometimes difficult to work with, particularly when you are multiplying and dividing them.

Review the definition and the examples of scientific notation. Ask: **Is 42×10^3 written in scientific notation?** (No) **Why?** (42 is not a number between 1 and 10)

Walk through the steps for writing numbers. Review the example and then work through it in the reverse order to arrive back at the original standard form.

PRACTICE ON YOUR OWN

In exercises 1–6, students write numbers in scientific notation.

In exercises 7–12, students write numbers in standard form.

CHECK

Determine that students know how to write numbers in scientific notation and standard form.

Students who successfully complete the **Practice on Your Own** and **Check** are ready to move on to the next skill.

COMMON ERRORS

Students may move the decimal in the wrong direction and may confuse whether the exponent of 10 should be positive or negative.

Students who made more than 3 errors in the **Practice on Your Own,** or who were not successful in the **Check** section, may benefit from the **Alternative Teaching Strategy.**

Alternative Teaching Strategy

Objective Write numbers in scientific notation.

Materials needed: multiple copies of game card and pennies

Tell students they are going to play Tic-Tac-Toe using scientific notation.

Give students a copy of the following game card and nine pennies.

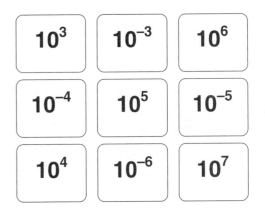

Review with students how to write a number in scientific notation.

Ask: **The 10 will have what kind of exponent if the original number is very small?** (negative) **The 10 will have what kind of exponent if the original number is very large?** (positive)

Write the numbers below on the board, one at a time. Instruct students to place a penny on the correct power of ten if the number is written in scientific notation. The student who calls out "Tic-Tac-Toe" first and correctly has three pennies in row (up, down, or diagonally) wins.

Game numbers: 4600 (10^3)
92,500,000 (10^7)
0.00049 (10^{-4})
0.0000055 (10^{-6})
824,000 (10^5)

Repeat the exercise using different numbers that you create to match the game board powers of 10.

Saxon Algebra 1

Name _____ Date _____ Class _____

Prerequisite Skills Intervention
Scientific Notation

Definition: A number is in scientific notation if it is written as the product of a number between 1 and 10 and a power of 10 ($a \times 10^n$).
Examples: 6×10^7 and 4.99×10^{-15}

To write from standard form to scientific notation
Step 1: Make sure the number has a decimal point. If it doesn't, place a decimal after the last digit in the number: $47,000,000 = 47,000,000.$
Step 2: Move the decimal point until the number is between 1 and 10.
Step 3: Count the number of places you moved the decimal point—this will be your exponent of 10. If the original number was a very large number, the exponent will be positive; if the number was a very small number, the exponent will be negative.
To write from scientific notation to standard form
Case 1: If the exponent of 10 is positive, move the decimal point to the right as many times as the value of the exponent. Fill in zeros as needed and drop the power of 10.
Case 2: If the exponent of 10 is negative, move the decimal point to the left as many times as the value of the exponent. Fill in zeros as needed and drop the power of 10.

Example: Write 46,000,000 in scientific notation. $4.6\,0\,0\,0\,0\,0\,0. = 4.6 \times 10^7$

Practice on Your Own
Write in scientific notation.

1. 5,400,000,000

2. 0.00026

3. 6 million

4. 0.00000000859

5. $112\frac{3}{4}$

6. $\dfrac{61}{100,000}$

Write in standard notation.

7. 4.22×10^6

8. 7.1×10^{-4}

9. 9×10^3

10. 1.365×10^{-9}

11. 6.84×10^8

12. 2×10^{-12}

Check
Write in scientific notation.

13. 0.00000000000012

14. 62,500,000,000

15. $206\frac{12}{25}$

Write in standard notation.

16. 4.1×10^2

17. 2.08×10^{-10}

18. 1.001×10^6

   Saxon Algebra 1

Teaching Skill 16

Objective Compare and order real numbers.

Point out that since fractions, decimals, and percents are just different ways of writing real numbers, they can be compared and ordered.

Review the comparison symbols: $<$, $>$, and $=$. Ask: **How do you read the "$<$" symbol?** (less than) **How do you read the "$>$" symbol?** (greater than)

Stress that the small, pointed end of the symbol always aims toward the smaller number.

Review the steps and the examples for comparing each pair of real number types: fractions and decimals; decimals and percents; and fractions and percents.

Ask: **What is the first step in comparing a fraction and a percent?** (You must change the fraction to a decimal.)

Remind students that a fraction greater than 1 will result in a decimal number greater than 1 and a percent greater than 100%.

PRACTICE ON YOUR OWN

In exercises 1–8, students compare real numbers.

In exercises 9–11, students order real numbers from least to greatest.

CHECK

Determine that students know how to compare and order real numbers.

Students who successfully complete the **Practice on Your Own** and **Check** are ready to move on to the next skill.

COMMON ERRORS

Students may confuse the $<$ and $>$ symbol.

Students who made more than 3 errors in the **Practice on Your Own,** or who were not successful in the **Check** section, may benefit from the **Alternative Teaching Strategy.**

Alternative Teaching Strategy

Objective Compare fractions using cross-multiplication.

Some students have not completely mastered long division and may benefit from using cross-multiplication to compare fractions.

Present the following example: $\frac{4}{7} \;\square\; \frac{9}{14}$.

Tell students they are going to compare the two fractions by cross-multiplying the numerators and the denominators.

Instruct students to rewrite the problem as follows:

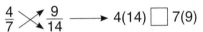 $\frac{4}{7} \diagdown \frac{9}{14} \longrightarrow 4(14)\;\square\;7(9)$

Next, have students multiply the numbers on the left side of the comparison and on the right side of the comparison.

The problem becomes $56\;\square\;63$. Ask: **Which symbol would you use to correctly complete this comparison?** (You would use $<$ since 56 is less than 63.)

Stress that this technique only works if you begin with the numerator in the <u>first</u> fraction.

Have students repeat the process above and complete the following comparisons:

$\frac{7}{10}\;\square\;\frac{13}{20}$; $(>)$ $\frac{4}{9}\;\square\;\frac{12}{27}$; $(=)$

$\frac{30}{54}\;\square\;\frac{5}{8}$; $(<)$ $\frac{2}{11}\;\square\;\frac{11}{54}$; $(<)$

When you feel comfortable that students are able to correctly compare fractions, ask: **How could you use this technique to compare decimals or percents?** (You could write the decimals as fractions with denominators of 10, 100, etc., and you could write the percents as fractions with denominators of 100.)

Saxon Algebra 1

Prerequisite Skills Intervention

Compare and Order Real Numbers

SKILL
16

To compare numbers, you must determine which number is smaller.

Symbols: < (less than), > (greater than), and = (equal to)

Fractions and Decimals	Decimals and Percents	Fractions and Percents
Change the fraction to a decimal by dividing. Then compare digits, beginning with tenths, moving to the right.	Change the percent to a decimal by moving the decimal point. Then compare digits.	Change both the fraction and the percent to decimals. Then compare digits.
Compare $\frac{4}{5}$ and 0.85. $\frac{4}{5} = 4 \div 5 = 0.80$ Compare 0.80 and 0.85. Tenths place: 8 = 8 Hundredths place: 0 < 5 so 0.80 < 0.85. $\frac{4}{5} < 0.85$	Compare 0.60 and 62%. $62\% = 0.62$ Compare 0.60 and 0.62. Tenths place: 6 = 6 Hundredths place: 0 < 2 so 0.60 < 0.62 $0.60 < 62\%$	Compare 10% and $\frac{2}{25}$. $10\% = 0.10; \frac{2}{25} = 0.08$ Compare 0.10 and 0.08. Tenths place: 1 > 0 so 0.10 > 0.08 $10\% > \frac{2}{25}$

Practice on Your Own

Compare. Write <, >, or =.

1. 9 ☐ 15

2. −5 ☐ −10

3. $\frac{1}{4}$ ☐ $\frac{1}{5}$

4. $\frac{11}{6}$ ☐ 2

5. 0.2 ☐ 0.202

6. 0.45 ☐ $\frac{9}{20}$

7. 50% ☐ 0.49

8. 75% ☐ $\frac{37}{50}$

Order the numbers from least to greatest.

9. $\frac{3}{4}$, 70%, $\frac{8}{12}$, 0.72 _____

10. 1.5, $\frac{8}{5}$, 140%, $1\frac{3}{7}$ _____

11. $\frac{3}{10}$, 35%, $\frac{1}{3}$, 0.33 _____

Check

Compare. Write <, >, or =.

12. 0.09 ☐ $\frac{1}{10}$

13. $\frac{5}{8}$ ☐ $\frac{9}{16}$

14. 0.33 ☐ 30%

15. $\frac{6}{5}$ ☐ 125%

Order the numbers from least to greatest.

16. $\frac{1}{5}$, 0.22, $\frac{3}{20}$, 16%, $\frac{1}{6}$, 0.165 _____

Saxon Algebra 1

Teaching Skill 17
Objective Classify real numbers.

Explain to students that the set of real numbers includes several smaller classifications of numbers.

Review each of the classifications. Ask: **Which classification includes the fewest number of elements?** (natural numbers) **Why?** (All the other classifications build on the natural number set. That is, they include all the natural numbers plus other numbers.)

Have students review the different classifications, looking for the number 5. Ask? **Is the number 5 a member of each of the sets of numbers?** (Yes) **Why is it a rational number?** (The number 5 can be written as $\frac{5}{1}, \frac{10}{2}, \frac{20}{4}$, etc.)

Point out that all integers, and therefore all whole numbers and all natural numbers, can be written as rational numbers. Also point out that all terminating decimals can be written as rational numbers. Review the example: $0.2 = \frac{2}{10}$ or $\frac{1}{5}$.

PRACTICE ON YOUR OWN
In exercises 1–9, students classify real numbers.

CHECK
Determine that students know how to classify real numbers.

Students who successfully complete the **Practice on Your Own** and **Check** are ready to move on to the next skill.

COMMON ERRORS
Students may not understand the difference between whole numbers and natural numbers.

Students who made more than 2 errors in the **Practice on Your Own**, or who were not successful in the **Check** section, may benefit from the **Alternative Teaching Strategy**.

Alternative Teaching Strategy
Objective Classify real numbers.

Materials needed: overhead transparency with the Venn Diagram shown below

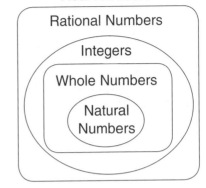

Explain to students that a Venn Diagram is a way of visually organizing sets of data that may overlap.

Display the overhead transparency. Ask: **Which set of numbers is the smallest?** (natural numbers) **Which set of numbers is the largest?** (real numbers)

Remind students that a natural number is also called a counting number. Ask? **When you count, what number do you begin with?** (1) Write the number 1 in the Natural Numbers section of the Venn Diagram. Write the next few natural numbers in the section, followed by three dots: (2, 3, 4, …)

Point out that the section for Natural Numbers is inside Whole Numbers, which is inside Integers, which is inside Rational Numbers, which is inside Real Numbers. Ask: **What does this mean with respect to the number 1?** (It is a natural number, a whole number, an integer, a rational number, and a real number.)

Work through the examples below, placing each one in the appropriate section of the diagram. Have students name all the classifications to which the numbers belong based on the way in which the sections of the Venn Diagram are nested.

$0, -5, \frac{4}{5}, 0.3, -\frac{7}{6}, \frac{20}{2}, 4\frac{1}{2}, 2.1, -\frac{42}{7}$

Saxon Algebra 1

Name _____ Date _____ Class _____

Prerequisite Skills Intervention

Classify Real Numbers

Natural Numbers	Whole Numbers
The set of natural numbers includes all counting numbers.	The set of whole numbers includes all natural numbers and zero.
{1, 2, 3, 4, 5, 6, 7, 8, 9, 10, ... }	{0, 1, 2, 3, 4, 5, 6, 7, 8, 9, 10, ... }
Integers	Rational Numbers
The set of integers includes all positive and negative whole numbers and zero.	A rational number is any number that can be written in the form $\frac{a}{b}$, where a and b are integers and b is not equal to 0.
{ ..., −5, −4, −3, −2, −1, 0, 1, 2, 3, 4, 5, ...}	Examples: $\frac{2}{3}$, $\frac{20}{4}$, $-\frac{9}{7}$, 0.5, 9.1, $2\frac{1}{3}$, etc.

Practice on Your Own

Tell if each number is a natural number, a whole number, an integer, or a rational number. Include all classifications that apply.

1. 5

2. −1

3. 0

_____

_____

_____

4. $\frac{11}{12}$

5. 25

6. $112\frac{3}{4}$

_____

_____

_____

7. 0.45

8. −4.8

9. 1,000,000

_____

_____

_____

Check

Tell if each number is a natural number, a whole number, an integer, or a rational number. Include all classifications that apply.

10. −6

11. 24

12. 12.5

_____

_____

_____

13. 0.0001

14. $-\frac{5}{9}$

15. $\frac{60}{5}$

_____

_____

_____

Saxon Algebra 1

Teaching Skill 18

Objective Graph numbers on a number line.

Draw a number line on the board and place 11 tick marks, evenly spaced, on the line. Do not label any of the tick marks.

Ask: **Without any labels, is it possible to determine what the tick marks represent?** (No) Add the labels −5, −4, ... 0, ... 4, 5 underneath the appropriate tick marks on the number line. Ask: **According to the labels, how is the line divided?** (Each tick mark represents one unit on the line.)

Add smaller tick marks between each pair of numbers. Ask: **What do these new marks represent?** (halves)

Stress that a number line can be divided in any way that is convenient as long as it is appropriately labeled.

Ask: **What kind of numbers are always to the left of 0?** (negative numbers)

Review the two examples with students, pointing out the differences in the way in which the lines are divided and labeled.

PRACTICE ON YOUR OWN

In exercises 1–10, students graph a variety of real numbers on a number line.

CHECK

Determine that students know how to graph numbers on a number line.

Students who successfully complete the **Practice on Your Own** and **Check** are ready to move on to the next skill.

COMMON ERRORS

Students may not pay attention to how a number line is divided or labeled and may incorrectly graph fractions and decimals.

Students who made more than 3 errors in the **Practice on Your Own**, or who were not successful in the **Check** section, may benefit from the **Alternative Teaching Strategy**.

Alternative Teaching Strategy

Objective Graph numbers on a number line.

Materials needed: several decks of cards

Have students work in pairs. Give each pair of students a deck of cards and ask them to remove all the face cards (J, Q, K and Joker).

Explain that the value of each card is the number on the face of the card. The Ace has a value of 1. If the card is red (hearts or diamonds), the number is a negative number; if the card is black (clubs or spades), the number is a positive number. For example, the 8 of hearts has a value of −8.

Draw the number line shown below on the board and have each student copy it on their paper.

Have each student draw a card from their deck and place a dot on their number line where that number value should be. Then place the card in a discard pile. Partners should check each other's answers.

Have students continue this exercise until each student has graphed 5 numbers. If you feel comfortable that students understand how to graph integers on a number line, move on to the exercise below.

Follow the same process as before, except the number line should be divided as follows: from −5 to 5, with 3 tick marks between each integer. Discuss with students what each tick mark represents (one fourth).

Have students remove the aces from the deck. In this exercise, students should draw two cards from the deck. The first card will be the ones value of a decimal and the second, the tenths value. If no cards or both cards are red, the number is positive; if one card is red, the number is negative. For example, if a student draws a 3 of clubs and a 5 of diamonds, the number is −3.5 Students should again place dots on the number line to indicate the number.

Name _____ Date _____ Class _____

Prerequisite Skills Intervention

Graph Numbers on a Number Line

To graph numbers on a number line:

• Step 1: Examine the number line and determine how it is divided.

• Step 2: Take note of whether the number is positive (located to the right of 0) or negative (located to the left of 0).

• Step 3: Move the appropriate number of spaces from 0 (or another integer) and place a point on the number line.

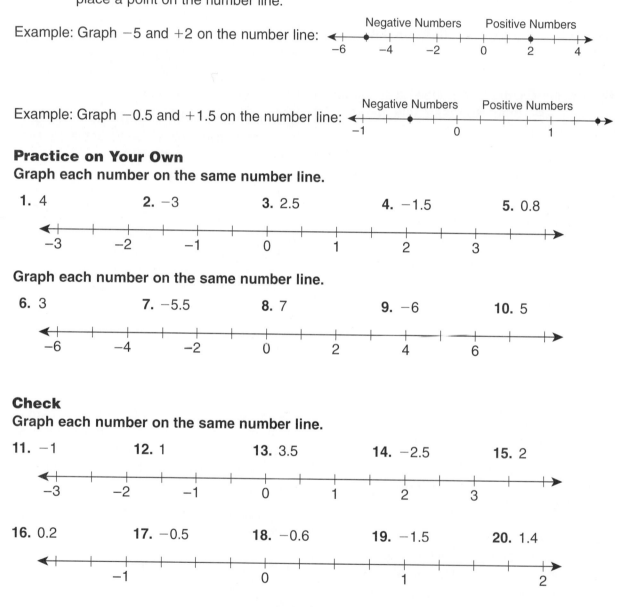

Example: Graph −5 and +2 on the number line:

Example: Graph −0.5 and +1.5 on the number line:

Practice on Your Own

Graph each number on the same number line.

1. 4	**2.** −3	**3.** 2.5	**4.** −1.5	**5.** 0.8

Graph each number on the same number line.

6. 3	**7.** −5.5	**8.** 7	**9.** −6	**10.** 5

Check

Graph each number on the same number line.

11. −1	**12.** 1	**13.** 3.5	**14.** −2.5	**15.** 2

16. 0.2	**17.** −0.5	**18.** −0.6	**19.** −1.5	**20.** 1.4

Saxon Algebra 1

Teaching Skill 19
Objective Choose an appropriate measure.

Explain to students that choosing an appropriate measure depends on the object being measured and what makes sense for that object.

Review the common units of measure for length. Ask: **About how long is a centimeter?** (A centimeter is a little more than a half an inch. There are 2.54 centimeters in one inch.) Ask: **About how long is a kilometer?** (A kilometer is about six-tenths of a mile.)

Point out that centimeters and inches can both be used to measure shorter objects. Ask: **Can kilometers and miles both be used to measure long distances?** (Yes) **Would centimeters or inches be used to measure long distances such as distances between cities?** (Neither)

Review the common units for weight and capacity with students. Discuss some examples of items that would be measured using each unit.

PRACTICE ON YOUR OWN
In exercises 1–8, students choose the best measurement for a variety of objects.

CHECK
Determine that students know how to choose appropriate measures.

Students who successfully complete the **Practice on Your Own** and **Check** are ready to move on to the next skill.

COMMON ERRORS
Students may not recall how certain measurements relate to each other, particularly when working with metric units.

Students who made more than 2 errors in the **Practice on Your Own**, or who were not successful in the **Check** section, may benefit from the **Alternative Teaching Strategy**.

Alternative Teaching Strategy
Objective Choose an appropriate measure.

Materials needed: several sets of the flashcards described below

Create flashcards (index cards are fine) for ten or more common items. Label the front and back with the name of the item. On one side of the card, write a reasonable measure; on the other side, write a less reasonable measure. For some cards, use two different units; for some, using the same units, but different number values.

For example, create the following cards:

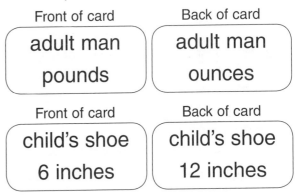

Make multiple copies of the flashcards. Give each student a set of cards. Tell students they are going to play "Speed Round" with the cards.

Before you begin, review with students common units of measure. Point to certain objects around the room and discuss which units of measure would be most appropriate to measure the length and the weight of each object.

Tell students you are going to give them 20 seconds to complete a task. The task is to choose the better measurement for the item on the card and place that side face up.

The student who is able to place the most cards correctly wins.

Have students shuffle the cards and repeat the exercise, allowing only 15 seconds to complete the task.

An extension of this exercise is to have students create their own cards.

Saxon Algebra 1

Name _____ Date _____ Class _____

Prerequisite Skills Intervention
Choose an Appropriate Measure

Choosing an appropriate measure depends on the object being measured and what makes sense for that object.

Most Common Units of Measure		
Length	**Weight (Mass)**	**Capacity**
inches (in.) feet (ft) yards (yd) miles (mi) centimeters (cm) meters (m) kilometers (km)	ounces (oz) pounds (lb) tons (T) grams (g) kilograms (kg)	fluid ounces (fl oz) cups (c) pints (pt) quarts (qt) gallons (gal) liters (L)

Example: What measure would you use to weigh an automobile?

Answer: Ounces and pounds do not make sense, because they are much too small. An automobile most likely weighs one to two tons, so tons is the better measure.

Practice on Your Own
For each object, circle the better measurement.

1. length of a football field: 100 ft or 100 yd

2. length of a sofa: 6 ft or 6 yd

3. height of a coffee table: 1.5 ft or 5 yd

4. mass of an ant: 0.1 g or 0.1 lb

5. airplane speed: 3000 mph or 300 mph

6. height of a 6-year old: 5 ft or 2.5 ft

7. diameter of a car tire: 3 ft or 15 in.

8. capacity of a teacup: 8 oz or 1 gal

Check
For each object, circle the better measurement.

9. height of a paperback book: 1 ft or 6 in.

10. length of a tropical fish: 6 ft or 6 in.

11. diameter of a dinner plate: 25 cm or 1 m

12. height of a cow: 5 ft or 5 yd

13. diameter of a wedding ring: 2 cm or 1 m

14. weight of a TV set: 30 lbs or 30 oz

15. capacity of a water tower: 50,000 gal or 50,000 pt

16. distance of a marathon: 26 mi or 2600 yd

Saxon Algebra 1

Teaching Skill 20

Objective Measure line segments using inches and centimeters.

Make sure each student has a ruler measured in inches and in centimeters.

Remind students that certain standard units are used to measure length. Point out that inches are the customary unit of measure and centimeters are the metric unit.

Review how a customary ruler is marked. Explain that in each inch there are a number of lines of different lengths. The longest line in the inch is in the middle. This is the half-inch mark.

The next shortest line is the $\frac{1}{4}$-inch mark;

the third shortest line is the $\frac{1}{8}$-inch mark;

and the fourth shortest is the $\frac{1}{16}$-inch mark.

Review the example with students.

Discuss how a centimeter ruler is marked. Remind students that metric units are divided into tens. The longest line in the middle represents a half of a centimeter and all the other lines represent tenths. Have students measure the line segment in the example using their centimeter ruler. (5.5 cm)

PRACTICE ON YOUR OWN

In exercises 1–8, students choose the best measurement for a variety of objects.

CHECK

Determine that students know how to choose appropriate measures.

Students who successfully complete the **Practice on Your Own** and **Check** are ready to move on to the next skill.

COMMON ERRORS

Students may not recall how certain measurements relate to each other, particularly when working with metric units.

Students who made more than 2 errors in the **Practice on Your Own**, or who were not successful in the **Check** section, may benefit from the **Alternative Teaching Strategy**.

Alternative Teaching Strategy

Objective Understand how a standard ruler is marked.

Materials needed: several rules and several sets of the flashcards shown below

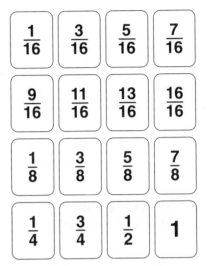

Give each student one set of cards. Have students shuffle their cards and turn them face down.

Tell students that they are going to race to organize the cards in the order in which they would find the numbers (markings) on a standard ruler.

When everyone is ready, say: **Go**. The first student to correctly arrange the cards wins.

Instruct students to leave their cards in the correct order. Ask: **If you were measuring a pencil to the nearest eighth of an inch, and the pencil was somewhere between $\frac{13}{16}$ and $\frac{7}{8}$, what would the correct measure be?** ($\frac{7}{8}$ in.)

Once you feel comfortable that students understand how a standard ruler is marked, have them use their own ruler to measure the length of their writing utensil to the nearest eight of an inch. Then have them trade writing utensils with another student and measure theirs to the nearest eighth of any inch. Have students check each other's measurements before moving on to another item.

Saxon Algebra 1

Prerequisite Skills Intervention
Measure with Customary and Metric Units

SKILL
20

Customary units include units such as inches, feet, yards, and miles.
Metric units include units such as centimeter, meter, and kilometer.

Example: What is the length of the segment shown to the nearest eighth of an inch?

Answer: The smallest tick mark represents $\frac{1}{16}$ of an inch. The line segment is slightly to the left of the $\frac{3}{16}$ mark, so the segment is $2\frac{1}{8}$ inch long, to the nearest eighth of an inch.

Practice on Your Own
Measure each segment to the nearest eighth of an inch and to the nearest half of a centimeter.

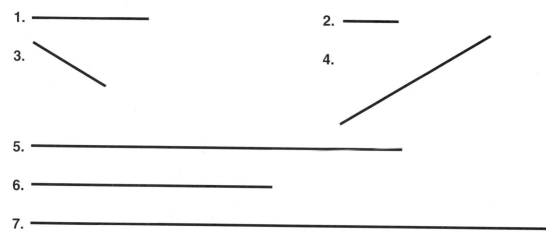

1. ————————

2. ———

3.

4.

5. ————————————————

6. ————————————

7. ————————————————————

Check
Measure each segment to the nearest eighth of an inch and to the nearest half of a centimeter.

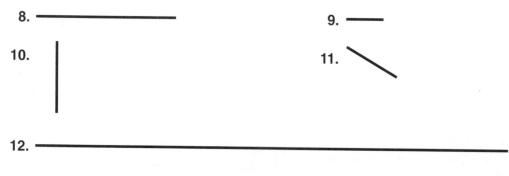

8. ————————————

9. ——

10.

11.

12. ————————————————————

Saxon Algebra 1

Teaching Skill 21
Objective Convert units of measure.

Point out to students that converting between units of measure always involves either multiplication or division. Ask: **Is it sometimes difficult to remember when to multiply and when to divide?** (Most students will probably say yes.)

Introduce the concept and review the definition of a conversion factor. Emphasize that you do not have to remember whether to multiply or divide if you use a conversion fact; it depends on the numerator and denominator of the fraction.

Have students look at the common conversion factors. Ask: **Why does a conversion factor equal 1?** (Because the measure in the numerator is equal to the measure in the denominator even though the units are different)

Instruct students to consider the example. Explain that the correct conversion factor is $\frac{1 \text{ yd}}{3 \text{ ft}}$ (not $\frac{3 \text{ ft}}{1 \text{ yd}}$) because you need feet in the denominator to cancel with the feet in the problem. Work through the example.

PRACTICE ON YOUR OWN
In exercises 1–9, students convert from one unit of measure to another.

CHECK
Determine that students know how to convert units of measure.

Students who successfully complete the **Practice on Your Own** and **Check** are ready to move on to the next skill.

COMMON ERRORS
Students may multiply when they should divide, or divide when they should multiply.

Students who made more than 2 errors in the **Practice on Your Own**, or who were not successful in the **Check** section, may benefit from the **Alternative Teaching Strategy**.

Alternative Teaching Strategy
Objective Convert units of measure.

Materials needed: multiple copies of the game cards shown below; copy of page 2 of this lesson (Common Conversion Factors)

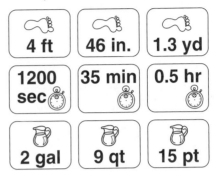

Have students review the chart of common conversion factors. Review with students how conversion factors are used when converting from one unit of measure to another.

Give each student a set of game cards. Have students briefly look at the cards and take note of the symbols on the cards. Explain that the footprint represents length; the clock represents time; and the pitcher represents capacity.

Have students shuffle their cards (face down). Tell students they are going to play "Speed."

Explain to students that when you say "Go," they are to flip their cards over, separate them into categories (length, time, and capacity), and put the cards in each category in order from least to greatest. Students should use scratch paper to convert to whichever units they believe will help them the most.

The student who correctly puts all the cards in order wins.

Answers: Length: 46 in., 1.3 yd, 4 ft; Time: 1200 sec, 0.5 hr, 35 min; and Capacity: 15 pt, 2 gal, 9 qt

An extension of this exercise is to have students create their own cards, using different units than the ones provided.

Saxon Algebra 1

Prerequisite Skills Intervention
Convert Units of Measure

To convert from one unit of measure to another, you can use a conversion factor and multiply.

Definition: a conversion factor is a fraction equal to 1 whose numerator and denominator have different units.

Common Conversion Factors		
Length	**Capacity**	**Weight**
$\dfrac{1\text{ ft}}{12\text{ in.}}$ or $\dfrac{12\text{ in.}}{1\text{ ft}}$	$\dfrac{1\text{ pt}}{2\text{ c}}$ or $\dfrac{2\text{ c}}{1\text{ pt}}$	
$\dfrac{1\text{ yd}}{3\text{ ft}}$ or $\dfrac{3\text{ ft}}{1\text{ yd}}$	$\dfrac{1\text{ qt}}{2\text{ pt}}$ or $\dfrac{2\text{ pt}}{1\text{ qt}}$	$\dfrac{1\text{ lb}}{16\text{ oz}}$ or $\dfrac{16\text{ oz}}{1\text{ lb}}$
$\dfrac{1\text{ mi}}{5280\text{ ft}}$ or $\dfrac{5280\text{ ft}}{1\text{ mi}}$	$\dfrac{1\text{ gal}}{4\text{ qt}}$ or $\dfrac{4\text{ qt}}{1\text{ gal}}$	$\dfrac{1\text{ T}}{2000\text{ lb}}$ or $\dfrac{2000\text{ lb}}{1\text{ T}}$
Time	**Metric**	
$\dfrac{1\text{ min}}{60\text{ sec}}$ or $\dfrac{60\text{ sec}}{1\text{ min}}$ $\dfrac{1\text{ hr}}{60\text{ min}}$ or $\dfrac{60\text{ min}}{1\text{ hr}}$	$\dfrac{1\text{ m}}{100\text{ cm}}$ or $\dfrac{100\text{ cm}}{1\text{ m}}$ $\dfrac{1\text{ m}}{1000\text{ mm}}$ or $\dfrac{1000\text{ mm}}{1\text{ m}}$	
$\dfrac{1\text{ day}}{24\text{ hr}}$ or $\dfrac{24\text{ hr}}{1\text{ day}}$ $\dfrac{1\text{ wk}}{7\text{ days}}$ of $\dfrac{7\text{ days}}{1\text{ wk}}$	$\dfrac{1\text{ km}}{1000\text{ m}}$ or $\dfrac{1000\text{ m}}{1\text{ km}}$	
$\dfrac{1\text{ yr}}{12\text{ mo}}$ or $\dfrac{12\text{ mo}}{1\text{ yr}}$	Note: All metric units have the same conversion factors based on the prefix.	

Example: Convert 12 feet to yards. $12\ \cancel{\text{ft}} \cdot \dfrac{1\text{ yd}}{3\ \cancel{\text{ft}}} = \dfrac{12\text{ yd}}{3} = 4\text{ yd}$

Practice on Your Own
Convert each unit of measure.

1. 30 months to years

2. 48 inches to feet

3. 3 pounds to ounces

4. 650 centimeters to meters

5. 1.5 days to hours

6. 16 quarts to gallons

7. 7000 pounds to tons

8. 2.2 liters to milliliters

9. 7 yards to feet

Check
Convert each unit of measure.

10. 9.2 meters to centimeters

11. 2.5 hours to minutes

12. 22 pints to quarts

13. 4500 milligrams to grams

14. 56 ounces to pounds

15. 4.5 years to months

Teaching Skill 22

Objective Identify points, segments, rays, lines, and planes.

Review with students the definitions provided on the worksheet of this lesson. Also review the notations.

Ask: **What is the difference between a segment and a ray?** (A segment only has one endpoint, while a ray has two.) Ask: **What is the difference between a ray and a line?** (A ray has one endpoint while a line does not have any.)

Review the example. Point out that there can be multiple rays or lines through any given point. Ask: **Can you write segment *BA* instead of segment *AB*?** (Yes) **Can you write ray *AB* instead of ray *BA*?** (No) **Why not?** (Because you must begin at the endpoint and proceed toward the arrow)

Ask: **Why are there no lines in the diagram?** (Because the series of points only extend in one direction, making them rays instead of lines)

PRACTICE ON YOUR OWN

In exercises 1–10, students identify points, segments, rays, lines, and planes on a diagram.

CHECK

Determine that students know how to identify points, segments, rays, lines, and planes.

Students who successfully complete the **Practice on Your Own** and **Check** are ready to move on to the next skill.

COMMON ERRORS

Students may confuse lines and rays or rays and segments because they do not pay attention to the arrows and endpoints.

Students who made more than 2 errors in the **Practice on Your Own**, or who were not successful in the **Check** section, may benefit from the **Alternative Teaching Strategy**.

Alternative Teaching Strategy

Objective Identify points, segments, rays, lines, and planes using a rectangular solid.

Give students an enlarged copy of a rectangular solid as shown below.

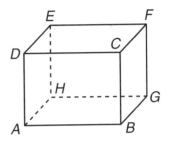

Remind students that a rectangular solid has faces, edges, and vertices. Give examples of each of these. For example, *ABCD* is a face; *AD* is an edge; and *A* is a vertex.

Ask: **Which of these is the same as a point?** (a vertex) **Which is the same as a segment?** (an edge) **Which is the same as a plane if it were extended in all directions?** (a face)

Have students count the number of vertices (8) and then name eight points. (*A, B, C, D, E, F, G,* and *H*)

Next have students count the number of edges (12) and name twelve segments. Remind students that segment *AB* is the same thing as segment *BA*. (*AB, AD, AH, BG, BC, CD, CF, DE, EF, EH, FG, GH*)

Ask: **How could you change any of the segments** (edges) **to make them rays?** (You could extend ONE of the sides without end.) **How could you change any of the segments to make them lines?** (You could extend both of the sides without end.)

Finally, have students count the number of faces (6) and then name six planes. (*ABCD, ABGH, ADEH, BCFG, CDEF,* and *EFGH*)

Repeat this exercise by pointing to the walls, edges, and corners of the classroom and having students identify them as points, segments, or planes.

Saxon Algebra 1

Name _____ Date _____ Class _____

Prerequisite Skills Intervention
Points, Lines, and Planes

SKILL
22

Object	Definition	Notation
Point	A location in space that has no size.	· A
Segment	A part of a line consisting of two endpoints and all the points between.	$\overline{AB}$
Ray	A part of a line consisting of one endpoint and all the points of the line on one side of the endpoint.	$\overrightarrow{AB}$
Line	A series of points that extends without end in opposite directions.	$\overleftrightarrow{AB}$
Plane	A flat (two-dimensional) surface that extends without end in all directions. A plane has no thickness.	$\mathcal{P}$

Example: Use the diagram to name a point, a segment, a ray, a line, and a plane (if possible).

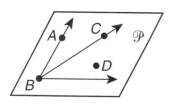

Answers
Any one of the following are points: *A*, *B*, *C*, or *D*.
There are two segments: $\overline{BA}$ and $\overline{BC}$.
There are two rays: $\overrightarrow{BA}$ and $\overrightarrow{BC}$.
There are no lines.
There is one plane: $\mathcal{P}$

Practice on Your Own
Use the diagram to the right to name each of the following.

1. a point _____

2. a line _____

3. a segment _____

4. a ray _____

5. a plane _____

6. a ray with endpoint *O* _____

7. the line that passes through the point *M* _____

8. the plane that contains the point *Q* _____

9. a segment with one endpoint at point *O* _____

10. the point where lines *MP* and *ON* meet _____

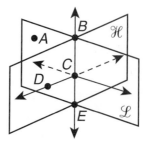

Check
Use the diagram to the right to name each of the following.

11. two points _____ and _____

12. a segment _____

13. two rays _____ and _____

14. a line _____

15. two planes _____ and _____

16. the plane that contains line *CD* _____

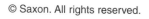

Saxon Algebra 1

Prerequisite Skills Intervention
Name and Classify Angles

SKILL 23

Teaching Skill 23
Objective Name and classify different types of angles.

Review with students how to name angles. Ask: **What letter is ALWAYS in the middle of a three letter angle name?** (the letter defining the vertex) **Is it okay to name the angle using only the letter at the vertex?** (No)

Cover each of the names and measures of the different types of classifications and the examples.

Ask: **How do you know if an angle is acute or obtuse just by looking at it?** (You can tell whether it is smaller or bigger than a right angle.)

Discuss the fact that a straight angle can be thought of as two right angles, side by side. Ask: **Does this make sense mathematically?** (Yes) **Why?** (Because $90 + 90 = 180$)

Have students complete the practice exercises.

PRACTICE ON YOUR OWN
In exercises 1–9, students name and classify different types of angles.

CHECK
Determine that students know how to name and classify angles.

Students who successfully complete the **Practice on Your Own** and **Check** are ready to move on to the next skill.

COMMON ERRORS
When naming angles, students may name the angle by the letter of the vertex only.

Students may confuse the definitions of acute and obtuse.

Students who made more than 2 errors in the **Practice on Your Own**, or who were not successful in the **Check** section, may benefit from the **Alternative Teaching Strategy**.

Alternative Teaching Strategy
Objective Classify different types of angles.

Instruct students to take out one clean sheet of paper. Have students fold the piece of paper in half vertically as shown below.

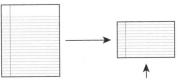

Have students consider the long edge of the folded sheet of paper. Ask: **What kind of angle is this?** (a straight angle)

Next, have students fold the piece of paper sideways as shown below.

Have students consider the angle around the corner of the folded paper. Ask: **What kind of angle is this?** (a right angle)

Finally, have students fold the piece of paper diagonally so that the top edge meets the side edge as shown.

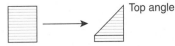

Top angle

Have students consider the top angle. Ask: **What kind of angle is this?** (an acute angle)

Have students unfold the piece of paper and trace each of the creases that were made by folding.

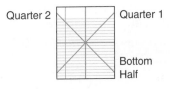

Quarter 2   Quarter 1

Bottom Half

Instruct students to shade an acute angle in Quarter 1, a right angle in Quarter 2, and an obtuse angle in the bottom half. (Answers may vary.)

Saxon Algebra 1

Name _____ Date _____ Class _____

Prerequisite Skills Intervention

Name and Classify Angles

SKILL 23

Angles are named using three letters. The vertex is ALWAYS in the middle.
Angles are classified by their measure according to the table below.

Classification	Measure	Example	Name
Acute	Less than 90°		∠ABC or ∠CBA
Right	90°		∠DEF or ∠FED
Obtuse	Greater than 90°		∠PQR or ∠RQP
Straight	180°		∠XYZ or ∠ZYX

Practice on Your Own
Name and classify each angle.

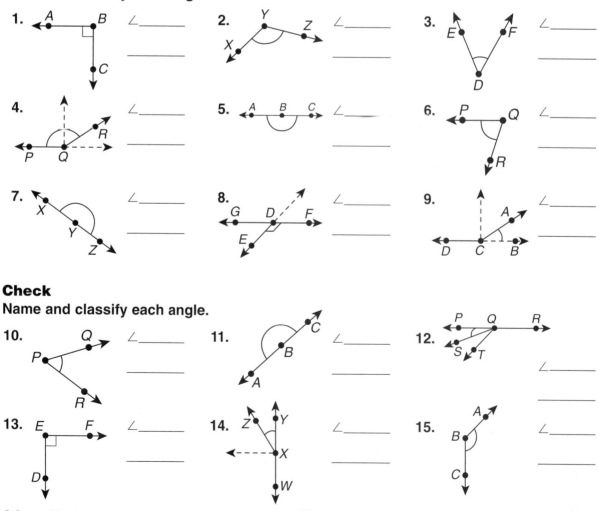

1. ∠_____ _____

2. ∠_____ _____

3. ∠_____ _____

4. ∠_____ _____

5. ∠_____ _____

6. ∠_____ _____

7. ∠_____ _____

8. ∠_____ _____

9. ∠_____ _____

Check
Name and classify each angle.

10. ∠_____ _____

11. ∠_____ _____

12. ∠_____ _____

13. ∠_____ _____

14. ∠_____ _____

15. ∠_____ _____

© Saxon. All rights reserved.

46

Saxon Algebra 1

Prerequisite Skills Intervention
Measure Angles

Teaching Skill 24
Objective Use a protractor to measure angles.

Draw a large acute angle on the board, approximately 45°. Point to the vertex of the angle and ask: **What is this point on the angle called?** (the vertex)

Using a board protractor and the angle you drew, demonstrate each of the steps for measuring an angle. Once you have arrived at a measure, which should be less than 90°, ask: **Is the angle I drew smaller than a right angle?** (Yes) **Does the measure I arrived at make sense?** (Yes) **Why?** (The angle measure should be less than 90°.)

Emphasize that students should always consider whether the measure they found makes sense in comparison to a right angle.

Have students look at their protractors. Point out that there are two sets of measures and that students should be careful to use the correct set, depending on which zero they use to line up the bottom edge of the angle they are measuring.

PRACTICE ON YOUR OWN
In exercises 1–6, students use a protractor to measure angles.

CHECK
Determine that students know how to use a protractor to measure an angle.

Students who successfully complete the **Practice on Your Own** and **Check** are ready to move on to the next skill.

COMMON ERRORS
Students may use the wrong set of measures on the protractor.

Students who made more than 1 error in the **Practice on Your Own**, or who were not successful in the **Check** section, may benefit from the **Alternative Teaching Strategy**.

Alternative Teaching Strategy
Objective Use a protractor to measure angles.

Materials needed: multiple copies of a circle that has a diameter of 6 inches and the center clearly marked

Tell students that they are going to construct a clock and use a protractor to confirm that their clock is fairly accurate. Give each student a circle.

Ask: **How many hours are represented on a clock?** (12) **How many degrees are in a circle?** (360°) **How many degrees should there be between each hour mark on a clock?** (360° ÷ 12 = 30°)

Have students draw a dotted vertical line from the top of the circle, through the center, to the bottom of the circle. Then have them draw a horizontal line from the left side of the circle, through the center, to the right side. Demonstrate on the board.

Ask: **If the lines you drew are truly vertical and horizontal, what should be the measures of the angles that are formed by the intersecting lines?** (90°) Have students use their protractors to measure the angles. If the angles are approximately 90°, move on to the next step. If they are not, have students erase their lines and try again. Instruct students to label 12:00, 3:00, 6:00, and 9:00.

Next have students draw a dotted line from the center of the circle to the upper right side of the circle, approximately one-third of the distance from 12:00 to 3:00. Demonstrate on the board.

Have students use their protractors to measure the angle formed. It should be approximately 30°. Repeat the steps outlined above, until students have drawn, measured, and labeled all 12 hours on the clock.

47 **Saxon** Algebra 1

Name _____ Date _____ Class _____

Prerequisite Skills Intervention

Measure Angles

Vocabulary: The vertex of an angle is the point where the two rays meet to form the angle.

To measure an angle:
- Step 1: Place the center hole on the straight edge of the protractor over the vertex of the angle.
- Step 2: Line up the zero on the straight edge of the protractor with one of the sides of the angle.
- Step 3: Locate the point where the second side of the angle intersects the curved edge of the protractor.
- Step 4: The number that is written on the protractor at the point of intersection is the measure of the angle.

Example: Find the measure of the angle shown.

Answer: Since one side of the angle is lined up with the zero along the inner set of measures, read the number on the same set of measures where the other side of the angle intersects the protractor; the measure of the angle is 35°.

Practice on Your Own
Use a protractor to measure each angle.

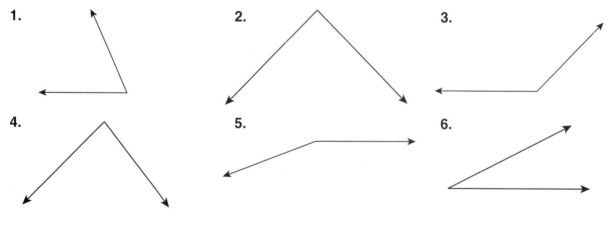

1.

2.

3.

4.

5.

6.

Check
Use a protractor to measure each angle.

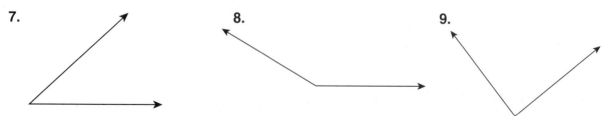

7.

8.

9.

48   **Saxon** Algebra 1

Prerequisite Skills Intervention

Angle Relationships

Teaching Skill 25

Objective Identify angle relationships.

Begin by explaining to students that angle relationships often provide information about the measure of the angles.

Point out that there are a number of angle postulates and theorems that establish congruence between certain types of angles. Emphasize that it is important to be able to identify angle relationships in order to apply those congruence postulates and theorems.

Review the definitions and examples of adjacent angles, vertical angles, complementary angles, and supplementary angles.

Point out the difference between complementary and supplementary angles. Ask: **Which pair of angles form a straight angle?** (supplementary)

Instruct students to complete the practice exercises.

PRACTICE ON YOUR OWN

In exercises 1–4, students choose which description best fits the angle relationships.

In exercises 5–8, students use a diagram to give examples of different types of angle relationships.

CHECK

Determine that students know how to identify angle relationships.

Students who successfully complete the **Practice on Your Own** and **Check** are ready to move on to the next skill.

COMMON ERRORS

Students may confuse the definitions of complementary and supplementary.

Students who made more than 2 errors in the **Practice on Your Own**, or who were not successful in the **Check** section, may benefit from the **Alternative Teaching Strategy**.

Alternative Teaching Strategy

Objective Identify angle relationships.

Materials needed: multiple enlarged copies of the game cards shown below

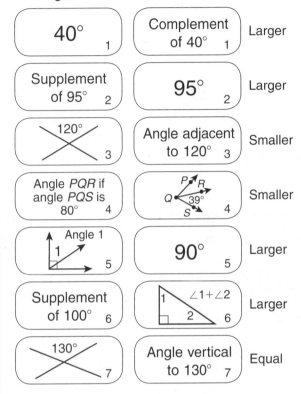

Tell students they are going to play "Larger, Smaller, or Equal."

Before you begin, review the definitions and a few examples of adjacent, vertical, complementary, and supplementary angles. Then, give each student a set of shuffled game cards.

Tell the students that when you say "Go," they should match their cards according to the small numbers in the lower right corner of the card. Then students should determine which card represents the smaller angle and which represents the larger angle. They should place the smaller angle in a pile on their left and the larger angle on their right. If the two angles are equal, they should place them both in a center pile.

The first student to correctly separate their cards wins.

© Saxon. All rights reserved.

49

Saxon Algebra 1

Name _____ Date _____ Class _____

Prerequisite Skills Intervention

Angle Relationships

Angle Relationships	
Adjacent Angles	**Vertical Angles**
Definition: two angles that share a side and a vertex, but no interior points	Definition: two angles whose sides are opposite rays
Example: 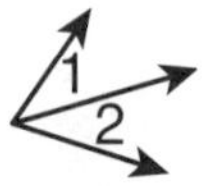	Example: 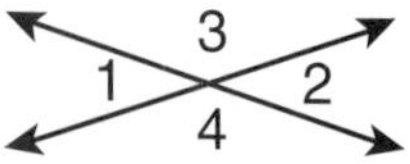 1 and 2 3 and 4
Complementary Angles	**Supplementary Angles**
Definition: two angles, the sum of whose measures is 90°	Definition: two angles, the sum of whose measures is 180°
Examples: 40° and 50°; 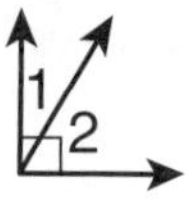	Examples: 60° and 120°; 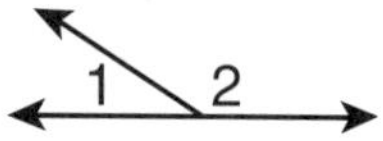

Practice on Your Own

Circle the better description for each labeled angle pair.

1. 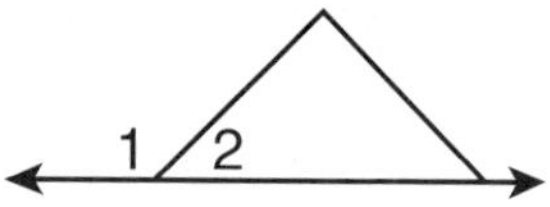
complementary angles
supplementary angles

2. 
vertical angles
supplementary angles

3. 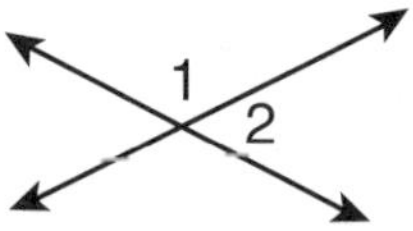
adjacent angles
vertical angles

4. 35° and 55°
complementary angles
supplementary angles

Use the diagram to the right to give an example of each angle pair.

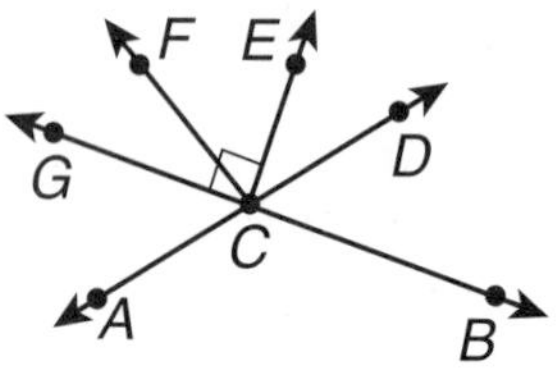

5. adjacent angles _____

6. complementary angles _____

7. vertical angles _____

8. supplementary angles _____

Check

Circle the better description for each labeled angle pair.

9. 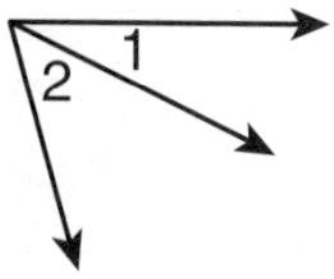
complementary angles
adjacent angles

10. 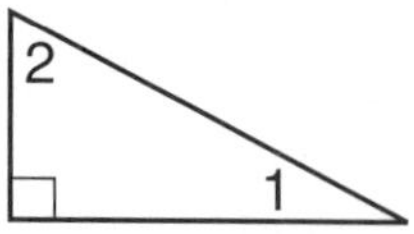
complementary angles
adjacent angles

Use the diagram to the right to give an example of each angle pair.

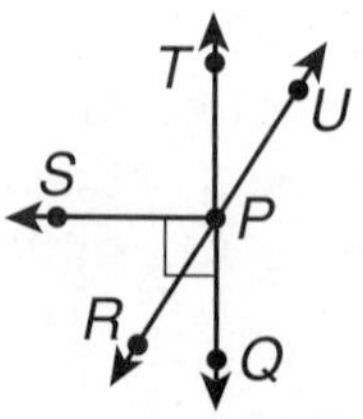

11. vertical angles _____

12. complementary angles _____

13. adjacent angles _____

14. supplementary angles _____

Saxon Algebra 1

Teaching Skill 26
Objective Find the measure of angles.

Begin the lesson by introducing the different angle relationships—corresponding, alternate interior, same-side interior, and vertical. Use the diagram to identify the different pairs of angles.

Point out that there are several pairs of vertical angles and several pairs of corresponding angles. Ask: **What is another way to describe corresponding angles?** (angles that "sit" in the same spot on both of the parallel lines)

Point out the difference between alternate interior angles and same-side interior angles.

Next, show students that they can trace an F to find corresponding angles, a Z for alternate interior angles, and an X for vertical angles.

Have students complete the practice exercises.

PRACTICE ON YOUR OWN
In exercises 1–5, students identify angle relationships when parallel lines are cut by a transversal.

In exercises 6–12, students find the measures of angles.

CHECK
Determine that students know what kind of angles are formed when parallel lines are cut by a transversal and how to find the measures of those angles.

Students who successfully complete the **Practice on Your Own** and **Check** are ready to move on to the next skill.

COMMON ERRORS
Students may confuse same-side interior angles and alternate interior angles.

Students who made more than 2 errors in the **Practice on Your Own**, or who were not successful in the **Check** section, may benefit from the **Alternative Teaching Strategy**.

Alternative Teaching Strategy
Objective Find the measure of angles.

Materials needed: wide-ruled lined paper, ruler, and a protractor

Have students use a ruler to draw two parallel horizontal lines, about eight to ten lines apart, on a piece of paper.

Review the definition of a transversal. Then, have students draw a diagonal transversal through the two parallel lines as shown below.

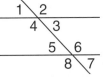

Instruct students to label each angle on their diagram, using the numbering system shown above.

Have students create the following table at the bottom of their sheet of paper:

Angle	1	2	3	4	5	6	7	8
Measure								

Instruct students to use their protractors to measure each angle on their diagram and record the measurements in the table.

Discuss with students the definitions of corresponding angles, alternate interior angles, same-side interior angles, and vertical angles.

Ask students to identify the following:

• The angle corresponding to $\angle2$; ($\angle6$)

• a same-side interior angle with $\angle4$; ($\angle5$)

• the angle that is vertical to $\angle2$; ($\angle4$)

• an alternate interior angle with $\angle3$; ($\angle5$).

Using the measurements students found and the angles identified above, have students make conjectures about what kinds of angles have congruent measures.

Discuss margins of error in measuring if students do not have equal measures where they should.

Prerequisite Skills Intervention

Parallel Lines and Transversals

SKILL **26**

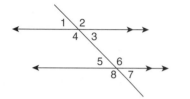

Corresponding angles: ∠1 and ∠5, ∠2 and ∠6, ∠3 and ∠7, ∠4 and ∠8

Alternate interior angles: ∠3 and ∠5, ∠4 and ∠6

Same-side interior angles: ∠3 and ∠6, ∠4 and ∠5

Vertical angles: ∠1 and ∠3, ∠2 and ∠4, ∠5 and ∠7, ∠6 and ∠8

Parallel line properties: If two parallel lines are cut by a transversal, then:

1. Corresponding angles are congruent;
2. Alternate interior angles are congruent; and
3. Same-side interior angles are supplementary.

Also recall: Vertical angles are congruent and straight angles have measures of 180°.

Example: If the measure of ∠2 above is 118°, what is the measure of ∠6? ∠4? ∠3?

Answers: ∠6 = 118° (corresponding); ∠4 = 118° (vertical); ∠3 = 62° (straight)

Practice on Your Own
Name the missing angle.

1. ∠d corresponds to ∠_____.

2. ∠b forms a straight angle with ∠_____ and ∠_____.

3. ∠c is a same-side interior angle with ∠_____.

4. ∠c is an alternate interior angle with ∠_____.

5. ∠f is vertical to ∠_____.

n   p   n ∥ p

a b   e f
d c   h g

Find the measure of each numbered angle.

6. ∠1 = _____

7. ∠2 = _____

8. ∠3 = _____

9. ∠4 = _____

10. ∠5 = _____

11. ∠6 = _____

12. ∠7 = _____

4 / 1
3 / 2

7 / 5
6 / 115°

Check
Name or find the measure of the angle as indicated.

13. ∠j is vertical to ∠_____.

14. ∠f corresponds to ∠_____.

15. ∠g is a same-side interior angle with ∠_____.

16. ∠k is an alternate interior angle with ∠_____.

17. The measure of ∠1 is _____.

18. The measure of ∠2 is _____.

19. The measure of ∠3 is _____.

20. The measure of ∠4 is _____.

75°
1 \ 2   g   f   ► p
           h k
3 \ 4   j   ► q

Saxon Algebra 1

Teaching Skill 27

Objective Name a polygon by the number of its sides.

Review with students the definition of a polygon. Stress that the figure must be closed and must NOT intersect itself.

Next, review each of the examples. Ask: **Why is the first figure not a polygon?** (The figure is not closed.) **Why is the third figure not a polygon?** (The figure intersects itself in the middle.)

Review with students the names of polygons identified in the table. Emphasize that the name depends on the number of sides. After reviewing the table, have students cover the right hand column and try to remember all the names.

Go over the definitions of equilateral, equiangular, and regular. Point out that a regular polygon cannot have an irregular shape, although an equilateral or equiangular polygon might.

Have students complete the practice exercises.

PRACTICE ON YOUR OWN

In exercises 1–8, students determine whether figures are polygons, name the polygons based on the number of sides, and identify figures that are regular polygons.

CHECK

Determine that students know how to identify polygons.

Students who successfully complete the **Practice on Your Own** and **Check** are ready to move on to the next skill.

COMMON ERRORS

Students may confuse the different names, particularly hexagon and heptagon.

Students who made more than 2 errors in the **Practice on Your Own,** or who were not successful in the **Check** section, may benefit from the **Alternative Teaching Strategy**.

Alternative Teaching Strategy

Objective Name a polygon by the number of its sides.

Materials needed: multiple copies of the game cards shown below—index cards work nicely.

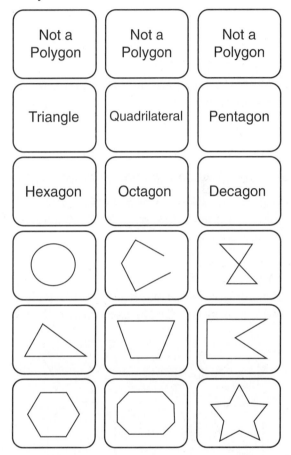

Have students work in pairs. Tell students they are going to play a memory game.

Instruct students to shuffle the cards and place them in rows, face down. Each student will flip over two cards. If one card has a polygon name on it and the other card has a matching figure, the student keeps the cards. If the name and the figure do not match, or there are two names or two figures, the student flips the cards back over. The winner is the student who has the most cards at the end of the game.

As an extension of this exercise, have students make their own game cards and play again.

Saxon Algebra 1

Prerequisite Skills Intervention

Identify Polygons

Definition: A polygon is a closed plane figure with at least three sides, none of which intersect other than at their endpoints.

Examples:

Not a polygon   Polygon

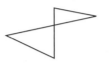

A polygon can be classified by its number of sides according to the table.

Definitions:

An equilateral polygon has all sides congruent.

An equiangular polygon has all angles congruent.

A regular polygon has all sides congruent and all angles congruent; that is, it is both equilateral and equiangular.

Number of Sides	Polygon
3	triangle
4	quadrilateral
5	pentagon
6	hexagon
7	heptagon
8	octagon
9	nonagon
10	decagon
12	dodecagon
n	n-gon

Practice on Your Own
Determine whether each figure is a polygon. If so, name it by its number of sides. Circle each figure that is a regular polygon.

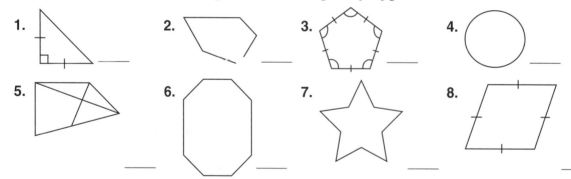

Check
Determine whether each figure is a polygon. If so, name it by its number of sides. Circle each figure that is a regular polygon.

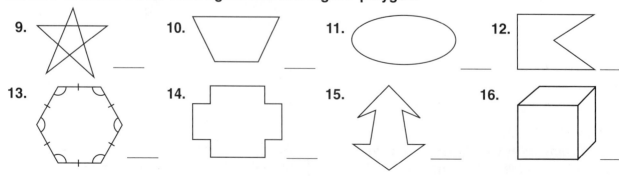

Saxon Algebra 1

Prerequisite Skills Intervention

Angles in Polygons

SKILL
28

Teaching Skill 28

Objective Find the measures of interior and exterior angles of polygons.

Begin by drawing a regular hexagon on the board. Extend one side of the hexagon, as shown below, to demonstrate examples of interior and exterior angles.

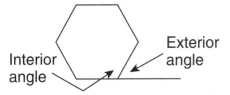

Ask: **If a figure has six sides, how many interior angles does it have?** (6) **How many exterior angles does it have?** (6)

Review the information provided in the table. As you move from one figure to the next, point out that the number of sides is increasing by 1, and the sum of the interior angles is increasing by 180°. Teach the formula for finding the sum and work examples using 3, 4, and 5 sides.

When you cover exterior angles, stress that the sum of the exterior angles is ALWAYS 360°, no matter how many sides there are.

PRACTICE ON YOUR OWN

In exercises 1–7, students find the measures of interior and exterior angles of polygons.

CHECK

Determine that students know how to find the measures of interior and exterior angles of polygons.

Students who successfully complete the **Practice on Your Own** and **Check** are ready to move on to the next skill.

COMMON ERRORS

Students may use the formula for finding the measures of interior angles incorrectly.

Students who made more than 2 errors in the **Practice on Your Own**, or who were not successful in the **Check** section, may benefit from the **Alternative Teaching Strategy**.

Alternative Teaching Strategy

Objective Find the measures of interior angles of polygons using triangles.

Materials needed: several sheets of paper, rulers

Begin by reminding students that the sum of the measures of the interior angles of a triangle is 180°.

Explain to students that they are going to complete the following table using triangles and multiples of 180.

Number of Sides	Sum of Interior Angles
3	180°
4	
5	
6	
8	

Have students draw a large rectangle, parallelogram, and trapezoid on a sheet of paper. Instruct students to choose a vertex and use a ruler to draw a line to each of the other vertices; this will divide the figure into triangles.

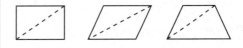

Ask: **How many triangles were formed in each of the quadrilaterals?** (2) **Since the sum of the measures of the interior angles of each triangle is 180°, what is the total sum for each of the quadrilaterals?** (2 × 180 = 360°) Add this sum to the table.

Have students repeat this exercise using a regular shaped pentagon and an irregular shaped pentagon.

$3 \times 180 = 540°$

Have students repeat the exercise using hexagons and octagons. They should draw both regular shapes and irregular shapes each time. Point out that the number of triangles is always two less than the number of sides.

Saxon Algebra 1

Name _____ Date _____ Class _____

Prerequisite Skills Intervention
Angles in Polygons

SKILL
28

Polygon Angle Measures				
Polygon	Triangle	Quadrilateral	Pentagon	General Polygon
Number of Sides	3	4	5	n
Sum of Interior Angles	180°	360°	540°	$180(n-2)$
Sum of Exterior Angles	360°	360°	360°	360
Regular Polygons (all sides and angles are congruent)				
Each Interior Angle	$\frac{180}{3}=60°$	$\frac{360}{4}=90°$	$\frac{540}{5}=108°$	$\frac{180(n-2)}{n}$
Each Exterior Angle	$\frac{360}{3}=120°$	$\frac{360}{4}=90°$	$\frac{360}{5}=72°$	$\frac{360}{n}$

Example: Find the value of x in pentagon *ABCDE*.

Answer: Since the polygon is a pentagon, the sum of the interior angles is 540°. Two of the angles are right angles (90° each) so the remaining three angles have a sum of $540 - 2(90) = 540 - 180 = 360$. With respect to x, the sum of the remaining three angles is $x + 2x + 2x = 5x$.

Solve $5x = 360$ by dividing both sides of the equation by 5: $\frac{5x}{5} = \frac{360}{5}$; $x = 72$.

Practice on Your Own
Find the indicated angle measure(s).

1. the sum of the interior angle measures of *PQRSTUVW* _____

2. the measure of each interior angle of *PQRSTUVW* _____

3. the sum of the exterior angle measures of *PQRSTUVW* _____

4. the measure of each exterior angle of *PQRSTUVW* _____

5. the measure of each interior angle of a regular polygon that has 7 sides _____

6. the measure of each exterior angle of a regular polygon that has 7 sides _____

7. the value of x in quadrilateral *ABCD* _____

Check
Find the indicated angle measure(s).

8. the sum of the interior angle measures of regular hexagon *JKLMNO* _____

9. the measure of each interior angle of regular hexagon *JKLMNO* _____

10. the sum of the exterior angle measures of regular hexagon *JKLMNO* _____

11. the measure of each exterior angle of regular hexagon *JKLMNO* _____

56   **Saxon** Algebra 1

Prerequisite Skills Intervention SKILL 29
Classify Triangles

Teaching Skill 29

Objective Classify triangles (right, acute, obtuse).

Begin the lesson by reminding students that angles can be classified as right, acute, or obtuse. Ask: **What is a right angle?** (an angle that has a measure of 90°) Draw a right angle on the board.

Remind students that an acute angle is one that has a measure less than 90°, and an obtuse angle is one that has a measure greater than 90°.

Point out that classifying triangles is similar to classifying angles. Review each of the types of triangles.

Ask: **Why does an obtuse triangle only have one obtuse angle?** (The sum of the angles cannot be greater than 180°.)

Point out that an angle may look like a right angle, but it is not a right angle unless one of the angles has a measure of 90° or the symbol in the corner of the two legs indicates that it is a right angle.

Have students complete the practice exercises.

PRACTICE ON YOUR OWN

In exercises 1–8, students classify triangles as acute, right, or obtuse triangles.

CHECK

Determine that students know how to classify triangles.

Students who successfully complete the **Practice on Your Own** and **Check** are ready to move on to the next skill.

COMMON ERRORS

Students may confuse acute and obtuse triangles because they do not pay attention to all three angles.

Students who made more than 1 error in the **Practice on Your Own,** or who were not successful in the **Check** section, may benefit from the **Alternative Teaching Strategy.**

Alternative Teaching Strategy

Objective Classify triangles (right, acute, obtuse).

Materials needed: game board shown below

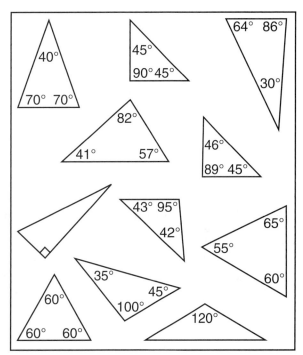

Review with students the three classifications of triangles.

Tell students they have a very difficult problem to solve. Hand out the following problem: "The angles of a particular obtuse triangle have the following properties: the measure of the largest angle is 5 times the measure of the smallest angle; the measure of the angle that is not the smallest or the largest is 40° bigger than the smallest angle and 40° smaller than the largest angle. What is the measure of the smallest angle?"

Tell students that they will find the answer to the problem by correctly classifying the triangles on their game boards, and that the answer to the problem is: the number of acute triangles times the number of obtuse triangles, plus the number of right triangles.

The first student to arrive at the correct answer wins. (20°) If time permits, have students try to find the measures of the other two angles using algebra. (60° and 100°)

57   **Saxon** Algebra 1

Name _____ Date _____ Class _____

Prerequisite Skills Intervention

Classify Triangles

Right Triangle	Acute Triangle	Obtuse Triangle

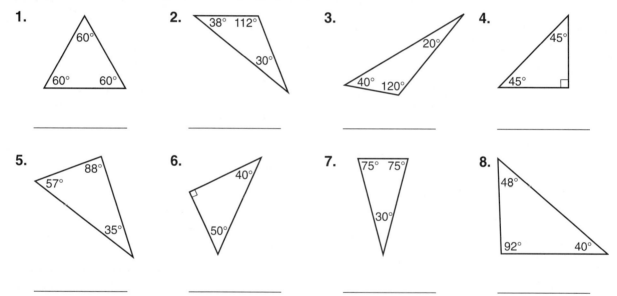

one right angle	three acute angles	one obtuse angle

Example: If a triangle has angles with measures of 98°, 52°, and 30°, what kind of triangle is it?

Answer: Since 98° > 90°, the triangle has one obtuse angle; the triangle is an obtuse triangle.

Practice on Your Own
Tell whether each triangle is acute, right, or obtuse.

1.   60° / 60° 60°

2.   38° 112° / 30°

3.   20° / 40° 120°

4.   45° / 45°

_____ _____ _____ _____

5.   88° / 57° / 35°

6.   40° / 50°

7.   75° 75° / 30°

8.   48° / 92° 40°

_____ _____ _____ _____

Check
Tell whether each triangle is acute, right, or obtuse.

9.   45° 100° / 35°

10.   58° / 32°

11.   60° / 49° 71°

12.   59° / 91° / 30°

_____ _____ _____ _____

58   **Saxon** Algebra 1

Teaching Skill 30

Objective Use the Triangle Sum Theorem to find the measures of missing angles.

Have students read the Triangle Sum Theorem. Point out that the theorem is easily stated in words or using symbols.

Ask: **What is the sum of the measures of the angles of a right triangle?** (180°) **An acute triangle?** (180°) **An obtuse angle?** (180°) **Does the kind of triangle determine the sum?** (No)

Draw a right triangle on the board. Be sure to include the symbol which indicates that the triangle is a right triangle. Ask: **Since one of the angles is 90° and the sum of all the angles is 180°, what is the sum of the other two angles?** (180° − 90° = 90°)

Work the example. Then have students look at, but not solve, problem 4. Point out that students will need to use algebra skills when there is more than one unknown angle. Write the following example on the board: $x + 3x = 140$. Remind students how to combine like terms and then solve the equation.

PRACTICE ON YOUR OWN

In exercises 1–8, students find the value of x using the Triangle Sum Theorem.

CHECK

Determine that students know how to use the Triangle Sum Theorem.

Students who successfully complete the **Practice on Your Own** and **Check** are ready to move on to the next skill.

COMMON ERRORS

Students may add or subtract incorrectly and arrive at the wrong angle measure.

Students who made more than 2 errors in the **Practice on Your Own,** or who were not successful in the **Check** section, may benefit from the **Alternative Teaching Strategy.**

Alternative Teaching Strategy

Objective Use the Triangle Sum Theorem to find the measures of missing angles.

Materials needed: multiple copies of game pieces and game boards (enlarged)

Review the Triangle Sum Theorem with students. Then hand out the game pieces.

Game pieces (first round)

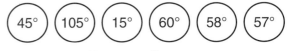

Game board (first round)

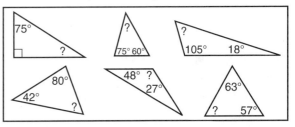

Tell students they are going to play "Find that Triangle" using the Triangle Sum Theorem. When you say "Go" students should try to match the correct game piece with the missing angle for each triangle. The first student to correctly match all the game pieces wins. (Answers from left to right: 15°, 45°, 57°, 58°, 105°, 60°)

For the second round, tell students they need to find the value of x to match the game pieces to the triangles. Remind them to set up equations and solve for the variable.

Game pieces (second round)

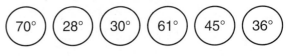

Game board (second round)

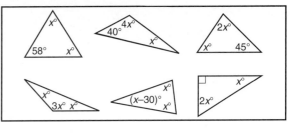

(Answers from left to right: 61, 28, 45, 36, 70, 30)

     Saxon Algebra 1

Name _____ Date _____ Class _____

Prerequisite Skills Intervention

Triangle Sum Theorem

Triangle Sum Theorem: The sum of the measures of the angles of a triangle is 180°.

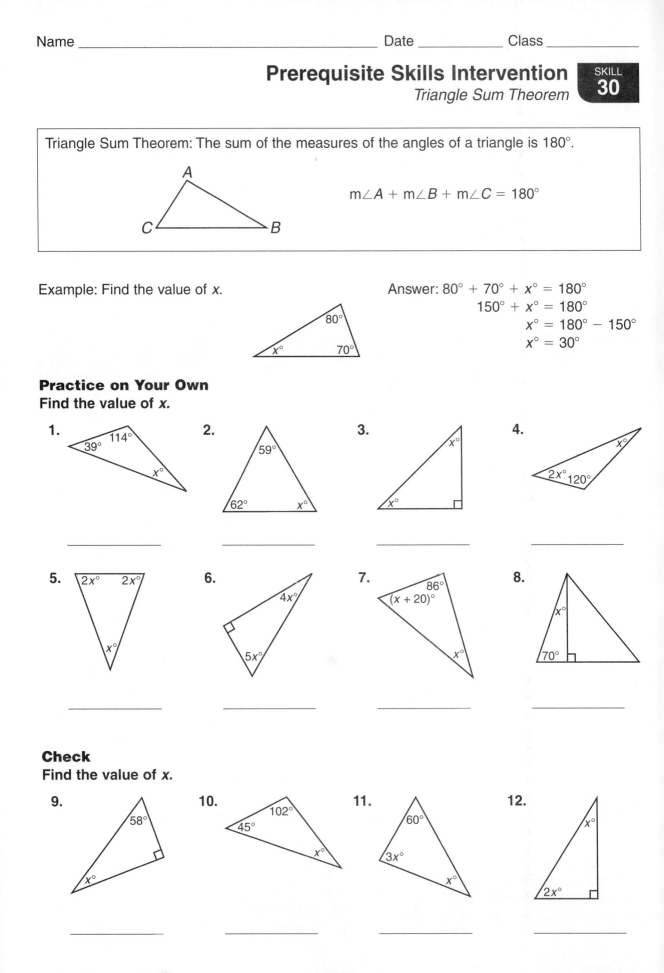

$$m\angle A + m\angle B + m\angle C = 180°$$

Example: Find the value of *x*.

Answer: $80° + 70° + x° = 180°$
$150° + x° = 180°$
$x° = 180° - 150°$
$x° = 30°$

Practice on Your Own
Find the value of x.

1. 39° 114° x°

2. 59° 62° x°

3. x°

4. 2x° 120° x°

5. 2x° 2x° x°

6. 4x° 5x°

7. 86° (x + 20)° x°

8. x° 70°

Check
Find the value of x.

9. 58° x°

10. 102° 45° x°

11. 60° 3x° x°

12. x° 2x°

Saxon Algebra 1

Prerequisite Skills Intervention

SKILL
31

Pythagorean Theorem

Teaching Skill 31
Objective Find the length of the hypotenuse of a right triangle.

Have students read the Pythagorean Theorem. Restate the theorem in words, as follows: the sum of the squares of the legs of a right triangle is equal to the square of the hypotenuse.

Emphasize that the hypotenuse of a right triangle is ALWAYS the side that is opposite the right angle. Ask: **If the lengths of all three sides are found correctly, which side will always be the longest side?** (the hypotenuse)

Point out that it does not matter which leg is represented by *a* and which is represented by *b*, but the hypotenuse must always be represented by *c*.

Work the example, stressing that you must square the legs first before you add them.

Since most numbers are not perfect squares, tell students that they may need to simply radicals. Work a few examples to remind them of the process.

PRACTICE ON YOUR OWN
In exercises 1–6, students find the length of the hypotenuse of several right triangles.

CHECK
Determine that students know how to use the Pythagorean Theorem to find the length of the hypotenuse of a right triangle.

Students who successfully complete the **Practice on Your Own** and **Check** are ready to move on to the next skill.

COMMON ERRORS
Students may add the lengths of the legs before squaring them.

Students who made more than 1 error in the **Practice on Your Own,** or who were not successful in the **Check** section, may benefit from the **Alternative Teaching Strategy.**

Alternative Teaching Strategy
Objective Verify the Pythagorean Theorem using a ruler.

Materials needed: several pieces of lined paper and a ruler

Remind students that the Pythagorean Theorem states that the sum of the squares of the legs of a right triangle is equal to the square of the hypotenuse. Tell students they are going to verify the theorem.

Have students take one piece of lined paper and fold it carefully in half (vertically), making a distinct crease in the paper. Instruct them to unfold the paper.

Instruct students to use a ruler to draw a vertical line up the crease 8 inches long, and a horizontal line at the bottom of the vertical line, 6 inches long. Next, have students connect the two lines with a diagonal, forming a right triangle.

Using a ruler, students should carefully measure the length of the hypotenuse. Instruct them to label the lengths of the legs, *a* and *b* (6 and 8), and the length of the hypotenuse, *c* (10).

Ask: **According to the Pythagorean Theorem, how are *a*, *b*, and *c* related?** ($a^2 + b^2 = c^2$). Have students confirm this by substituting their values into the equation.

Repeat the exercise above on separate sheets of paper using the following measurements:

1) vertical line 4 inches; horizontal, 3 inches (hypotenuse should equal 5 inches)

2) vertical line 12 cm; horizontal, 5 cm (hypotenuse should equal 13 cm)

3) vertical line 15 cm; horizontal, 8 cm (hypotenuse should equal 17 cm)

When you feel comfortable that students know how to use the Pythagorean Theorem, move on to examples that do not require measurements.

Name _____ Date _____ Class _____

Prerequisite Skills Intervention

Pythagorean Theorem

SKILL **31**

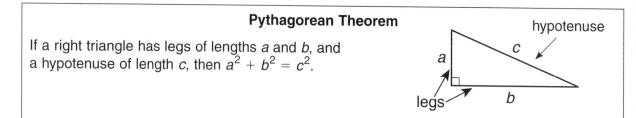

Pythagorean Theorem

If a right triangle has legs of lengths a and b, and a hypotenuse of length c, then $a^2 + b^2 = c^2$.

Example: Find the length of the hypotenuse of the right triangle.

Answer:
$$a^2 + b^2 = c^2$$
$$3^2 + 4^2 = c^2$$
$$9 + 16 = c^2$$
$$25 = c^2$$
$$c = \sqrt{25} = 5 \quad \text{The length of the hypotenuse is 5.}$$

Practice on Your Own

Find the length of the hypotenuse in each right triangle. If the length is not a whole number, give the answer in simplest radical form.

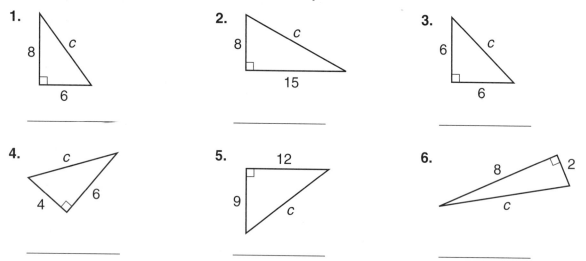

1. 8, 6, c

2. 8, 15, c

3. 6, 6, c

4. 4, 6, c

5. 12, 9, c

6. 8, 2, c

Check

Find the length of the hypotenuse in each right triangle. If the length is not a whole number, give the answer in simplest radical form.

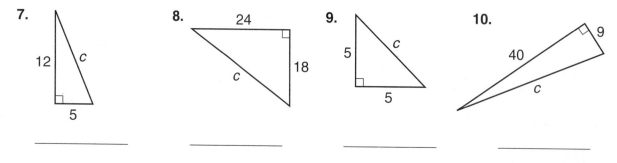

7. 12, 5, c

8. 24, 18, c

9. 5, 5, c

10. 40, 9, c

Saxon Algebra 1

Teaching Skill 32

Objective Find the length of a side of a special right triangle.

Review with students the properties and the diagrams of the special right triangles.

Point out that for a 45°-45°-90° triangle, if the length of either leg is given, then finding the lengths of the other leg and the hypotenuse is easy. However, if the hypotenuse is given (and does not have a $\sqrt{2}$ in it), then finding the lengths of the two legs is not as easy. Stress that students will need to set up and solve an equation. Work an example like problem 7 to demonstrate how to do this.

Approach 30°-60°-90° triangles the same way. Point out that if the shorter leg or the hypotenuse is given, the calculations are easy; if the longer leg is given (and does not have a $\sqrt{3}$ in it), students will need to use an equation. Work an example to demonstrate.

PRACTICE ON YOUR OWN

In exercises 1–8, students use properties of 30°-60°-90° and 45°-45°-90° triangles to find the length of an unknown side of the triangle.

CHECK

Determine that students know how to use special right triangle properties to find the length of a side.

Students who successfully complete the **Practice on Your Own** and **Check** are ready to move on to the next skill.

COMMON ERRORS

Students may confuse the order in which the $1 : \sqrt{3} : 2$ ratio applies to the sides of a 30°-60°-90° triangle.

Students who made more than 2 errors in the **Practice on Your Own,** or who were not successful in the **Check** section, may benefit from the **Alternative Teaching Strategy.**

Alternative Teaching Strategy

Objective Verify the ratios of the sides of special right triangles.

Materials needed: two pieces of lined paper, a ruler, and a protractor

Draw a 45°-45°-90° triangle on the board. Remind students that the two legs should be equal and the hypotenuse should be $\sqrt{2}$ times the lengths of the legs.

Have students take one piece of lined paper and fold it carefully in half (vertically), making a distinct crease in the paper. Instruct them to unfold the paper.

Instruct students to use a ruler to do the following:

1) Draw a 4-inch line along the crease, beginning at any line near the bottom of the sheet of paper.
2) At the bottom of the line they drew, draw a horizontal line that is 4 inches long.
3) Connect the two lines with a diagonal, forming a right triangle.

Ask: **Since the two legs are equal (4 inches), what should the measure of the two smaller angles be?** (45°) Have students use protractors to verify this.

Next, tell students that $\sqrt{2}$ is approximately equal to 1.4. Have the students use their ruler to measure the length of the hypotenuse. Ask: **Is the length of the hypotenuse approximately 4 × 1.4?** (It should be.)

Next, have students fold the other piece of paper in the same way, forming a crease. Remind students of the properties of a 30°-60°-90° triangle. Tell students that $\sqrt{3}$ is approximately equal to 1.75. Have students draw a horizontal line near the bottom of the page that is 3 inches long and vertical line up the crease that is 3×1.75 or 5.25 inches long. Instruct students to use a protractor to measure the angles of the triangle and a ruler to measure the length of the hypotenuse. (The angles should be roughly 30° and 60° and the hypotenuse 6 inches.)

Saxon Algebra 1

Prerequisite Skills Intervention

Special Right Triangles

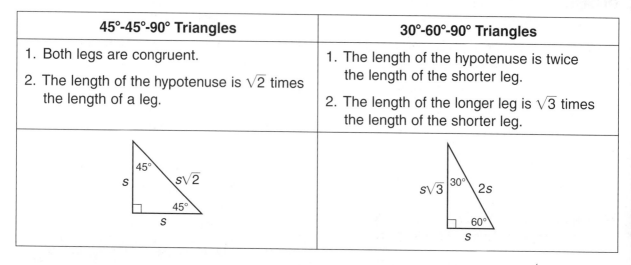

45°-45°-90° Triangles	30°-60°-90° Triangles
1. Both legs are congruent.	1. The length of the hypotenuse is twice the length of the shorter leg.
2. The length of the hypotenuse is $\sqrt{2}$ times the length of a leg.	2. The length of the longer leg is $\sqrt{3}$ times the length of the shorter leg.

Example: Find the value of *x*. Give the answer in simplest radical form.

Answer: In a 30°-60°-90° triangle, the length of the hypotenuse is twice the length of the shorter leg. So solve: $x = 2(5)$ or $x = 10$.

Practice on Your Own

Find the value of *x*. Give the answer in simplest radical form.

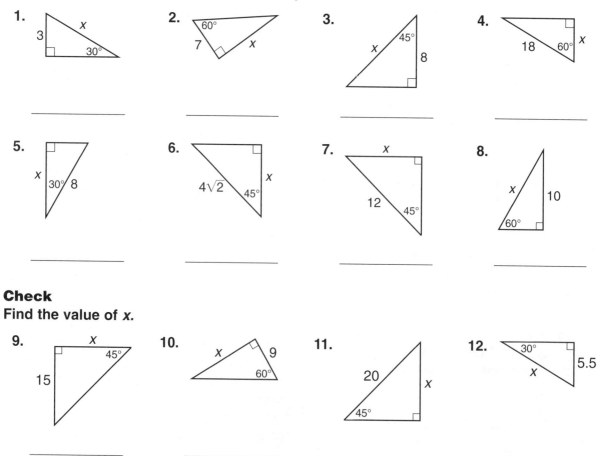

1.

2.

3.

4.

5.

6.

7.

8.

Check

Find the value of *x*.

9.

10.

11.

12.

Saxon Algebra 1

Teaching Skill 33

Objective Determine whether given triangles are congruent.

Instruct students to read the definition at the top of the page. Ask: **Are all squares congruent?** (No) **Are all triangles congruent?** (No)

Have students complete the following statement: "Congruent figures have the same _____ and are the same _____." (shape, size)

Review with students each of the triangle congruence theorems and postulates. Stress the meaning of "included angle."

Have students read through the example. Encourage students to mark the diagram according to which angles and/or sides are congruent.

Before moving on to the practice exercises, review with students the properties of parallel lines cut by a transversal. These will be helpful in determining congruence.

PRACTICE ON YOUR OWN

In exercises 1–6, students determine whether given triangles are congruent and if they are, explain why.

CHECK

Determine that students know how to establish congruence between given triangles.

Students who successfully complete the **Practice on Your Own** and **Check** are ready to move on to the next skill.

COMMON ERRORS

Students may not pay attention to whether an angle is an included angle when using the SAS postulate.

Students who made more than 2 errors in the **Practice on Your Own**, or who were not successful in the **Check** section, may benefit from the **Alternative Teaching Strategy**.

Alternative Teaching Strategy

Objective Fill in information so that two triangles are congruent.

Materials needed: enlarged versions of the following figures

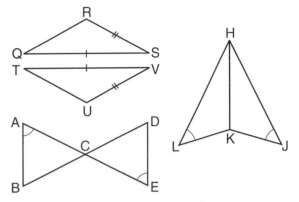

Some students may benefit from working backwards and figuring out what additional information would make two triangles congruent.

Distribute copies of the figures above. Have students look at triangles *QRS* and *TUV*. Point out that two sides are already marked as being congruent. Ask: **If you want to use SSS to show that the triangles are congruent, what additional information is needed?** (Side *QR* is equal to side *TU*.)

Ask: **If you want to use SAS to show that the triangles are congruent, what additional information is needed?** (Angle *RSQ* is equal to angle *UVT*.)

Ask: **Are there any other postulates that you can use given that we can add only one piece of additional information?** (No)

Have students look at triangles *ABC* and *EDC*. Ask: **Which unmarked angles must be congruent and why?** (angle *ACB* and angle *ECD* because they are vertical angles) Instruct students to mark the angles with double arcs. Ask: **If you want to use ASA to show that the triangles are congruent, what additional information is needed?** (Side *AC* is equal to side *CE*.)

Follow a similar process for triangles *HLK* and *HJK* using ASA.

Saxon Algebra 1

Name _____ Date _____ Class _____

Prerequisite Skills Intervention

Congruent Figures

Definition: Two triangles are congruent if corresponding sides are congruent and corresponding angles are congruent.

Triangle Congruence Theorems and Postulates				
SSS	**SAS**	**ASA**	**AAS**	**HL**
all three sides	two sides and the included angle	two angles and the included side	two angles and a nonincluded side	hypotenuse and leg (right triangles)

Example: Determine whether $\triangle ABC$ and $\triangle EBD$ are congruent. If they are, explain why.

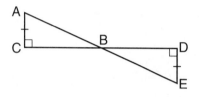

Answer: Yes, they are congruent by AAS.

$\angle ACB \cong \angle EDB$ because they are both right angles.
$\angle ABC \cong \angle EBD$ because they are vertical angles.
The markings on the triangles indicate that side AC is congruent to side DE.

Practice on Your Own

Determine whether the given triangles are congruent. If they are, explain why.

1. $\triangle ABD$ and $\triangle ACD$

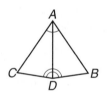

_____

2. $\triangle PQR$ and $\triangle RSP$

_____

3. $\triangle MNP$ and $\triangle VTU$

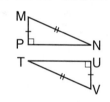

_____

4. $\triangle FGH$ and $\triangle HJK$

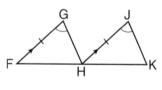

_____

5. $\triangle ABC$ and $\triangle DEF$

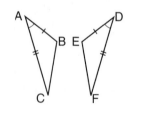

_____

6. $\triangle LMN$ and $\triangle PNM$

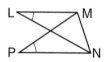

_____

Check

Determine whether the given triangles are congruent. If they are, explain why.

7. $\triangle DEF$ and $\triangle SRT$

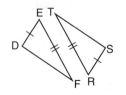

_____

8. $\triangle ABD$ and $\triangle CDB$

_____

9. $\triangle PRQ$ and $\triangle SQR$

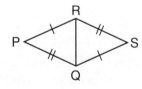

_____

Saxon Algebra 1

Teaching Skill 34

Objective Identify similar figures.

Instruct students to read the definition at the top of the page. Ask: **What is the difference between similar figures and congruent figures?** (The sides of congruent figures are equal while the sides of similar figures are only proportional.)

Ask: **Are all triangles similar?** (No) **Are all right triangles similar?** (No) **Are all equilateral triangles similar?** (Yes) Explain why the last question is yes while the first two are no.

Draw two triangles on the board—one with sides of lengths 1, 2, and 3, and a larger one with sides of lengths 3, 6, and 9. Make the angles approximately equal. Point out that all the lengths of the sides of the larger triangle are three times the lengths of the sides of the smaller triangle. Explain that this means the sides are proportional with a ratio of 1 to 3, and the triangles are similar.

Have students read the Similarity Theorem and then complete the practice exercises.

PRACTICE ON YOUR OWN

In exercises 1–6, students determine if geometric figures are similar.

CHECK

Determine that students know how to determine whether geometric figures are similar.

Students who successfully complete the **Practice on Your Own** and **Check** are ready to move on to the next skill.

COMMON ERRORS

Students may not be able to correctly determine if the sides are proportional.

Students who made more than 2 errors in the **Practice on Your Own**, or who were not successful in the **Check** section, may benefit from the **Alternative Teaching Strategy**.

Alternative Teaching Strategy

Objective Identify similar figures.

Materials needed: centimeter graph paper, centimeter ruler, protractors

Some students may benefit from constructing and measuring similar figures.

Have students draw two right triangles on graph paper. One should have a base of 3 units and a height of 4 units and the other a base of 6 units and a height of 8 units.

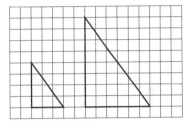

Ask: **What is the ratio of the smaller base to the larger base?** (3 to 6 or 1 to 2). **What is the ratio of the smaller height to the larger height?** (4 to 8 or 1 to 2)

Ask: **What should be the ratio of the smaller hypotenuse to the larger hypotenuse?** (1 to 2) Have students use a ruler to measure and confirm that the ratio is 5 to 10 which is the same as 1 to 2.

Explain that since the ratios are all equal, the sides of the two triangles are proportional and the triangles are therefore similar.

Have students use a protractor to measure and label each angle (not including the right angle) of the smaller triangle. Ask: **Since the triangles are similar, what should the angles of the larger triangle be?** (They should be congruent to the corresponding angles of the smaller triangle.)

Repeat the exercise by having students draw two rectangles, one that is 2 by 3 and one that is 6 by 9.

An extension of this exercise is to have students explore how the perimeters and areas of similar figures are related.

Saxon Algebra 1

Name _____ Date _____ Class _____

Prerequisite Skills Intervention

Identify Similar Figures

Definition: Two polygons are similar if corresponding angles are congruent and corresponding sides are proportional.

Similarity Theorem (SSS): If the corresponding sides of two figures are proportional, then the figures are similar.

Practice on Your Own
Identify which figures appear to be similar.

1. Figure A   Figure B   Figure C   Figure D   Answer: _____ and _____

2. Figure A   Figure B   Figure C   Figure D   Answer: _____ and _____

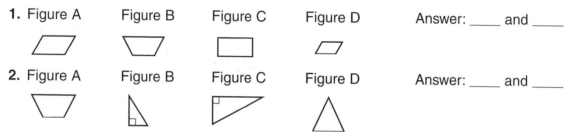

Determine if the given figures are similar. If so, explain why.

3. $\triangle DEF$ and $\triangle GDF$

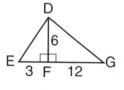

_____

4. parallelograms *ABCD* and *PQRS*

_____

5. Figures *ABCDE* and *RSTUV*

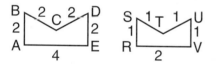

_____

6. $\triangle HJK$ and $\triangle RST$

_____

Check
Identify which figures appear to be similar.

7. Figure A   Figure B   Figure C   Figure D   Answer: _____ and _____

Determine if the given figures are similar. If so, explain why.

8. regular pentagons *HJKLM* and *RSTUV*

9. $\triangle FGH$ and $\triangle FKL$

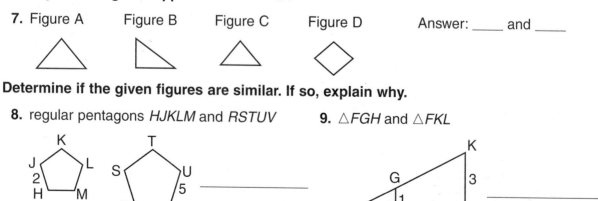

_____

_____

Saxon Algebra 1

Teaching Skill 35

Objective Find missing measures in similar figures.

Instruct students to read the statement at the top of the page and the similarity proportion statements.

Remind students that a proportion is a statement that two ratios are equal. Emphasize that the order in which the proportion is written depends on the order of the letters in the figure names.

Have students look at the example and consider the sides of the figures that are given and the side that is missing. Point out that *H and J* are the first two letters in the name of the figure and *H and L* are the first and last letters. Ask: **Which letters are P and S?** (first and last) **And the missing side, PQ?** (first and second) Stress that this matters when setting up the proportion. Write on the board:

$$\frac{\text{first two}}{\text{first and last}} = \frac{\text{first two}}{\text{first and last}}$$

Encourage students to write proportions using this method.

PRACTICE ON YOUR OWN

In exercises 1–7, students determine which sides and angles of similar figures can be found, and find the missing measures.

CHECK

Determine that students know how to find the missing measure in similar figures.

Students who successfully complete the **Practice on Your Own** and **Check** are ready to move on to the next skill.

COMMON ERRORS

Students may not pay attention to the order of the letters in figure names and may "mismatch" sides or angles.

Students who made more than 2 errors in the **Practice on Your Own**, or who were not successful in the **Check** section, may benefit from the **Alternative Teaching Strategy**.

Alternative Teaching Strategy

Objective Find missing measures in similar figures.

Draw the triangles shown below on the board. One triangle should be about 3 times the size of the other. Have the students draw approximately the same triangles on their paper.

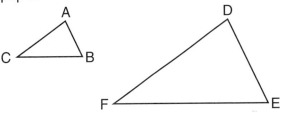

Next, write the following statement on the board in large letters:

$$\triangle ABC \sim \triangle DEF$$

Ask: **According to the diagram, which angle of triangle DEF corresponds to angle ABC?** (*DEF*) Ask: **If the measure of angle ABC is 40°, what is the measure of angle DEF?** (40°)

Repeat the question for each of the angles. Point out that the letters of corresponding angles are written in the same order as in the names of the triangles.

Have students label the diagram as follows: *AB* = 2, *BC* = 5, *EF* = 15, and *DE* = ?

Ask: **According to the diagram, which side corresponds to AB?** (*DE*) **Which side corresponds to BC?** (*EF*) Again, point out the relevance of the order in which the letters are written in the names of the triangles.

Review with students how to set up and solve a proportion. Have students set up the following proportion. Then substitute appropriate values and solve.

$$\frac{AB}{BC} = \frac{DE}{EF} \qquad \left(\frac{2}{5} = \frac{?}{15}, DE = 6\right)$$

Repeat this exercise using diagrams of similar rectangles. Be sure to emphasize the order of the letters each time.

Saxon Algebra 1

Prerequisite Skills Intervention
Find Missing Measures in Similar Figures

Corresponding sides of similar polygons are proportional. Corresponding angles of similar polygons are congruent.

> Notation: $\triangle ABC \sim \triangle DEF$ Remember: order matters!
>
> Similarity proportion statements: $\dfrac{AB}{BC} = \dfrac{DE}{EF}$; $\dfrac{AC}{BC} = \dfrac{DF}{EF}$; $\dfrac{AB}{AC} = \dfrac{DE}{DF}$; etc.

Example: $\square HJKL \sim \square PQRS$. $HJ = 6$, $HL = 2$, and $PS = 7$. What is PQ?

- Step 1: Write a proportion using letters; use the sides given and the missing side:

  $$\frac{HJ}{HL} = \frac{PQ}{PS}$$

- Step 2: Replace the given sides with the appropriate values: $\dfrac{6}{2} = \dfrac{PQ}{7}$.

- Step 3: Solve the proportion using cross-multiplication:

  $$6(7) = 2(PQ); \quad PQ = \frac{6(7)}{2} = \frac{42}{2} = 21$$

Practice on Your Own

1. $\triangle RST \sim \triangle XYZ$. Complete the congruence statement: $m\angle TSR \cong m\angle \boxed{}$

2. $\triangle ABC \sim \triangle STU$. $m\angle BCA = 62°$. What other angle has a measure of $62°$? _____

3. $\square AGPS \sim \square DHNZ$. $m\angle GPS = 65°$ and $m\angle PSA = 115°$.

   What is the measure of $\angle NZD$? _____

4. $\square DEFG \sim \square LMNO$. If you know the values of DE, DF, and LN, for which other side is it

   possible to find the length? _____

5. $\pentagon ABCDE \sim \pentagon LMNOP$. Complete the proportion: $\dfrac{BE}{AC} = \dfrac{\boxed{}}{LN}$

6. $\triangle HPV \sim \triangle UBK$. $UB = 18$, $HP = 2$, and $BK = 90$. What is PV? _____

7. $\square WXYZ \sim \square PQRS$. $XY = 5$, $YZ = 12$, and $QR = 30$. What is RS? _____

Check

8. $\triangle FGH \sim \triangle LMN$. $m\angle HFG = 84°$. What other angle has a measure of $84°$? _____

9. $\square ABCD \sim \square PQRS$. $m\angle ABC = 80°$ and $m\angle DAB = 100°$.

   What is the measure of $\angle PQR$? _____

10. $\square JKLM \sim \square DEFG$. If you know the values of DF, DG, and JL, for which other

    side is it possible to find the length? _____

11. $\triangle CDE \sim \triangle HJK$. $DE = 24$, $JK = 3$, and $CE = 64$. What is HK? _____

12. $\triangle UVWX \sim \triangle CDEF$. $WX = 9$, $VW = 11$, and $EF = 36$. What is DE? _____

Saxon Algebra 1

Teaching Skill 36

Objective Find the perimeter of figures.

Instruct students to read the definition at the top of the page. Stress that the shape of the figure does not matter—the method for finding the perimeter will be the same: add the lengths of all the sides.

Ask: **What is true about a regular figure?** (All the sides of a regular figure are equal.) **What is true about the sides of a rectangle or a parallelogram?** (Opposite sides are equal.) **What is true about the sides of an isosceles triangle or an isosceles trapezoid?** (The two sides that are not parallel are equal.)

Point out that when working with figures that have equal sides, it is a good idea to label all the sides. This will remind students to add <u>all</u> of the sides to correctly find the perimeter.

Instruct students to work through the example, step by step. Remind them to always include units when given.

PRACTICE ON YOUR OWN

In exercises 1–6, students find the perimeter of the given figure.

CHECK

Determine that students know how to find the perimeter of various figures.

Students who successfully complete the **Practice on Your Own** and **Check** are ready to move on to the next skill.

COMMON ERRORS

Students may not include all sides when finding the perimeter of a figure.

Students who made more than 1 error in the **Practice on Your Own**, or who were not successful in the **Check** section, may benefit from the **Alternative Teaching Strategy**.

Alternative Teaching Strategy

Objective Find the perimeter of figures.

Materials needed: a ruler, a yardstick and a flexible measuring tape

Have the students measure the length and width of their math textbook. Then have them sketch a diagram of the book on a piece of paper and label the sides according to the measurements they took.

Remind students that perimeter is equal to the distance around a figure. Have the students use a flexible tape measure to measure around the entire book and record their answer.

Next, instruct the students to use the formula for finding perimeter to confirm their answer: $P = s_1 + s_2 + s_3 + s_4$

Repeat the exercise by having the students measure the sides of their desktop and find the perimeter using both the tape measure and the addition formula.

Ask: **Can you find the perimeter of triangles using the same method?** (Yes) **How about pentagons or hexagons?** (Yes) **And circles?** (No) **Why not?** (A circle does not have sides that you can add up.)

Instruct students to choose other objects in the room to practice measuring, sketching, and finding perimeter. Have the students compare their answers with other students who measured the same objects.

Saxon Algebra 1

Name _____ Date _____ Class _____

Prerequisite Skills Intervention

Find Perimeter

Definition: The perimeter of a figure is the distance around the figure. The shape of the figure is not important.

To find the perimeter of any figure:

- Step 1: Label all the sides with the correct lengths.
- Step 2: Write an equation: $P = s_1 + s_2 + s_3 + \ldots$
- Step 3: Find P by adding the values. Don't forget to include units.

Example: Find the perimeter of the regular pentagon.

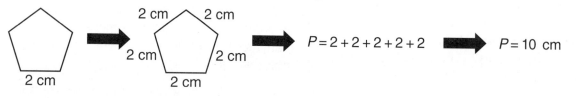

$P = 2 + 2 + 2 + 2 + 2$ $P = 10$ cm

Practice on Your Own
Find the perimeter of each figure.

1. triangle *ABC*

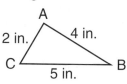

$P =$ _____

2. square *DEFG*

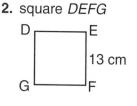

$P =$ _____

3. regular octagon *MNPQRSTU*

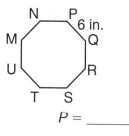

$P =$ _____

4. parallelogram *WXYZ*

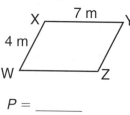

$P =$ _____

5. pentagon *DEFGH*

$P =$ _____

6. isosceles triangle *LMN*

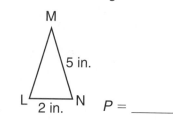

$P =$ _____

Check
Find the perimeter of each figure.

7. equilateral triangle *RST*

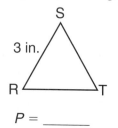

$P =$ _____

8. hexagon *EFGHJK*

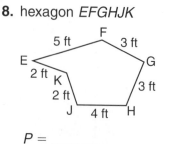

$P =$ _____

9. isosceles trapezoid *ABCD*

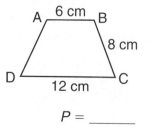

$P =$ _____

Saxon Algebra 1

Teaching Skill 37

Objective Use formulas to find the area of polygons.

Review with students the definition of area. Ask: **What is the difference between perimeter and area?** Guide students to the correct answer if necessary. (Perimeter is the distance around the <u>outside</u> of a figure, while area is the amount of space that covers the <u>inside</u> of the figure.)

Review with students each of the polygons and the associated area formula.

Point out that for a rectangle, it does not matter which dimension is labeled the base and which is labeled the height. However, for a parallelogram, the base is always one of the parallel sides and the height is the perpendicular height (the distance between the two parallel sides).

Point out that calculating the area of a triangle (and a trapezoid) involves multiplying by one-half.

Review the example and then have students complete the practice exercises.

PRACTICE ON YOUR OWN

In exercises 1–8, students find the area of the given polygon.

CHECK

Determine that students know how to use formulas to find area.

Students who successfully complete the **Practice on Your Own** and **Check** are ready to move on to the next skill.

COMMON ERRORS

When finding the area of a triangle or a trapezoid, students may forget to multiply by $\frac{1}{2}$.

Students who made more than 2 errors in the **Practice on Your Own,** or who were not successful in the **Check** section, may benefit from the **Alternative Teaching Strategy.**

Alternative Teaching Strategy

Objective Use formulas to find the area of polygons.

Materials needed: multiple copies of the game cards shown below. Index cards cut in half work nicely.

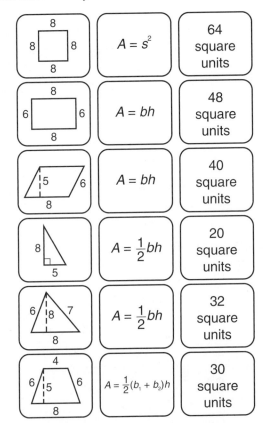

Have students work in pairs. Tell students they are going to play "Go Fish." Shuffle each deck of cards well before giving them to students.

Each student is dealt 4 cards. The remaining cards in their deck are placed face down between the students.

The goal of the game is to get the most sets of three matching cards; one with a figure, one with the correct formula for finding the area of that figure, and one with the correct area calculation for that figure.

Students take turns asking their partner for a specific card or drawing one card from the "Go Fish" pile until all the cards have been drawn and correctly matched.

 Saxon Algebra 1

Name _____ Date _____ Class _____

Prerequisite Skills Intervention
Area of Polygons

Definition: The area of a plane figure is the number of square units needed to cover the surface of the figure.

Example: The area of a 3 by 4 rectangle ( ) is 12 square units or 12 units^2.

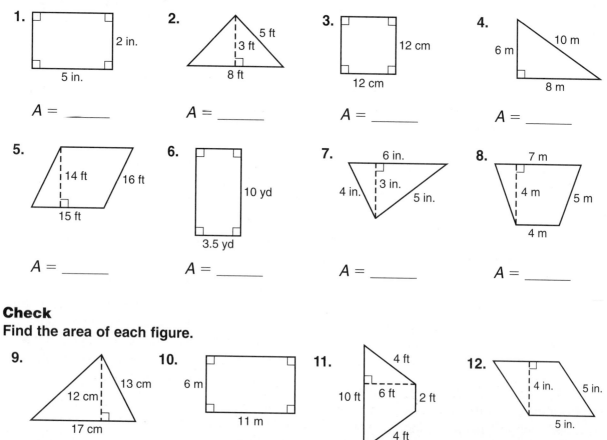

Area Formulas				
Square	Rectangle	Parallelogram	Triangle	Trapezoid
s	h, b	h, b	h, b	b_1, h, b_2
$A = s^2$	$A = bh$	$A = bh$	$A = \frac{1}{2}bh$	$A = \frac{1}{2}(b_1 + b_2)h$

Example: Find the area of the triangle.

7 m, 6 m, 10 m

Answer: $A = \frac{1}{2}bh$

$A = \frac{1}{2}(10)(6) = \frac{1}{2}(60) = 30$ m^2

Practice on Your Own
Find the area of each figure.

1. 2 in., 5 in.

$A = $ _____

2. 5 ft, 3 ft, 8 ft

$A = $ _____

3. 12 cm, 12 cm

$A = $ _____

4. 10 m, 6 m, 8 m

$A = $ _____

5. 14 ft, 16 ft, 15 ft

$A = $ _____

6. 10 yd, 3.5 yd

$A = $ _____

7. 6 in., 4 in., 3 in., 5 in.

$A = $ _____

8. 7 m, 4 m, 5 m, 4 m

$A = $ _____

Check
Find the area of each figure.

9. 13 cm, 12 cm, 17 cm

$A = $ _____

10. 6 m, 11 m

$A = $ _____

11. 4 ft, 10 ft, 6 ft, 2 ft, 4 ft

$A = $ _____

12. 4 in., 5 in., 5 in.

$A = $ _____

Saxon Algebra 1

Teaching Skill 38

Objective Find the areas of figures in the coordinate plane.

Review with students the definition of area. **Ask: Is the definition different when dealing with the coordinate plane as compared to dealing with polygons in general?** (No)

Remind students how to correctly plot coordinates in the coordinate plane. Then, review each of the steps for finding area in the coordinate plane.

Point out that it is possible to simply count the number of square units inside a square or rectangle, but when working with parallelograms, triangles, circles, and trapezoids, students must use area formulas.

Practice with students how to subtract negative numbers. Stress that it is critical to include the negative when working with coordinates of points on the left side of the *y*-axis and below the *x*-axis. Review the example with students.

PRACTICE ON YOUR OWN

In exercises 1–6, students find the area of the given polygon.

CHECK

Determine that students know how to find the area of a figure in the coordinate plane.

Students who successfully complete the **Practice on Your Own** and **Check** are ready to move on to the next skill.

COMMON ERRORS

Students may not add or subtract correctly when one or more of the coordinates of the figure is a negative coordinate.

Students who made more than 2 errors in the **Practice on Your Own,** or who were not successful in the **Check** section, may benefit from the **Alternative Teaching Strategy.**

Alternative Teaching Strategy

Objective Find the areas of figures in the coordinate plane.

Materials needed: Grid paper

Some students may find it difficult to work with coordinates in the coordinate plane. It may be simpler for them to count to determine dimensions of figures for which they are calculating area.

Have students draw several sets of *x*- and *y*-axes on a piece of a grid paper. Instruct them to label the axes 1 through 5 in the positive directions and −1 through −5 in the negative directions. Next, have students plot the following points on one of the sets of axes: (−4, 2), (3, 2), (3, −3) and (−4, −3) and connect them to form a rectangle.

Tell students that rather than subtracting coordinates to find dimensions, they are going to count by placing small dots on the grid as shown below. Demonstrate on an overhead transparency.

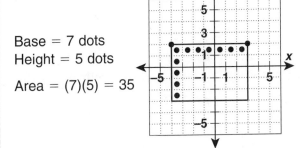

Base = 7 dots
Height = 5 dots

Area = (7)(5) = 35

Point out that for some figures, students must be careful choosing where they count. As an example, have students plot the points (−4, 4), (−4, −2) and (5, 2) and connect them to form a triangle. Then have them find the area by counting.

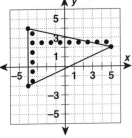

Base = 6 dots
Height = 9 dots

Area = $\frac{1}{2}(6)(9) = 27$

Have students plot a variety of figures and find area using the counting technique.

Saxon Algebra 1

Name _____ Date _____ Class _____

Prerequisite Skills Intervention
Find Area in the Coordinate Plane

Definition: The area of a plane figure is the number of square units needed to cover the surface of the figure.

To find the area of a figure in the coordinate plane:
Step 1: If the figure is not already graphed, graph it.
Step 2: Determine the dimensions of the figure by subtracting the appropriate coordinates.
Step 3: Substitute the appropriate dimensions into the formula for the area of the figure.
Step 4: Calculate the area.

Example: Find the area of the rectangle with vertices $(-3, 2)$, $(2, 2)$, $(2, -2)$ and $(-3, -2)$.

Step 1

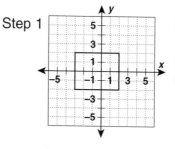

Step 2: Base $= 2 - (-3) = 5$
       Height $= 2 - (-2) = 4$
Step 3: $A = bh = (5)(4)$
Step 4: $A = (5)(4) = 20$

Practice on Your Own
Find the area of each figure.

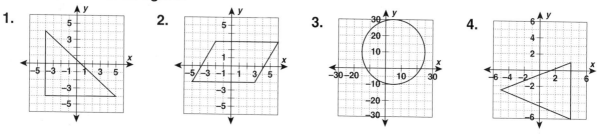

1. _____   2. _____   3. _____   4. _____

Find the area of each figure with the given vertices.

5. rectangle $ABCD$ with $A(-1, 6)$, $B(4, 6)$, $C(4, 2)$, and $D(-1, 2)$ _____

6. right triangle PQR with $P(-1, 1)$, $Q(5, 1)$, and $R(-1, 4)$ _____

Check
Find the area of each figure.

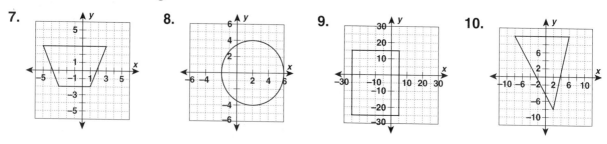

7. _____   8. _____   9. _____   10. _____

Find the area of each figure with the given vertices.

11. parallelogram $JKLM$ with $J(-4, 3)$, $K(1, 3)$, $L(5, -1)$, and $M(0, -1)$ _____

12. circle C whose diameter passes through the points $(-2, -3)$ and $(4, -3)$ _____

76   **Saxon** Algebra 1

Prerequisite Skills Intervention

Circumference and Area of Circles

Teaching Skill 39

Objective Find the circumference and area of circles.

Remind students that perimeter is the distance around a figure and that it can be found by finding the sum of the lengths of the sides of the figure.

Point out that circumference has the same meaning as perimeter. Ask: **How many sides does a circle have?** (Some students may say 1, some may say infinitely many.) Explain that not being able to count the "sides" of a circle requires that there be a formula for finding the circumference.

Review with students the formulas for finding circumference. Point out that either formula may be used, depending on which dimension is given (radius or diameter).

Review with students the formula for finding area. Emphasize that students MUST use the length of the radius to calculate area. Ask: **How do you find the radius, given the diameter?** (divide by 2)

Review each of the examples and have students complete the practice exercises.

PRACTICE ON YOUR OWN

In exercises 1–8, students find the circumference and area of the given circle.

CHECK

Determine that students know how to find the circumference and area of a circle.

Students who successfully complete the **Practice on Your Own** and **Check** are ready to move on to the next skill.

COMMON ERRORS

Students may forget to divide the diameter in half before finding area.

Students who made more than 2 errors in the **Practice on Your Own,** or who were not successful in the **Check** section, may benefit from the **Alternative Teaching Strategy.**

Alternative Teaching Strategy

Objective Estimate the area of a circle using circumscribed and inscribed squares.

Materials needed: compass and ruler

Tell students they are going to learn to estimate the area of a circle.

Have the students use a compass to draw a circle of radius 3 in. Instruct them to label the center and lightly draw a diameter inside the circle that is parallel to the bottom edge of their piece of paper. Ask: **What is the length of the diameter?** (6 in.)

Next, have them circumscribe a square around the circle. Ask: **What is the length of a side of the square?** (6 in.) Instruct students to erase the diameter.

Finally, have them inscribe a square in the circle, being as precise as possible. Students' drawings should look like the following:

Have students draw a diagonal for the smaller, inside square. Ask: **Is the diagonal also a diameter of the circle?** (Yes) **What is the length of the diagonal?** (6 in.)

Discuss with students how to find the length of the side of the smaller square using the fact that the diagonal they drew divides the square into two triangles, each of which is a 45°-45°-90° triangle with a hypotenuse of 6 in. (The length of the side is $\frac{6}{\sqrt{2}}$.)

Next, have students calculate the area of each square. (36 in.^{2} and 18 in.^{2}) Ask: **How does the area of the circle compare to the areas of the squares?** (It is smaller than the largest area and larger than the smallest area.) Have students average the two areas together. ($36 + 18 = 54 \div 2 = 27$) Then have students find the area of the circle using the area formula and compare.

Have students repeat the exercise using circles of different radii.

     Saxon Algebra 1

Name _____ Date _____ Class _____

Prerequisite Skills Intervention
Circumference and Area of Circles

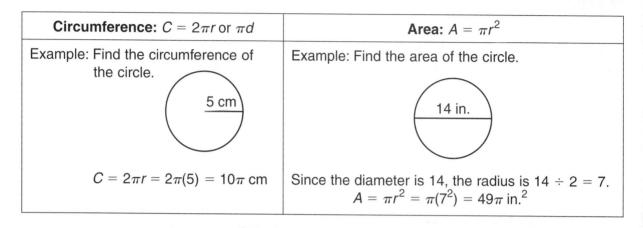

Circumference: $C = 2\pi r$ or πd	Area: $A = \pi r^2$
Example: Find the circumference of the circle. 5 cm	Example: Find the area of the circle. 14 in.
$C = 2\pi r = 2\pi(5) = 10\pi$ cm	Since the diameter is 14, the radius is $14 \div 2 = 7$. $A = \pi r^2 = \pi(7^2) = 49\pi$ in.^{2}

Practice on Your Own
Find the circumference and area of each circle. Give your answers in terms of π.

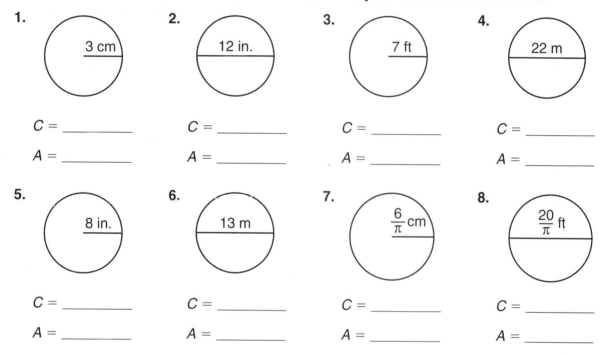

1. 3 cm

C = _____

A = _____

2. 12 in.

C = _____

A = _____

3. 7 ft

C = _____

A = _____

4. 22 m

C = _____

A = _____

5. 8 in.

C = _____

A = _____

6. 13 m

C = _____

A = _____

7. $\frac{6}{\pi}$ cm

C = _____

A = _____

8. $\frac{20}{\pi}$ ft

C = _____

A = _____

Check
Find the circumference and area of each circle. Give your answers in terms of π.

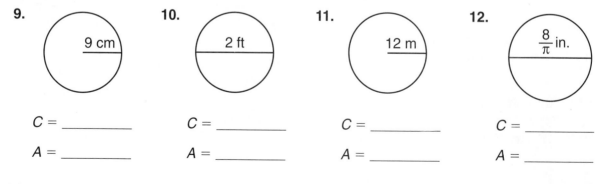

9. 9 cm

C = _____

A = _____

10. 2 ft

C = _____

A = _____

11. 12 m

C = _____

A = _____

12. $\frac{8}{\pi}$ in.

C = _____

A = _____

78   **Saxon** Algebra 1

Prerequisite Skills Intervention

Symmetry

Teaching Skill 40

Objective Draw symmetric figures using a given line of symmetry.

Review with students the definition of line symmetry.

Draw a scalene triangle on the board. Then draw a line approximately through the center of the triangle. Ask: **Is one half of the triangle identical to the other half?** (No) **Is the triangle symmetric?** (No)

Draw a rectangle on the board. Then draw a vertical line approximately through the center of the rectangle. Ask: **Is one half of the rectangle identical to the other half?** (Yes) **Is the rectangle symmetric?** (Yes)

Point out that using the coordinate plane is one way to draw symmetric figures. Review the example. Stress that if the line of symmetry is horizontal, the top half of the image will be identical to the bottom half. Ask: **If the line of symmetry is vertical, which halves of the image will be identical?** (the left and right)

PRACTICE ON YOUR OWN

In exercises 1–6, students use a given line of symmetry to draw a symmetric figure.

CHECK

Determine that students know how to draw symmetric figures using a given line of symmetry.

Students who successfully complete the **Practice on Your Own** and **Check** are ready to move on to the next skill.

COMMON ERRORS

Students may incorrectly draw the other half of a figure when the line of symmetry is not vertical or horizontal.

Students who made more than 1 error in the **Practice on Your Own,** or who were not successful in the **Check** section, may benefit from the **Alternative Teaching Strategy.**

Alternative Teaching Strategy

Objective Find the lines of symmetry of given figures.

Some students may benefit from finding lines of symmetry given a symmetric figure.

Provide students with copies of the figures described below. (Figures should be drawn as precisely as possible.)

1) a square with sides of length 6 inches
2) a 6-inch by 4-inch rectangle
3) a parallelogram with a base of 6 inches and a height of approximately 4 inches
4) a 45°-45°-90° triangle with sides of length 6 inches
5) an isosceles triangle with a height of 6 inches and a base of 4 inches
6) a scalene triangle with sides of length 4, 5, and 6 inches
7) a circle with a diameter of 6 inches

Remind students that figures may have exactly one line of symmetry, more than one, or none.

Have students consider the square. Instruct them to fold the square in half, from top to bottom (vertically) and then unfold it. Next, have students trace the crease with a pen or pencil. Ask: **Is this a line of symmetry?** (Yes) **Why?** (The top of the square is identical to the bottom of the square.)

Next, have students fold the square in half from left to right (horizontally) and then unfold it. Repeat the instructions above to arrive at a horizontal line of symmetry.

Repeat the exercise by having students fold the square diagonally one way, and then diagonally the other way. When finished, ask: **How many lines of symmetry does a square have?** (4)

Have students follow this process to find the number of lines of symmetry for each of the figures provided. (rectangle = 2; parallelogram = 0; 45°-45°-90° triangle = 1; isosceles triangle = 1; scalene triangle = 0; and circle = infinitely many)

© Saxon. All rights reserved.

79

Saxon Algebra 1

Name _____ Date _____ Class _____

Prerequisite Skills Intervention
Symmetry

Definition: If a plane figure can be folded across a line so that its two halves are exactly the same, then the figure has line symmetry. Some figures have only one line of symmetry, some have more than one, and some have none.

Example: Copy the graph and use the line of symmetry to complete the figure.

Answer: Copy the figure so that the image below the line is exactly the same as the image above the line.

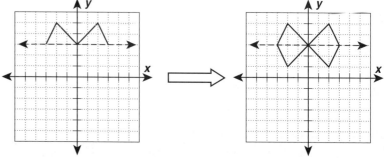

Practice on Your Own
Copy the graph and use the line of symmetry to complete the figure.

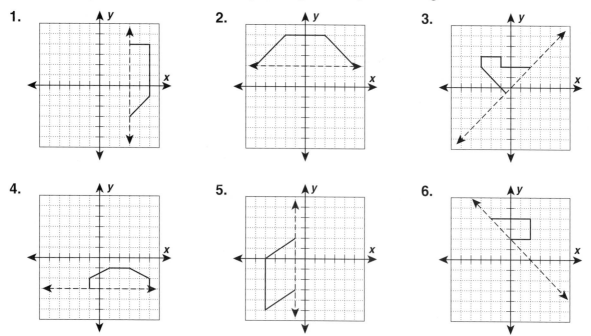

1.

2.

3.

4.

5.

6.

Check
Copy the graph and use the line of symmetry to complete the figure.

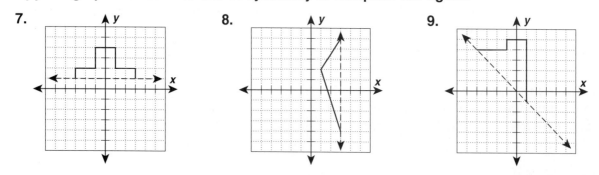

7.

8.

9.

Saxon Algebra 1

Teaching Skill 41

Objective Find the surface area of cubes and rectangular prisms.

Review with students the definition of surface area. Discuss the following example: the amount of wrapping paper needed to cover a gift box. Point out that all six sides of the gift box need to be covered. Ask a student to describe the six sides of any box. (A box has a front and back, two ends, and a top and bottom.)

Draw and label a cube on the board. Ask: **Are the dimensions of all the sides the same?** (Yes) **How many sides are there?** (6) Guide students to see the connection between these facts and the formula for finding the surface area of a cube.

Draw a rectangular prism on the board. Ask: **Do the front and back of the prism have the same dimensions?** (Yes) **Do the two ends have the same dimensions?** (Yes) **And the top and bottom?** (Yes) Explain that this is why each of the products in the formula is multiplied by 2. Work through the example with students.

PRACTICE ON YOUR OWN

In exercises 1–6, students find the surface area of the given cube or rectangular prism.

CHECK

Determine that students know how to find surface area.

Students who successfully complete the **Practice on Your Own** and **Check** are ready to move on to the next skill.

COMMON ERRORS

Students may forget to multiply each of the "sides" by 2 when finding the surface area of a rectangular prism.

Students who made more than 1 error in the **Practice on Your Own**, or who were not successful in the **Check** section, may benefit from the **Alternative Teaching Strategy**.

Alternative Teaching Strategy

Objective Find the surface area of rectangular prisms.

Materials needed: ruler, scissors, scotch tape, and stiff drawing paper

Tell students that they are going to verify that the formula for finding the surface area of a rectangular prism is correct.

Instruct students to draw two identical rectangles with length 4 inches and height 3 inches. Students should label one of the rectangles *Front* and the other *Back*. Have students calculate the area of both rectangles and write it on each of the rectangles. (12 in.^{2})

Next, have students repeat this exercise, drawing two 4 by 2 rectangles with the labels *Top* and *Bottom* and the area written on each. (8 in.^{2})

Finally, have students repeat this exercise one last time, drawing two 3 by 2 rectangles with the labels *Left* and *Right* and the area written on each. (6 in.^{2})

Instruct students to find the sum of all the areas. (52 in.^{2})

Draw the following diagram on the board and instruct the students to lay their rectangles out in the same way on their desks.

	Top	
	Back	
	Bottom	
L	Front	R

Instruct students to tape together any rectangles that are touching. Then they should "roll" the sides and tape the *Top* to the *Front*. Finally, fold up the *Left* and *Right* ends and tape them to the *Back*.

Ask: **What kind of solid have you created?** (a rectangular prism) **What are the dimensions of the prism?** (4 by 3 by 2) **What was the total area of the individual rectangles you drew?** (52 in.^{2})

Have students use the formula for surface area to confirm that 52 in.^{2} is also the surface area of the prism they have created.

Saxon Algebra 1

Name _____ Date _____ Class _____

Prerequisite Skills Intervention

Surface Area

Definition: The surface area of a solid is the number of square units needed to cover the entire surface of the solid. Surface area is the sum of the areas of all the sides and the bases of the solid. Surface area units are always square units.

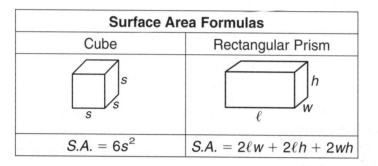

Surface Area Formulas	
Cube	Rectangular Prism
$S.A. = 6s^2$	$S.A. = 2\ell w + 2\ell h + 2wh$

Example: Find the surface area of a rectangular prism with height 2 cm, width 7 cm, and length 10 cm.

Answer: Since each of the dimensions is given, substitute the values into the equation for surface area and simplify:

$$S.A. = 2\ell w + 2\ell h + 2wh \text{ (with } \ell = 10, w = 7, \text{ and } h = 2)$$
$$= 2(10)(7) + 2(10)(2) + 2(7)(2)$$
$$= 140 + 40 + 28$$
$$= 208 \text{ cm}^2$$

Practice on Your Own
Find the surface area of each solid.

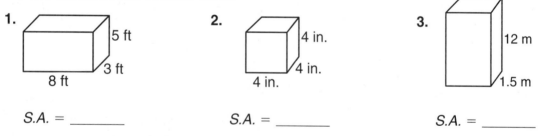

1.

5 ft
3 ft
8 ft

S.A. = _____

2.

4 in.
4 in.
4 in.

S.A. = _____

3.

6 m
12 m
1.5 m

S.A. = _____

4. A rectangular prism with height 9 m, width 7 m, and length 1 m _____

5. A cube with side length 5 in. _____

6. A rectangular prism with height 6 cm and a square base with side length 3 cm _____

Check
Find the surface area of each solid.

7.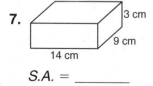

3 cm
9 cm
14 cm

S.A. = _____

8. A rectangular prism with height 2.5 ft, width 8 ft, and length 16 ft _____

9. A cube with side length 10 in. _____

Saxon Algebra 1

Teaching Skill 42

Objective Find the volume of cubes and rectangular prisms.

Review with students the definition of volume. Discuss the following examples: the amount of water needed to completely fill a rectangular swimming pool and the amount of sand needed to fill a child's sandbox. Have students give other examples of volume.

Ask: **When trying to find volume, does it matter if the space has a top?** (No)

Review the volume formulas for a cube and a rectangular prism. Ask: **Are the two formulas basically the same?** (Yes) **Why?** (If you label each of the sides of the cube with one of ℓ, w, or h, the formulas are the same—the product of the three dimensions.)

Emphasize that units of volume are always cubic units, since volume is calculated by multiplying three dimensions.

Review the example and then have students complete the practice exercises.

PRACTICE ON YOUR OWN

In exercises 1–6, students find the volume of the given solid.

CHECK

Determine that students know how to find volume.

Students who successfully complete the **Practice on Your Own** and **Check** are ready to move on to the next skill.

COMMON ERRORS

Students may forget to cube the units of measure.

Students who made more than 1 error in the **Practice on Your Own**, or who were not successful in the **Check** section, may benefit from the **Alternative Teaching Strategy**.

Alternative Teaching Strategy

Objective Find the volume of cubes and rectangular prisms.

Materials needed: connecting cubes (at least 30)

Show students a connecting cube. Inform them that each cube represents one cubic unit of volume, each with length 1 unit, width 1 unit, and height 1 unit.

Connect 4 cubes horizontally.
Ask: **What are the dimensions of the prism created by connecting the four cubes?** (4 by 1 by 1) **If you count the unit cubes, how many are there?** (4)

Review how to use the volume formula ($V = \ell \times w \times h$). Ask: **If you use the volume formula, how many cubic units are there?** ($4 \times 1 \times 1 = 4$)

Next, connect four sets of three cubes horizontally. Have students count the cubes as you connect them. (12)

Connect two of the sets so they are side by side, and place the other two sets directly on top of them. This should form a 3 by 2 by 2 prism.

Ask: **What are the dimensions of the prism created by connecting all the cubes?** (3 by 2 by 2) **How many cubes did you count?** (12) **If you use the formula for finding volume, how many cubic units are there?** ($3 \times 2 \times 2 = 12$)

Have students work in pairs. Give each pair of students 20 connecting cubes. Instruct them to build different sized rectangular prisms. Then have students find the volume of each by counting the cubes and by using the volume formula. Students should build at least one prism that is a cube.

Saxon Algebra 1

Prerequisite Skills Intervention

Volume

SKILL **42**

Definition: Volume is a measure of the amount of space a solid, liquid or gas occupies. Volume units are always cubic units.

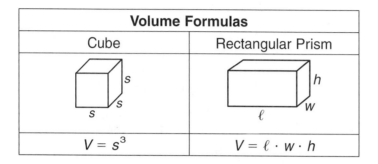

Volume Formulas	
Cube	Rectangular Prism
$V = s^3$	$V = \ell \cdot w \cdot h$

Example: Find the volume of a rectangular prism with height 2 cm, width 7 cm, and length 10 cm.

Answer: Since each of the dimensions is given, substitute the values into the equation for volume and simplify:

$$V = \ell \cdot w \cdot h \text{ (with } \ell = 10, w = 7, \text{ and } h = 2)$$
$$= 10 \cdot 7 \cdot 2$$
$$= 140 \text{ cm}^3$$

Practice on Your Own
Find the volume of each solid.

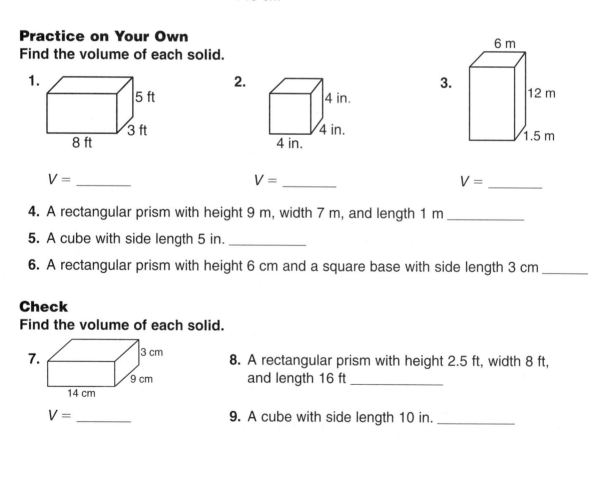

1. 5 ft, 3 ft, 8 ft

   $V = $ _____

2. 4 in., 4 in., 4 in.

   $V = $ _____

3. 6 m, 12 m, 1.5 m

   $V = $ _____

4. A rectangular prism with height 9 m, width 7 m, and length 1 m _____

5. A cube with side length 5 in. _____

6. A rectangular prism with height 6 cm and a square base with side length 3 cm _____

Check
Find the volume of each solid.

7. 3 cm, 9 cm, 14 cm

   $V = $ _____

8. A rectangular prism with height 2.5 ft, width 8 ft, and length 16 ft _____

9. A cube with side length 10 in. _____

       Saxon Algebra 1

Prerequisite Skills Intervention

Whole Number Operations

SKILL
43

Teaching Skill 43

Objective Add, subtract, multiply, and divide
whole numbers.

Make sure students are familiar with the
appropriate symbols and terminology for
the four basic operations ($+$, $-$, $\times$, $\div$, sum,
difference, product, and quotient).

Direct students' attention to the addition
example; remind them that when the digits
in any given "place" (e.g. ones, tens, etc.)
have a sum greater than 9, the sum must be
regrouped and it is necessary to "rename"
a portion of the grouping. Work through the
example. Point out that "renaming" may
also be necessary when multiplying large
numbers.

Next have students consider the subtraction
example. Remind students of when it is
necessary to regroup and how to do so.
Work through the example. Point out that
"renaming" may also be necessary when
dividing numbers, since subtraction is used.

Work through the other two examples,
emphasizing each step of the process.
Then have students complete the practice
exercises.

PRACTICE ON YOUR OWN

In exercises 1–12, students add, subtract,
multiply, and divide whole numbers.

CHECK

Determine that students know how to add,
subtract, multiply, and divide whole numbers.

Students who successfully complete the
Practice on Your Own and **Check** are ready
to move on to the next skill.

COMMON ERRORS

Students may incorrectly "rename" when
adding or subtracting.

Students who made more than 3 errors in
the **Practice on Your Own**, or who were not
successful in the **Check** section, may benefit
from the **Alternative Teaching Strategy**.

Alternative Teaching Strategy

Objective Add, subtract, multiply, and divide
whole numbers.

Materials needed: multiple copies of the
crossword puzzle below

Some students may find basic operations
tedious and therefore may tend to make
careless errors when performing them.

First, review with students the appropriate
symbols and terminology for the four basic
operations ($+$, $-$, $\times$, $\div$, sum, difference,
product, and quotient). Then, have students
practice performing the basic operations
by completing the following crossword
puzzle. Point out that careless errors will
affect multiple answers. The first student to
correctly complete the puzzle wins.

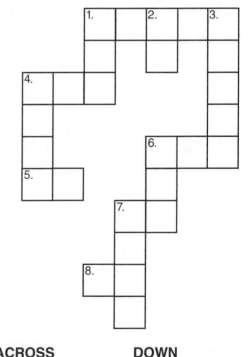

ACROSS
1. 86×122
4. $316 + 218$
5. $203 \div 7$
6. $812 - 92$
7. $224 \div 14$
8. $105 - 37$

DOWN
1. $212 - 108$
2. $492 \div 12$
3. 245×86
4. $4216 + 896$
6. $439 + 277$
7. 12×99

Answers: Across 1) 10492; 4) 534; 5) 29;
6) 720; 7) 16; 8) 68 Down 1) 104; 2) 41;
3) 21070; 4) 5112; 6) 716; 7) 1188

Name _____ Date _____ Class _____

Prerequisite Skills Intervention

Whole Number Operations

SKILL 43

		General Operation Reminders		
Addition	**Subtraction**	**Multiplication**	**Division**
Align place values and don't forget to "rename" when needed.	Align place values and don't forget to "rename" when needed.	Align place values, shift to the left as you work through each place value, and don't forget to "rename" when needed.	Divide and subtract one step at a time, don't forget to bring numbers down as you move to the next step, and "rename" when needed.
Example: $\overset{1\,1}{128}$ $+77$ 205	Example: $\overset{8\,12}{9\!\!\!/2}$ -38 54	Example: $\overset{2}{24}$ $\times 17$ $\overset{1}{168}$ 24 408	Example: 51 $8\overline{)408}$ -40 08 -08 0

Practice on Your Own
Add, subtract, multiply or divide.

1. 46
   + 8

2. 23
   × 9

3. 126
   − 52

4. 7)182

5. 95 − 67

6. 125 + 62

7. 948 ÷ 12

8. 31 × 45

9. 528 ÷ 48

10. 209 − 115

11. 56 × 19

12. 88 + 14

Check
Add, subtract, multiply or divide.

13. 27
    + 9

14. 35
    × 7

15. 99
    − 38

16. 9)486

17. 87 + 63

18. 372 ÷ 12

19. 106 − 78

20. 29 × 56

Saxon Algebra 1

Teaching Skill 44

Objective Add and subtract decimals.

Remind students that when adding and subtracting decimals, it is necessary to first rewrite the problem vertically in order to align the decimal points. It is also helpful to add zeros as placeholders so that all the numbers have the same number of digits behind the decimal point.

Point out that all the same rules apply to working with decimals as they do to working with whole numbers. For example, if the sum of the digits in any given "place" (e.g. ones, tens, etc.) is greater than 9, the sum must be regrouped and it is necessary to "rename" a portion of the grouping to the next "place." Work through the addition example with students.

Next have students consider the subtraction example. Remind students of when it is necessary to regroup and "rename" and how to do so. Work through the example.

Have students complete the practice exercises.

PRACTICE ON YOUR OWN

In exercises 1–8, students add and subtract decimals.

CHECK

Determine that students know how to add and subtract decimals.

Students who successfully complete the **Practice on Your Own** and **Check** are ready to move on to the next skill.

COMMON ERRORS

Students may forget to align decimal points, or misalign them, when adding or subtracting.

Students who made more than 2 errors in the **Practice on Your Own**, or who were not successful in the **Check** section, may benefit from the **Alternative Teaching Strategy**.

Alternative Teaching Strategy

Objective Add and subtract decimals.

Materials needed: multiple copies of the cards shown below (index cards cut in quarters work nicely)

Some students may benefit from arranging the steps in the addition or subtraction process.

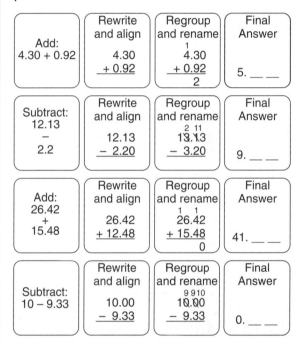

Give each student a set of well-shuffled cards, face down. Instruct students to leave the cards face down until you say "Go."

After you say "Go", students are to separate the cards into four sets (four different addition or subtraction problems) based on the numbers that appear on the cards. Then, students should place the cards in the correct order, based on how each problem would be solved sequentially.

After students place the cards in the correct order, they should solve the final step of the problem. The first student to solve all four problems correctly wins.

Note: the cards are in the correct order as shown above.

Answers: 5.22; 9.93; 41.9; and 0.67

Saxon Algebra 1

Prerequisite Skills Intervention

Add and Subtract Decimals

SKILL
44

General Operation Reminders	
Addition	**Subtraction**
Rewrite the problem vertically, align the decimals, fill in zeros if necessary, and don't forget to regroup and "rename" when needed.	Rewrite the problem vertically, align the decimals, fill in zeros if necessary, and don't forget to regroup and "rename" when needed.
Example: Add 42.62 + 9.7 $\quad$ 1 1 $\quad$ 42.62 $\quad$ + 9.70 $\quad$ 52.32	Example: Subtract 19 − 7.2 $\quad$ 8 10 $\quad$ 19.0 $\quad$ − 7.2 $\quad$ 11.8

Practice on Your Own
Add or subtract.

1. 4.6
$\quad$ + 2.8

_____

2. 43.60
$\quad$ −29.57

_____

3. 15.62
$\quad$ + 0.88

_____

4. 1.82
$\quad$ −0.95

_____

5. 9.5 + 4.13

_____

6. 1.24 − 0.66

_____

7. 92.5 + 16.5

_____

8. 11 − 8.43

_____

Check
Add or subtract.

9. 2.79
$\quad$ + 7.42

_____

10. 23.0
$\quad$ − 8.5

_____

11. 50.34
$\quad$ + 37.80

_____

12. 1.60
$\quad$ − 0.99

_____

13. 8.7 + 12.23

_____

14. 13 − 8.49

_____

15. 68.48 − 67.86

_____

16. 43.47 + 28.53

_____

Saxon Algebra 1

Teaching Skill 45
Objective Multiply decimals.

Remind students that multiplying decimals works just like multiplying whole numbers. The only difference is the decimal point.

Review with students the steps for multiplying decimals. Point out that it is not necessary to line up the decimal points when rewriting the problem, as it is when adding or subtracting decimals. Review Example 1 with students.

Next, review the steps for multiplying by powers of 10. Ask: **What are the first five powers of 10?** (10, 100, 1000, 10,000, and 100,000)

Work through the example. Emphasize that as long as the power of 10 is a whole number, the decimal point will always move to the right.

You may also want to work through an example in which additional zeros are needed. For example, have students multiply 14.25 by 1000. (14,250)

Have students complete the practice exercises.

PRACTICE ON YOUR OWN
In exercises 1–8, students multiply decimals.

CHECK
Determine that students know how to multiply decimals.

Students who successfully complete the **Practice on Your Own** and **Check** are ready to move on to the next skill.

COMMON ERRORS
Students may misplace the decimal in the final product.

Students who made more than 2 errors in the **Practice on Your Own,** or who were not successful in the **Check** section, may benefit from the **Alternative Teaching Strategy.**

Alternative Teaching Strategy
Objective Multiply decimals.

Materials needed: multiple copies of the maze shown below

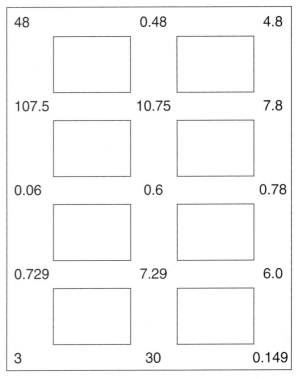

FINISH

Review with students the steps for multiplying decimals. Then give each student a copy of the maze.

Tell the students they are going to work their way through the maze by finding the correct product to each of the problems you write on the board. Students may pass through a number, but not through a line. The student to find the correct path through the maze first wins.

Problems:
1. 0.12 × 40 (4.8)
2. 1.3 × 6 (7.8)
3. 2.5 × 4.3 (10.75)
4. 12 × 0.05 (0.6)
5. 0.4 × 0.15 (0.06)
6. 0.09 × 8.1 (0.729)
7. 0.006 × 500 (3)
8. 1.5 × 20 (30)
9. 2.98 × 0.05 (0.149)

Saxon Algebra 1

Name _____ Date _____ Class _____

Prerequisite Skills Intervention

Multiply Decimals

General Operation Reminders	
Multiplying Decimals	**Multiplying by Powers of 10**
Step 1: Rewrite the problem vertically. Step 2: Multiply the numbers just as you would multiply whole numbers. Step 3: Count the total number of decimal places in the two factors. Step 4: The product must have the same number of decimal places as the total found in Step 3. You may need to add zeros as placeholders.	Step 1: Count the number of zeros in the power of 10. Step 2: Move the decimal point in the other factor to the right the same number of places as the number you counted in Step 1.
Example 1: Multiply 9.27×0.6. Total of 3 decimal places $$\begin{array}{r} 1\,4 \\ 9.27 \\ \times\ \ 0.6 \\ \hline 5.562 \end{array}$$ Also needs 3 decimal places	Example 2: Multiply 0.735×100. There are two zeros in the power of 10, so move the decimal point in 0.735 two places to the right and drop the zero. $0.735 \longrightarrow 73.5$

Practice on Your Own
Multiply.

1. 0.5×0.9 **2.** 4.2×0.3 **3.** 1.3×1.3 **4.** 7.3×0.25

_____   _____   _____   _____

5. 0.4×5.62 **6.** 2.5×0.065 **7.** 5.62×10 **8.** 0.493×100

_____   _____   _____   _____

Check
Multiply.

9. 0.2×0.7 **10.** 7.9×0.5 **11.** 2.2×2.2 **12.** 0.36×6.1

_____   _____   _____   _____

13. 3.5×0.071 **14.** 96×0.1 **15.** 4622×100 **16.** 0.09×10

_____   _____   _____   _____

         Saxon Algebra 1

Teaching Skill 46

Objective Divide decimals.

Review with students the different terms in a division problem: dividend, divisor, and quotient.

Point out that when written horizontally, the dividend is the first term, the divisor is the second term, and the quotient is the final answer.

Review Step 1 with students. Ask: **When using a "division box," which term is written inside the box?** (the dividend)

Review Steps 2 and 3. Ask: **Which term determines how many places to move the decimals?** (the divisor) **When are no moves needed?** (when the divisor is a whole number)

Review Steps 4 and 5. Emphasize that it is absolutely necessary to include the decimal point in the quotient directly above the "new" decimal point in the dividend.

Work through the example with students and then have them complete the practice exercises.

PRACTICE ON YOUR OWN

In exercises 1–8, students divide decimals.

CHECK

Determine that students know how to divide decimals.

Students who successfully complete the **Practice on Your Own** and **Check** are ready to move on to the next skill.

COMMON ERRORS

Students may forget to place the decimal point in the quotient.

Students who made more than 2 errors in the **Practice on Your Own,** or who were not successful in the **Check** section, may benefit from the **Alternative Teaching Strategy.**

Alternative Teaching Strategy

Objective Divide decimals.

Materials needed: multiple copies of the game cards shown below (index cards work nicely)

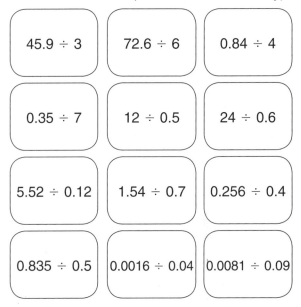

$45.9 \div 3$	$72.6 \div 6$	$0.84 \div 4$
$0.35 \div 7$	$12 \div 0.5$	$24 \div 0.6$
$5.52 \div 0.12$	$1.54 \div 0.7$	$0.256 \div 0.4$
$0.835 \div 0.5$	$0.0016 \div 0.04$	$0.0081 \div 0.09$

Have students work in pairs. Give each pair of students one set of game cards and instruct them to shuffle the cards. With the cards face down, students should take turns selecting one card from the deck until each student has 6 cards.

Instruct the students to turn their cards over and rewrite their problems on the back of each card using a "division box" and shifting the decimal point to the correct spot in the divisor, the dividend, and the quotient. Tell students they are NOT to solve the problems. When both students in each pair have rewritten all of their problems, they should trade cards and check each other's work, discussing any errors they find.

Next, instruct the students to complete their partner's problems and trade cards back when all the problems are complete. The students should once again check their partner's work and discuss any errors they find.

Answers (in the order the cards appear left to right, top to bottom): 15.3, 12.1, 0.21, 0.05, 24, 40, 46, 2.2, 0.64, 1.67, 0.04, 0.09)

 Saxon Algebra 1

Prerequisite Skills Intervention
Divide Decimals

General Operation Reminders
Dividing Decimals

Step 1: Rewrite the problem using a "division box."
Step 2: If the divisor is not a whole number, change it to a whole number by moving the decimal point to the right.
Step 3: Move the decimal point in the dividend to the right the same number of places as you moved it in Step 2.
Step 4: Place a decimal point in the quotient directly above the decimal point in the dividend.
Step 5: Divide the numbers just as you would divide whole numbers.

Example 1: Divide $7.68 \div 0.8$.

$$0.8\overline{)7.68} \longrightarrow 8\overline{)76.8} \longrightarrow \begin{array}{r} 9.6 \\ 8\overline{)76.8} \\ -72 \\ \hline 48 \\ -48 \\ \hline 0 \end{array}$$

The quotient is 9.6.

Practice on Your Own
Divide.

1. $11.2 \div 7$

2. $8.12 \div 4$

3. $4.96 \div 2$

4. $0.85 \div 5$

_____ _____ _____ _____

5. $7.8 \div 0.2$

6. $4.32 \div 0.6$

7. $18.75 \div 0.5$

8. $0.508 \div 0.4$

_____ _____ _____ _____

Check
Divide.

9. $22.5 \div 9$

10. $6.64 \div 4$

11. $7.47 \div 3$

12. $0.58 \div 2$

_____ _____ _____ _____

13. $16.8 \div 0.8$

14. $4.59 \div 0.9$

15. $11.2 \div 0.7$

16. $0.528 \div 0.6$

_____ _____ _____ _____

Saxon Algebra 1

Teaching Skill 47

Objective Multiply and divide fractions.

Review with students the steps for multiplying fractions. Point out that it is a good idea to write fraction multiplication problems horizontally, rather than vertically, to keep the numerators and the denominators lined up.

Remind students that simplest form means no common factors in the numerator and denominator and no improper fractions. Review with students how to rewrite an improper fraction as a mixed number.

Work through the multiplication example.

Next review the steps for dividing fractions. Point out that the only difference between multiplying and dividing is Step 1. Ask: **How do you find the reciprocal of a fraction?** (Invert or "flip" it) **How do you find the reciprocal of a whole number?** (Write the whole number as a fraction with a denominator of 1 and then invert it.)

Work through the division example and have students complete the practice exercises.

PRACTICE ON YOUR OWN

In exercises 1–8, students multiply and divide fractions.

CHECK

Determine that students know how to multiply and divide fractions.

Students who successfully complete the **Practice on Your Own** and **Check** are ready to move on to the next skill.

COMMON ERRORS

Students may forget to use the reciprocal when dividing.

Students who made more than 2 errors in the **Practice on Your Own,** or who were not successful in the **Check** section, may benefit from the **Alternative Teaching Strategy.**

Alternative Teaching Strategy

Objective Use modeling to multiply fractions.

Some students may benefit from being able to visualize multiplication.

Tell students they are going to practice multiplying fractions using models. Write the following problem on the board:

$$\frac{3}{4} \times \frac{5}{7}$$

Instruct students to draw a rectangle and divide it into 4 rows of equal height. Explain that each row represents one-fourth. Have students shade 3 of the 4 rows to represent three-fourths.

Next instruct students to divide the rectangle into 7 columns of equal width. Ask: **Why 7 columns?** (to represent sevenths) **How many columns should you shade?** (5) Encourage students to shade differently (dots, diagonal lines, etc.) than before.

Ask: **How many small rectangles are there in the diagram?** (28) **How many of the rectangles have both types of shading?** (15) Explain to students that the product of the two fractions is

$$\frac{\text{\# with both shadings}}{\text{total \#}} = \frac{15}{28}.$$

Have students repeat this exercise to find the products below. Remind them to simplify where appropriate.

$$\frac{5}{9} \times \frac{1}{4}; \frac{5}{6} \times \frac{7}{8}; \frac{2}{5} \times \frac{3}{4}; \frac{4}{5} \times \frac{1}{6}; \text{ and } \frac{2}{3} \times \frac{5}{8}$$

$$\left(\frac{5}{36}; \frac{35}{48}; \frac{3}{10}; \frac{2}{15}; \text{ and } \frac{5}{12}\right)$$

Saxon Algebra 1

Prerequisite Skills Intervention

Multiply and Divide Fractions

SKILL 47

General Operation Reminders	
Multiplying Fractions	**Dividing Fractions**
Step 1: Multiply the numerators. Multiply the denominators. Step 2: Write the answer in simplest form. Divide by the greatest common factor if needed.	Step 1: Find the reciprocal of the divisor (the second fraction) and rewrite the problem as a multiplication problem. Step 2: Multiply the numerators. Multiply the denominators. Step 3: Write the answer in simplest form. Divide by the greatest common factor if needed.
Example 1: Multiply $\frac{2}{5} \times \frac{3}{4}$. $\frac{2}{5} \times \frac{3}{4} = \frac{2 \times 3}{5 \times 4} = \frac{6}{20}$ GCF of 6 and 20 is 2. $\frac{6}{20} = \frac{6 \div 2}{20 \div 2} = \frac{3}{10}$. The product is $\frac{3}{10}$.	Example 2: Divide $\frac{1}{6} \div \frac{3}{4}$. $\frac{1}{6} \div \frac{3}{4} = \frac{1}{6} \times \frac{4}{3} = \frac{4}{18}$ GCF of 4 and 18 is 2. $\frac{4}{18} = \frac{4 \div 2}{18 \div 2} = \frac{2}{9}$. The product is $\frac{2}{9}$.

Practice on Your Own
Multiply or divide. Give your answer in simplest form.

1. $\frac{4}{5} \times \frac{1}{3}$

2. $\frac{3}{4} \div \frac{1}{4}$

3. $\frac{2}{9} \times \frac{1}{2}$

4. $\frac{3}{5} \div \frac{2}{5}$

_____   _____   _____   _____

5. $\frac{4}{7} \times \frac{1}{4}$

6. $\frac{4}{11} \div 4$

7. $\frac{9}{10} \times 5$

8. $8 \div \frac{4}{3}$

_____   _____   _____   _____

Check
Multiply or divide. Give your answer in simplest form.

9. $\frac{1}{9} \times \frac{1}{2}$

10. $\frac{2}{5} \div \frac{3}{5}$

11. $\frac{5}{8} \times \frac{4}{7}$

12. $\frac{9}{11} \div \frac{1}{11}$

_____   _____   _____   _____

13. $\frac{7}{12} \times \frac{1}{7}$

14. $\frac{6}{7} \div 6$

15. $\frac{3}{4} \times 2$

16. $12 \div \frac{4}{5}$

_____   _____   _____   _____

Saxon Algebra 1

Teaching Skill 48

Objective Add and subtract fractions.

Review with students the meaning of "like fractions" and "unlike fractions."

Point out that adding and subtracting like fractions (fractions with the same denominators) requires simple addition or subtraction of the numerators; the denominator in the answer does not change.

Remind students that simplest form means no common factors in the numerator and denominator and no improper fractions. Review with students how to convert an improper fraction to a mixed number.

Work through the addition example.

Review with students the steps for adding or subtracting unlike fractions. Point out that in some cases, one of the denominators may be the LCD, in which case only the other fraction must be rewritten. Work through the subtraction example.

Ask: **When subtracting a fraction from a mixed number, what should you do first?** (Convert the mixed number to an improper fraction.)

Have students complete the exercises.

PRACTICE ON YOUR OWN

In exercises 1–8, students add and subtract fractions.

CHECK

Determine that students know how to add and subtract fractions.

Students who successfully complete the **Practice on Your Own** and **Check** are ready to move on to the next skill.

COMMON ERRORS

Students may add or subtract the denominators.

Students who made more than 2 errors in the **Practice on Your Own,** or who were not successful in the **Check** section, may benefit from the **Alternative Teaching Strategy.**

Alternative Teaching Strategy

Objective Add like fractions.

Some students may benefit from a visual model of adding like fractions. Encourage students to use a model until they are comfortable without it.

To create a model for fifths, have students draw a rectangle and divide it into 5 columns of equal length. Explain that each column represents one-fifth.

Tell students they are going to find the sum of $\frac{3}{5} + \frac{4}{5}$. Instruct students to begin by shading 3 of the five columns in their rectangle.

Since there are not enough fifths to shade 4 more, draw a second rectangle with 5 columns. Instruct students to shade the remaining 2 fifths in the first rectangle and 2 more in the second rectangle.

Instruct students to count the shaded fifths. (7) Show that the sum is $\frac{7}{5}$. Remind students that they can rewrite this as a mixed number. $\left(1\frac{2}{5}\right)$

Ask: **How would you model fourths?** (Draw a rectangle with 4 columns.) **Tenths?** (Draw a rectangle with 10 columns.)

Have student practice this technique by find the sums $\frac{3}{7} + \frac{6}{7}$ $\left(1\frac{2}{7}\right)$ and $\frac{5}{12} + \frac{7}{12}$ $\left(\frac{12}{12} = 1.\right)$

As an extension of this exercise, have students consider the example $\frac{1}{4} + \frac{7}{8}$. Ask:

Could you use this technique to add the fractions as they are written? (No) **What would you need to do first?** $\left(\text{Rewrite } \frac{1}{4}\right.$ as $\left.\frac{2}{8}.\right)$ Have students complete this problem.

Saxon Algebra 1

Name _____ Date _____ Class _____

Prerequisite Skills Intervention

Add and Subtract Fractions

SKILL 48
SKILL
48

General Operation Reminders	
Adding and Subtracting Fractions	
Like Fractions (same denominators)	Unlike Fractions (different denominators)
Step 1: Add or subtract the numerators. Step 2: Write the sum or difference of the numerators over the denominator. Step 3: Write the answer in simplest form.	Step 1: Find the least common denominator (LCD) and then rewrite each fraction so that its denominator is the LCD. Step 2: Follow the steps for adding or subtracting like fractions.
Example 1: Add $\frac{1}{8} + \frac{5}{8}$. $\frac{1}{8} + \frac{5}{8} = \frac{1+5}{8} = \frac{6}{8}$ (GCF of 6 and 8 is 2.) $\frac{6}{8} = \frac{6 \div 2}{8 \div 2} = \frac{3}{4}$ The sum is $\frac{3}{4}$.	Example 2: Subtract $1\frac{1}{2} - \frac{3}{4}$. Rewrite $1\frac{1}{2}$ as $\frac{3}{2}$. The LCD of 2 and 4 is 4. $\frac{3}{2} \times \frac{2}{2} = \frac{6}{4}$ $\frac{6}{4} - \frac{3}{4} = \frac{3}{4}$ The difference is $\frac{3}{4}$.

Practice on Your Own
Add or subtract. Give your answer in simplest form.

1. $\frac{2}{5} + \frac{1}{5}$

2. $\frac{5}{7} - \frac{2}{7}$

3. $\frac{2}{5} + \frac{1}{10}$

4. $\frac{4}{9} - \frac{1}{3}$

_____   _____   _____   _____

5. $1\frac{5}{9} - \frac{2}{9}$

6. $\frac{7}{8} + \frac{3}{4}$

7. $1\frac{2}{3} - \frac{5}{6}$

8. $\frac{2}{3} + \frac{1}{6} + \frac{5}{12}$

_____   _____   _____   _____

Check
Add or subtract. Give your answer in simplest form.

9. $\frac{6}{11} + \frac{3}{11}$

10. $\frac{8}{9} - \frac{2}{9}$

11. $\frac{3}{14} + \frac{1}{7}$

12. $\frac{7}{12} - \frac{1}{4}$

_____   _____   _____   _____

13. $1\frac{7}{8} - \frac{3}{8}$

14. $\frac{7}{10} + \frac{3}{5}$

15. $1\frac{1}{8} - \frac{3}{4}$

16. $\frac{1}{5} + \frac{4}{15} + \frac{3}{10}$

_____   _____   _____   _____

Saxon Algebra 1

Teaching Skill 49
Objective Find the percent of a number.

Review with students how to change a percent to a decimal. Point out that if the percent is a one digit number (e.g. 7%), they will need to add a zero as a placeholder (e.g. 7% = 0.07).

Ask: **What do you have to remember when multiplying by a decimal?** (The number of decimal places in the final product must equal the number of decimal places in the factors.)

Tell students that percent problems can easily be converted into equations. Review the translation chart with students. Ask: **How can you represent an unknown quantity?** (You can use any variable, such as *n* or *x*.)

Work through the example with students. Point out that the percent must be converted to a decimal before multiplying.

Have students complete the exercises. Encourage the students to estimate the products before multiplying so they will know if their answers make sense.

PRACTICE ON YOUR OWN
In exercises 1–4, students find the product of a decimal and a whole number.

In exercises 5–10, students find the percent of a number.

CHECK
Determine that students know how to find the percent of a number.

Students who successfully complete the **Practice on Your Own** and **Check** are ready to move on to the next skill.

COMMON ERRORS

Students may forget to change the percent to a decimal before multiplying.

Students who made more than 2 errors in the **Practice on Your Own,** or who were not successful in the **Check** section, may benefit from the **Alternative Teaching Strategy.**

Alternative Teaching Strategy
Objective Find the percent of a number.

Explain to students that they can find percents using proportions.

Write the following words on the board: cents, century, centipede, and centimeter. Ask: **What does "cent" mean?** (100) Ask: **What does percent mean?** (per 100)

Ask: **Is 25% the same as $\frac{25}{100}$?** (Yes)

Remind students that a proportion is two ratios that are equal to each other. Write on the board this proportion: $\frac{is}{of} = \frac{\%}{100}$. Tell students that they can use this proportion to solve percent problems. For example, have students consider the following question: What is 25% of 200? Have students underline "what is" once, "25%" twice, and "200" three times.

$$\underline{\text{What is}} \quad \underline{\underline{25\%}} \quad \text{of} \ \underline{\underline{\underline{200}}}?$$

Explain that "what" (or *n* since "what" is an unknown quantity) should be substituted for "is"; 200 should be substituted for "of"; and 25 should be substituted for %.

$$\frac{n}{200} = \frac{25}{100}$$

Ask: **How do you solve a proportion?** (Find the cross products.) **What are the cross products?** (100*n* and 5000).

Write the equation 100*n* = 5000 on the board. Ask: **How do you solve for the variable?** (Divide both sides of the equation by 100.) Solve the equation:

$\frac{100n}{100} = \frac{5000}{100}$; *n* = 50. So, 50 is 25% of 200.

Have students use this strategy to answer the following questions:

What is 80% of 50? (40);
What is 15% of 400? (60);
What is 35% of 120? (42); and
What is 90% of 440? (396)

Saxon Algebra 1

Name _____ Date _____ Class _____

Prerequisite Skills Intervention

Percent Problems

Multiplying by percents:

Step 1: Change the percent to a decimal by dropping the % symbol and
moving the decimal point two places to the left.
Step 2: Multiply using rules for decimal multiplication.

Translating a percent problem into an equation:

Rewrite the percent as a decimal and then use the translations at the right to rewrite the problem as an equation.

Word	Mathematical Translation
what	an unknown quantity, such as n or x
is	equals or =
of	multiplication or $\cdot$ or $\times$ or ( )

Example: What is 30% of 90?

$$n = 0.30 \times 90$$

$$n = 27$$

Practice on Your Own
Multiply.

1. 0.25×72 **2.** 0.15×60 **3.** 0.20×1400 **4.** 0.06×500

_____   _____   _____   _____

Answer each question.

5. What is 12% of 50?   _____   **6.** What is 70% of 30?   _____

7. What is 22% of 150?   _____   **8.** What is 10% of 450?   _____

9. What is 50% of 168?   _____   **10.** What is 65% of 4000?   _____

Check
Multiply.

11. 0.08×250 **12.** 0.35×60 **13.** 0.40×600 **14.** 0.75×480

_____   _____   _____   _____

Answer each question.

15. What is 3% of 200?   _____   **16.** What is 20% of 115?   _____

17. What is 45% of 180?   _____   **18.** What is 95% of 300?   _____

Saxon Algebra 1

Teaching Skill 50

Objective Calculate simple interest.

Review with students the formula for finding simple interest. Point out that *principle* is always a dollar amount, *rate* is always a percent (but should be rewritten as a decimal), and *time* is always the number of years. Ask: **What if the time is given in months?** (It must be converted to years before substituting the value into the formula.)

Work through Example 1 with students. Explain that each given value should be substituted into the formula. Make sure students understand that they will be multiplying the three values.

Next, review with students how to find the interest rate when the amount of simple interest is already known. Point out that the same formula is used; it is simply solved for *r* and rewritten for convenience.

Have students complete the exercises.

PRACTICE ON YOUR OWN

In exercises 1–3, students find the products and quotients of decimals and whole numbers.

In exercises 4–8, students calculate simple interest and find simple interest rates.

CHECK

Determine that students know how to calculate simple interest and find simple interest rates.

Students who successfully complete the **Practice on Your Own** and **Check** are ready to move on to the next skill.

COMMON ERRORS

Students may forget to change the percent to a decimal before multiplying.

Students who made more than 2 errors in the **Practice on Your Own,** or who were not successful in the **Check** section, may benefit from the **Alternative Teaching Strategy.**

Alternative Teaching Strategy

Objective Calculate simple interest.

Materials needed: multiple copies of the game cards shown below (index cards cut in fourths work nicely)

Tell students they are going to play "Match Them Up."

Give each student a set of well-shuffled game cards and instruct them to leave the cards face down.

Explain that there are four sets of four numbers that correctly complete the formula for simple interest.

Remind students that the formula for finding simple interest is $I = Prt$, where I represents the amount of simple interest; P is the amount of principle; r is the interest rate; and t is the number of years.

Ask: **What does *Prt* mean?** (the product of P times r times t)

Tell the students that when you say "Go," they are to turn their cards over and try to match the correct cards. The first student to find all four sets wins.

Answers:
Set 1: $630 = ($7000)(3%)(3)
Set 2: $450 = ($9000)(1%)(5)
Set 3: $640 = ($4000)(8%)(2)
Set 4: $2000 = ($5000)(4%)(10)

Name _____ Date _____ Class _____

Prerequisite Skills Intervention

Simple Interest

SKILL
50

Finding the Amount of Interest	Finding the Interest Rate
Simple Interest Formula: $I = Prt$ P = principle (the amount invested) r = interest rate (written as a decimal) t = time (number of <u>years</u>)	Solve the Simple Interest Formula for r by dividing both sides of the equation by Pt. $$\frac{I}{Pt} = \frac{Prt}{Pt} \longrightarrow r = \frac{I}{Pt}$$
Example 1: What is the simple interest on an investment of $3000 at 4% for 5 years? $$I = Prt$$ $P = \$3000; r = 4\% = 0.04; t = 5$ $$I = (3000)(0.04)(5)$$ $$I = \$600$$	Example 2: A savings account of $1000 earned $120 simple interest in 4 years. Find the interest rate. $$r = \frac{I}{Pt}$$ $I = \$120; P = \$1000; t = 4$ $$r = \frac{120}{1000(4)} = 0.03 = 3\%$$

Practice on Your Own
Evaluate.

1. (500)(0.03)(5) _____

2. (4000)(0.02)(10) _____

3. $\dfrac{120}{(1500)(4)}$ _____

Use the formula for simple interest, $I = Prt$, to answer the question.

4. What is the simple interest on an investment of $5000 at 2% for 3 years? _____

5. What is the simple interest on an investment of $1800 at 4% for 2 years? _____

6. What is the simple interest on an investment of $10,000 at 4% for 5 years? _____

7. A savings account of $2500 earned $225 simple interest in 3 years. Find the interest rate. _____

8. A certificate of deposit in the amount of $25,000 earned $2000 simple interest in 2 years. Find the interest rate. _____

Check
Evaluate.

9. (1000)(0.05)(4) _____

10. (2500)(0.04)(5) _____

11. $\dfrac{180}{(6000)(2)}$ _____

Use the formula for simple interest, $I = Prt$, to answer the question.

12. What is the simple interest on an investment of $8000 at 6% for 5 years? _____

13. What is the simple interest on an investment of $75,000 at 8% for 2 years? _____

14. A savings account of $50,000 earned $25,000 simple interest in 10 years. Find the interest rate. _____

Saxon Algebra 1

Prerequisite Skills Intervention

Add and Subtract Integers

Teaching Skill 51

Objective Add and subtract integers.

Explain to students that adding and subtracting integers is best understood by thinking about absolute values, that is, the numbers without the negative signs.

Review with students how to add integers with the same signs. Ask: **If both signs are positive, what will be the sign of the sum?** (positive) **If both signs are negative, what will be the sign of the sum?** (negative) **Does it matter which number is larger?** (No) Work through Example 1.

Review with students how to add integers with opposite signs. Stress that the sign of the sum is determined by the larger number. Work through Example 2.

Review with students how to subtract integers. Ask: **What is the opposite of 5?** (−5) **What is the opposite of −8?** (+8) Work through Example 3.

Remind students that zero is neither positive nor negative. Ask: **When is the sum of two integers zero?** (when the numbers are opposites, e.g. 4 and −4)

Have students complete the exercises.

PRACTICE ON YOUR OWN

In exercises 1–12, students add and subtract integers.

CHECK

Determine that students know how to add and subtract integers.

Students who successfully complete the **Practice on Your Own** and **Check** are ready to move on to the next skill.

COMMON ERRORS

Students may confuse a subtraction sign with a negative sign.

Students who made more than 2 errors in the **Practice on Your Own,** or who were not successful in the **Check** section, may benefit from the **Alternative Teaching Strategy.**

Alternative Teaching Strategy

Objective Add and subtract integers using a number line.

Materials needed: copies of the number lines shown below.

Some students may benefit from visualizing addition and subtraction using a number line. Give each student copies of the number lines. Tell students they are going to add integers using the number lines.

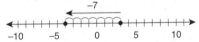

Write "3 + (−7)" on the board. Direct students' attention to the first number line. Ask: **What do each of the tick marks represent on the number lines?** (one unit)

Instruct students to place a dot on the number 3. Ask: **If you were going to add 7 to 3, which direction would you move on the number line?** (right) **Since you are adding −7 instead, which way do you move?** (left) Instruct students to move 7 units to the left. Ask: **What is the result?** (−4)

Next, have students use the second number line to add −13 + 15. Ask: **Where do you place your first dot?** (−13) **In which direction should you move?** (right) Make sure students arrive at 2 as an answer.

After students have a good understanding of adding integers, explain how to use the number line to subtract integers. Have students use the third and fourth number lines to practice the following: 8 − 14 and −2 − (−9). Make sure students know to move to the left when subtracting positive numbers and to the right when subtracting negative numbers (the opposite of when adding).

Have the students make up additional problems and draw their own number lines.

101   **Saxon** Algebra 1

Name _____ Date _____ Class _____

Prerequisite Skills Intervention
Add and Subtract Integers

Adding Integers		Subtracting Integers
Same Signs	Opposite Signs	
Step 1: Ignore the signs.	Step 1: Ignore the signs.	Instead of subtracting, add the opposite of the second number and then use the rules for adding integers.
Step 2: Add the two numbers.	Step 2: Subtract the smaller number from the larger number.	
Step 3: Add the sign of the larger number to the answer.	Step 3: Add the sign of the larger number to the answer.	
Example 1: Add $-3 + (-9)$. $3 + 9 = 12$ Since both numbers are negative, the answer is also negative. $-3 + (-9) = -12$	Example 2: Add $7 + (-12)$. $12 - 7 = 5$ Since the larger number is negative $(12 > 7)$, the answer is also negative. $7 + (-12) = -5$	Example 3: Subtract $6 - (-3)$. The opposite of -3 is 3. $6 + 3 = 9$

Practice on Your Own
Perform each indicated operation.

1. $-11 + 16$

2. $-22 + 18$

3. $15 - (-10)$

4. $-3 - 14$

_____

5. $20 + (-9)$

6. $-6 + (-5)$

7. $6 - (-13)$

8. $8 - 14$

_____

9. $-100 + 95$

10. $-7 + (-10)$

11. $-10 - (-10)$

12. $-25 - (-40)$

_____

Check
Perform each indicated operation.

13. $-2 + 8$

14. $10 - 18$

15. $14 + (-21)$

16. $7 - (-3)$

_____

17. $40 + (-35)$

18. $-17 - 4$

19. $-12 + 12$

20. $18 - (-13)$

_____

Saxon Algebra 1

Teaching Skill 52

Objective Multiply and divide integers.

Inform students that multiplying and dividing integers is just like multiplying and dividing whole numbers; the only difference is determining the sign of the final product or quotient.

Review with students the rule for multiplying and dividing integers with like signs. Point out that the sign of the answer is determined by the number of factors that have a negative sign. If none (0) of the factors are negative, the product or quotient is positive. Likewise, if both (2) of the factors are negative, the product or quotient is positive. Ask: **Does it matter which number is larger or if the two numbers have the same value?** (No)

Next, review the rule for multiplying and dividing integers with unlike signs. Ask: **What does "unlike" mean?** (One of the signs is negative and the other is positive.) Ask: **Does it matter which number is larger or if the two numbers have the same value?** (No)

Have students complete the exercises.

PRACTICE ON YOUR OWN

In exercises 1–12, students multiply and divide integers.

CHECK

Determine that students know how to multiply and divide integers.

Students who successfully complete the **Practice on Your Own** and **Check** are ready to move on to the next skill.

COMMON ERRORS

Students may forget to include the negative sign when multiplying or dividing integers with unlike signs.

Students who made more than 2 errors in the **Practice on Your Own,** or who were not successful in the **Check** section, may benefit from the **Alternative Teaching Strategy.**

Alternative Teaching Strategy

Objective Multiply and divide integers using flashcards.

Materials needed: multiple copies of the flashcards shown below

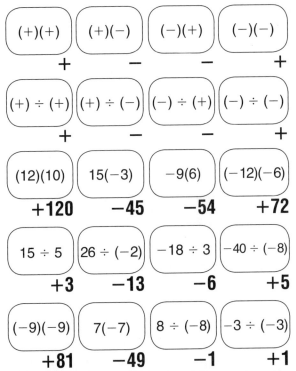

Have students work in pairs. Give each pair of students one set of flashcards. Have them divide the cards into two groups; one group with positive and negative signs only, and one group with both numbers and signs.

Instruct students to shuffle the group of cards that has signs only. Students should take turns drawing a card and stating a rule such as "positive times negative is negative."

When students show an understanding of how the products and quotients of signs work, instruct them to switch to the cards that have numbers.

Again, students should shuffle the cards and repeat the process described above.

As an extension of this exercise, have students create additional cards with a variety of sign combinations.

Saxon Algebra 1

Name _____ Date _____ Class _____

Prerequisite Skills Intervention
Multiply and Divide Integers

Multiplying and Dividing Integers	
Like Signs	Unlike Signs
Rule: When multiplying or dividing two integers with like signs (both positive or both negative), the product or quotient is always positive.	Rule: When multiplying or dividing two integers with unlike signs (one positive and one negative), the product or quotient is always negative.
Example 1: Multiply $-5(-10)$. The signs are the same so the product is $+50$.	Example 2: Divide $27 \div (-9)$. The signs are different so the quotient is -3.

Practice on Your Own
Perform each indicated operation.

1. $5(-3)$

2. $24 \div (-6)$

3. $-11(5)$

4. $-40 \div 5$

_____ _____ _____ _____

5. $-9(-7)$

6. $-18 \div (-3)$

7. $-25(6)$

8. $\dfrac{-60}{4}$

_____ _____ _____ _____

9. $13(2)$

10. $\dfrac{-49}{-7}$

11. $-8(4)$

12. $\dfrac{48}{-16}$

_____ _____ _____ _____

Check
Perform each indicated operation.

13. $7(-10)$

14. $-42 \div (-7)$

15. $-8(9)$

16. $35 \div (-5)$

_____ _____ _____ _____

17. $-4(-16)$

18. $-144 \div 12$

19. $-3(-3)$

20. $\dfrac{-120}{-10}$

_____ _____ _____ _____

Saxon Algebra 1

Prerequisite Skills Intervention
Simplify Radical Expressions

SKILL 53

Teaching Skill 53
Objective Simplify radical expressions.

Review with students the definition of simplest form. Ask: **Is $\sqrt{4}$ written in simplest form?** (No) **Why or why not?** (4 is a perfect square factor.) **Is $\sqrt{\dfrac{1}{7}}$ written in simplest form?** (No, because there is a fraction under the radical sign.) **Is $\dfrac{\sqrt{5}}{3}$ written in simplest form?** (Yes, even though there is a fraction, the denominator does not have a radical in it.)

Next, review with students how to simplify radical expressions. Work through each example. Point out that when the expression involves a product or a fraction, it may be more convenient to multiply or divide first, then simplify. Provide the following example: $\sqrt{20}\sqrt{5}$. Ask: **Is 20 or 5 a perfect square?** (No) **If you multiply first, do you get a perfect square inside the radical?** (Yes, 100) Provide a similar example using a fraction (e.g. $\sqrt{\dfrac{45}{5}}$).

Have students complete the exercises.

PRACTICE ON YOUR OWN
In exercises 1–8, students simplify radical expressions.

CHECK
Determine that students know how to simplify radical expressions.

Students who successfully complete the **Practice on Your Own** and **Check** are ready to move on to the next skill.

COMMON ERRORS
Students may leave a radical expression in the denominator of a fraction.

Students who made more than 2 errors in the **Practice on Your Own,** or who were not successful in the **Check** section, may benefit from the **Alternative Teaching Strategy.**

Alternative Teaching Strategy
Objective Simplify radical expressions.

Some students may benefit from seeing the connection between square roots and squares more directly.

Remind students that the first step in simplifying a radical is to check for perfect squares. If the number inside the radical is the square of an integer, it can be simplified. Write the following problem on the board:
$$\sqrt{49} = \sqrt{7 \cdot 7} = \sqrt{7^2}$$

Ask: **Since taking the square root of a number is the inverse of squaring the number, what can be said about the square root of a number squared?** (It is equal to the number.)

Have students complete the following table.

n	n^2	$\sqrt{}$	$\sqrt{n^2} = n$
1	1	$\sqrt{1}$	$\sqrt{1^2} = 1$
2	4	$\sqrt{4}$	$\sqrt{2^2} = 2$
3	9	$\sqrt{9}$	$\sqrt{3^2} = 3$
4		$\sqrt{}$	$\sqrt{} =$
5		$\sqrt{}$	$\sqrt{} =$
6		$\sqrt{}$	$\sqrt{} =$
7		$\sqrt{}$	$\sqrt{} =$
8		$\sqrt{}$	$\sqrt{} =$
9		$\sqrt{}$	$\sqrt{} =$
10		$\sqrt{}$	$\sqrt{} =$

Write the problems below on the board. Have students rewrite the problems as n^2 and then simplify. Remind students that if the expression is a product, they can simplify each term separately and then multiply. Likewise, if the expression is a fraction, they can simplify the numerator and the denominator one at a time.

$\sqrt{16}\ \left(\sqrt{4^2} = 4\right)$; $\sqrt{81}\ \left(\sqrt{9^2} = 9\right)$;

$\sqrt{36}\sqrt{100}\ \left(\sqrt{6^2} = 6,\ \sqrt{10^2} = 10,\ 6 \cdot 10 = 60\right)$

$\sqrt{\dfrac{9}{25}}\ \left(\dfrac{\sqrt{9}}{\sqrt{25}} = \dfrac{\sqrt{3^2}}{\sqrt{5^2}} = \dfrac{3}{5}\right)$

Saxon Algebra 1

Prerequisite Skills Intervention

Simplify Radical Expressions

SKILL 53

Definition: A radical expression is in *simplest form* when all of the following conditions are met.

1. The number, or expression, under the radical sign contains no perfect square factors (other than 1).

2. The expression under the radical sign does not contain a fraction.

3. If the expression is a fraction, the denominator does not contain a radical expression.

How to Simplify Radical Expressions		
Look for perfect square factors and simplify these first. If the radical expression is preceded by a negative sign, then the answer is negative.	If the expression is a product, simplify then multiply, or multiply then simplify, whichever is most convenient.	If the expression is (or contains) a fraction, simplify then divide, or divide then simplify, whichever is most convenient.
Example 1: Simplify $\sqrt{81}$. Since 81 is a perfect square factor, simplify the expression to 9. $\sqrt{81} = \sqrt{9 \cdot 9} = 9$ $-\sqrt{81} = -\sqrt{9 \cdot 9} = -9$	Example 2: Simplify $\sqrt{25}\sqrt{16}$. Since both numbers are perfect squares, simplify then multiply: $\sqrt{5 \cdot 5}\sqrt{4 \cdot 4} = 5 \cdot 4 = 20$	Example 3: Simplify $-\sqrt{\dfrac{4}{49}}$. $-\sqrt{\dfrac{4}{49}} = -\dfrac{\sqrt{2 \cdot 2}}{\sqrt{7 \cdot 7}} = -\dfrac{2}{7}$

Practice on Your Own

Simplify each expression.

1. $\sqrt{25}$

2. $\sqrt{9}\sqrt{36}$

3. $\sqrt{\dfrac{81}{121}}$

4. $-\sqrt{81}$

_____ _____ _____ _____

5. $\sqrt{100}\sqrt{4}$

6. $\sqrt{2(32)}$

7. $\sqrt{169}$

8. $-\sqrt{\dfrac{1}{625}}$

_____ _____ _____ _____

Check

Simplify each expression.

9. $\sqrt{16}$

10. $\sqrt{81}\sqrt{64}$

11. $-\sqrt{49}$

12. $\sqrt{\dfrac{4}{25}}$

_____ _____ _____ _____

13. $\sqrt{2}\sqrt{50}$

14. $-\sqrt{144}$

15. $-\sqrt{9}\sqrt{4}$

16. $\sqrt{\dfrac{9}{36}}$

_____ _____ _____ _____

Saxon Algebra 1

Teaching Skill 54

Objective Find the absolute value of numbers and expressions.

Review with students the definition of absolute value at the top of the page.

Have students read the statement that begins with $|6|$. Ask: **What other number is 6 units from 0?** (-6) **Does that mean that $|-6|$ is also 6?** (Yes)

Review the general rule with students. Ask: **Can the statement $|n| = -2$ ever be true?** (No) **Why not?** (The general rule tells us that the absolute value of any nonzero number is always a positive value.) Point out that this makes sense, since distance is always positive as well.

Review with students the steps for evaluating an absolute value expression. Point out that the expression inside the absolute value symbols should be evaluated first, then find the distance from zero.

Review each of the examples with students and have them complete the practice exercises.

PRACTICE ON YOUR OWN

In exercises 1–12, students find the absolute value of numbers and expressions.

CHECK

Determine that students know how to find absolute value.

Students who successfully complete the **Practice on Your Own** and **Check** are ready to move on to the next skill.

COMMON ERRORS

Students may change negative numbers to positive numbers inside the absolute value symbols before performing the indicated operation.

Students who made more than 2 errors in the **Practice on Your Own,** or who were not successful in the **Check** section, may benefit from the **Alternative Teaching Strategy.**

Alternative Teaching Strategy

Objective Find the absolute value of numbers and expressions.

Draw the table below on the board and instruct the students to duplicate it on their paper.

Negative Value	Distance from 0	Positive Value
−1	(1)	1
−2	(2)	2
−3	(3)	3
−4	(4)	4
−5	(5)	5

Remind students that the absolute value of a number is the distance between that number and zero.

Tell students they are going to complete the center column by using a number line. Instruct students to draw a number line and label it from −5 to 5. For each of the values in the table, instruct students to count the number of jumps (the distance) between that value and zero. Encourage students to make conjectures about the relationship between $|-n|$ and $|n|$. (They are equal.)

Draw the table below on the board and instruct students to duplicate it.

Expression	Simplified	Distance from 0
$|7 - 4|$	$(|3|)$	(3)
$|5 - 12|$	$(|-7|)$	(7)
$|-10 + 6|$	$(|-4|)$	(4)
	$|-1|$	(1)
	$|12|$	(12)
	$|-15|$	(15)

For the first three rows, instruct students to complete the second column for each of the expressions. Then they should use number lines to find the distance to zero and complete the third column. For the last three rows, have students make up expressions that would result in column 2, and then complete column 3. (Answers may vary in column 1.)

     Saxon Algebra 1

Name _____ Date _____ Class _____

Prerequisite Skills Intervention

Absolute Value

Definition: The *absolute value* of a number is the distance between that number and zero on a number line.

$|6|$ is read as "the absolute value of 6" and means the distance between 6 and 0 on a number line.

$|6| = 6$

General rule: The absolute value of any nonzero number is always a positive value.

To evaluate an expression that contains an absolute value:

- Step 1: Evaluate the expression inside the absolute value symbols (as if they were parentheses).

- Step 2: Take the absolute value of the final result (make it positive).

Example 1: $|-7| = 7$ Example 2: $|-14 + 9| = |-5| = 5$

Example 3: $|0.5| = 0.5$ Example 4: $|20 - 23| = |-3| = 3$

Practice on Your Own
Find the absolute value of each expression.

1. $|-15|$ **2.** $|8|$ **3.** $|0.4|$ **4.** $|-1.19|$

_____ _____ _____ _____

5. $|25 - 15|$ **6.** $|18 - 22|$ **7.** $|0.25 - 1|$ **8.** $|4.6 - 3.9|$

_____ _____ _____ _____

9. $|-8 + 14|$ **10.** $|-9 + 2|$ **11.** $|5 - 12 + 7|$ **12.** $|23 + 7 - 42|$

_____ _____ _____ _____

Check
Find the absolute value of each expression.

13. $|-11|$ **14.** $|2.3|$ **15.** $|-50 + 40|$ **16.** $|100 - 75|$

_____ _____ _____ _____

17. $|80 - 93|$ **18.** $|-2.5 + 2.5|$ **19.** $|-5.2 + 4.1|$ **20.** $|11 - 14 + 2|$

_____ _____ _____ _____

          Saxon Algebra 1

Teaching Skill 55

Objective Use the correct order of operations to evaluate expressions.

Explain to students that order of operations gives us a set of rules as to which operations are carried out first when an expression involves more than one operation.

Review the correct order of operations with students and the trick for remembering the order.

Direct students' attention to the first example. Demonstrate why having a set of rules is necessary by working out the problem left to right instead of using the correct order of operations. ($8 - 2 \cdot 3 = 6 \cdot 3 = 18$) Ask: **Do you get the same result?** (No)

Have students consider the second and third examples. Before working through the examples, ask a volunteer to list the operations they see in each problem, in the order in which they would be performed.

Have students complete the exercises.

PRACTICE ON YOUR OWN

In exercises 1–12, students evaluate expressions using order of operations.

CHECK

Determine that students know how to use the correct order of operations to evaluate expressions.

Students who successfully complete the **Practice on Your Own** and **Check** are ready to move on to the next skill.

COMMON ERRORS

Students may always work from left to right and forget to follow the correct order of operations.

Students who made more than 2 errors in the **Practice on Your Own,** or who were not successful in the **Check** section, may benefit from the **Alternative Teaching Strategy.**

Alternative Teaching Strategy

Objective Use the correct order of operations to evaluate expressions.

Some students may benefit from manipulating numbers and the order of operations.

Write the following numbers on the board: 2, 3, 4, 5, and 6. Tell students that you are going to use each number exactly once, along with one set of parentheses and one each of $+$, $-$, $\cdot$, and $\div$ to arrive at a final result of 4.

Write: $6 - (2 \cdot 3 + 4) \div 5$. Work through the correct order of operations to demonstrate that the result is 4.

$$6 - (2 \cdot 3 + 4) \div 5$$
$$= 6 - (6 + 4) \div 5$$
$$= 6 - 10 \div 5$$
$$= 6 - 2$$
$$= 4$$

Instruct students to repeat this exercise using the same numbers and the same rules to arrive at a result of 3. Point out that they can have as many, or as few, numbers inside the parentheses as they need. (Students may arrive at different results; one possible result is $(2 + 3) \div 5 + 6 - 4$.)

If students have trouble reaching an answer, have them work in pairs. As students become more comfortable, use larger numbers and mix up the operations. For example, require the use of one exponent, two additions, and two subtractions. Be sure to specify whether any parentheses are allowed.

Sample problems:

1) Use the numbers 1, 2, 3, 4, and 5 with one exponent, and one each of $+$, $-$, and $\cdot$ to arrive at a result of 13. No parentheses allowed. Possible answer: $5 \cdot 4 - 2^3 + 1$.

2) Use the numbers 2, 3, 4, 6, and 10 with one exponent, one set of parentheses, and one each of $+$, $-$, and $\div$ to arrive at a result of 14. Possible answer: $3^2 + 10 \div (6 - 4)$.

Saxon Algebra 1

Prerequisite Skills Intervention

Order of Operations

The Correct Order of Operations			
1. **P**arentheses	2. **E**xponents	3. **M**ultiply / **D**ivide (left to right)	4. **A**dd / **S**ubtract (left to right)

One way to remember the correct order: **P**lease **e**xcuse **m**y **d**ear **A**unt **S**ally.

Example 1	Example 2	Example 3
Evaluate $8 - 2 \cdot 3$. $8 - 6$ ②	Evaluate $(6 + 4)^2 \div 5$. $10^2 \div 5$ $100 \div 5$ ⑳	Evaluate $2^3 + 4 \cdot 3 - 6$. $8 + 4 \cdot 3 - 6$ $8 + 12 - 6$ $20 - 6$ ⑭

Practice on Your Own

Evaluate each expression.

1. $(5 + 1) - 3$

2. $8 \cdot 8 \div 16$

3. $6 \cdot 5 + 1$

_____

_____

_____

4. $24 \div 3 - 5$

5. $(8 + 10) \div 3$

6. $20 + 1 - 7$

_____

_____

_____

7. $7^2 + 1$

8. $72 \div 2^3$

9. $21 + 15 \div 3$

_____

_____

_____

10. $8 + 7 \cdot 5$

11. $3 \cdot 6 - 2 \cdot 9$

12. $(4 + 2)^2 \div 9$

_____

_____

_____

Check

Find the absolute value of each expression.

13. $(6 + 10) \div 4$

14. $40 - 4 \cdot 10$

15. $5 \cdot 10 \div 2$

_____

_____

_____

16. $15 - 3 + 10$

17. $4 \cdot 8 \div 4^2$

18. $8 \cdot 5 + 3 \cdot 6$

_____

_____

_____

Saxon Algebra 1

Teaching Skill 56

Objective Use the Distributive Property to simplify expressions.

Explain to students that multiplying a sum (or difference) by a number is the same as multiplying each of the addends by the number and then adding the products.

To demonstrate, write the following on the board: $7 \times (3 + 2)$. Ask: **If you follow the correct order of operations, how would you rewrite this problem?** (7×5) **What is the solution?** (35)

Write the problem on the board again. This time, demonstrate the Distributive Property by rewriting the problem as $7(3) + 7(2)$. Ask: **What is the solution to the problem written this way?** $(21 + 14 = 35)$

Review with students how to represent the Distributive Property in rule form. Point out that the property works the same whether there are numbers or variables, or both, inside the parentheses.

Work through each example. Point out that the placement of the parentheses does not affect the way in which the property works.

Have students complete the exercises.

PRACTICE ON YOUR OWN

In exercises 1–12, students use the Distributive Property to simplify expressions.

CHECK

Determine that students know how to use the Distributive Property.

Students who successfully complete the **Practice on Your Own** and **Check** are ready to move on to the next skill.

COMMON ERRORS

Students may try to combine the terms inside the parentheses before multiplying.

Students who made more than 2 errors in the **Practice on Your Own,** or who were not successful in the **Check** section, may benefit from the **Alternative Teaching Strategy.**

Alternative Teaching Strategy

Objective Use modeling to understand the Distributive Property.

Materials needed: grid paper

Some students may benefit from visualizing the Distributive Property.

Draw a rectangle on the board with length 9 inches and width 4 inches. Label the width 4 and the length $6 + 3$.

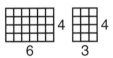

Have students draw a 4×9 rectangle on their grid paper and label it the same way. Instruct students to count the total number of small rectangles. (36)

Next, have students break apart the grid to show a 4×6 rectangle and a 4×3 rectangle.

Have students count the total number of small rectangles in each of the larger rectangles and add. $(24 + 12 = 36)$

Explain to students that the Distributive Property works just like breaking apart the grids. Have students rewrite the problem $4(6 + 3)$ using the Distributive Property and the grids they drew. $[4(6 + 3) = 4(6) + 4(3)]$

Instruct students to use grids to rewrite the following problems using the Distributive Property: $5(2 + 1)$; $8(4 + 3)$; and $6(7 + 2)$. $[5(2) + 5(1); 8(4) + 8(3);$ and $6(7) + 6(2)]$

When students are comfortable working with grids and numbers, have them draw a rectangle with length $5 + x$ and width 3. Have them break the rectangle in two and re-label each of the smaller rectangles.

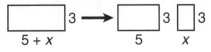

Ask: **How do you rewrite $3(5 + x)$ using the Distribute Property?** $[3(5) + 3(x)]$ Work a few additional examples if time permits.

 Saxon Algebra 1

Prerequisite Skills Intervention

Distributive Property

SKILL
56

The Distributive Property of Multiplication	
Multiplying a sum by a number: $a(b + c) = ab + ac$	Multiplying a difference by a number: $a(b - c) = ab - ac$
Example 1: Simplify $7(2x + 3)$. $7\,(2x + 3) = 7(2x) + 7(3) = 14x + 21$	Example 2: Simplify $15(3 - 4m)$. $15\,(3 - 4m) = 15(3) - 15(4m) = 45 - 60m$
Note: Remember, if a variable does not have a coefficient, assume the coefficient is 1. Example 3: Simplify $11(5 + y)$. $11\,(5 + 1y) = 11(5) + 11(1y) = 55 + 11y$	

Practice on Your Own
Simplify each expression.

1. $5(x + 6)$

2. $5(z - 7)$

3. $(n - 2)2$

4. $4(3 + k)$

_____   _____   _____   _____

5. $8(6 - y)$

6. $(m + 3)6$

7. $10(p + 1)$

8. $(20 - c)3$

_____   _____   _____   _____

9. $(q - 1)7$

10. $11(5 + t)$

11. $(7 + b)2$

12. $9(4 - w)$

_____   _____   _____   _____

Check
Simplify each expression.

13. $12(c + 2)$

14. $(3 - a)5$

15. $25(1 + d)$

16. $10(5 - j)$

_____   _____   _____   _____

17. $(x + 3)4$

18. $15(2 + y)$

19. $3(g - 25)$

20. $(m - 1)9$

_____   _____   _____   _____

Saxon Algebra 1

Prerequisite Skills Intervention

Combine Like Terms

Teaching Skill 57

Objective Simplify expressions by combining like terms.

Discuss with students that combining like terms simply means adding or subtracting terms that are alike.

Point out that terms can be constants (numbers), variables (letters), or a combination of both. Stress that in order to be like terms, the "variable factors" must be the same. That is, the exponent of the variables must be the same. Ask: **Are $3x$ and $3x^2$ like terms?** (No) **Why not?** (Because the first term has an exponent of 1 and the second term has an exponent of 2.) Give several examples of like terms and unlike terms.

Remind students that a coefficient is the number that precedes the variable. Ask: **In the term $7x$, what is the coefficient?** (7) Explain that if a variable does not have a coefficient, it is understood to be 1. Explain to students that combining like terms is achieved by adding (or subtracting) the coefficients of the like terms.

Review both examples and then have students complete the exercises.

PRACTICE ON YOUR OWN

In exercises 1–14, students simplify expressions by combining like terms.

CHECK

Determine that students know how to combine like terms.

Students who successfully complete the **Practice on Your Own** and **Check** are ready to move on to the next skill.

COMMON ERRORS

Students may forget that when a variable does not have a coefficient, it is understood to be 1.

Students who made more than 3 errors in the **Practice on Your Own,** or who were not successful in the **Check** section, may benefit from the **Alternative Teaching Strategy.**

Alternative Teaching Strategy

Objective Simplify expressions by combining like terms.

Some students may benefit from physically matching like terms using circles, squares, triangles, etc.

Remind students that like terms must have identical variable factors.

Write the following problem on the board:

$$12x + 1 + 7x + 19$$

Circle the constants and draw a square around the terms with x's.

Ask: **Can you add circles and squares and get a common term?** (No) **Can you add constants and variables and get a common term?** (No) **What is the sum of the terms that have squares around them?** ($19x$) **What is the sum of the terms that have circles around them?** (20) **What is the simplified form of the expression?** ($19x + 20$)

Point out that this method works well when there are multiple types of terms. Write the following problem on the board:

$$7n + 13m - 6 - 3n + 2m + 10 - n$$

Ask: **How many different types of terms are part of this problem?** (3; constants, m's, and n's) Circle the constants, draw squares around the m's, and draw triangles around the n's. Remind students to include the negatives.

Before simplifying, ask: **What is the coefficient of the last term?** (-1)

Instruct students to simplify the expression. Emphasize that they should be careful with negatives. ($3n + 15m + 4$)

Have students work a number of problems using this technique.

     Saxon Algebra 1

Prerequisite Skills Intervention

Combine Like Terms

Definition: An algebraic term is a number, a variable, or the product of numbers and variables. *Like terms* are those terms that have exactly the same variable factor. For example, $2x$ and $7x$ are like terms because they both have the variable factor, x.

Combining like terms means adding or subtracting them. To combine like terms:

- Step 1: Reorder the terms so that like terms are together.
- Step 2: Add (or subtract) the coefficients of the like terms. If a variable does not have a coefficient, it is understood to be 1.

Example 1	$7x - 5 + 2x + 15$	Example 2	$6 + 2a - 8b + 4a - 11$
Reorder:	$7x + 2x - 5 + 15$	Reorder:	$6 - 11 + 2a + 4a - 8b$
Add:	$7x + 2x = (7 + 2)x = 9x$	Subtract:	$6 - 11 = -5$
Add:	$-5 + 15 = 10$	Add:	$2a + 4a = (2 + 4)a = 6a$
		Single term:	$-8b$
Answer:	$9x + 10$	Answer:	$-5 + 6a - 8b$

Practice on Your Own
Simplify each expression by combining like terms.

1. $2x + 10x$

2. $9m + (-5m)$

3. $6a^2 + a^2$

4. $-10t + 3t$

5. $14b + (-17b)$

6. $12d^2 - 4d^2$

7. $6x - 7x$

8. $-5f + 5f$

9. $8.2h + 2.8h$ _____

10. $4y - 9 - 13y$ _____

11. $3 + 6x + 7 + 4x$ _____

12. $2 + 4u - 7 + 3u + 10 - 12u$ _____

13. $9y - 2x + 4y + 11x - 3x$ _____

14. $16j + 8 - 9j - 4 - 7j$ _____

Check
Simplify each expression by combining like terms.

15. $9x + x$

16. $-5c + 2c$

17. $a^2 - 4a^2$

18. $11.5z - 3.1z$

19. $22m + 16 - m - 5 - 11m$ _____

20. $7q + 3r - 2r + q - 6r$ _____

Saxon Algebra 1

Teaching Skill 58

Objective Connect words and algebra.

Point out to students that an algebraic expression (or equation) is simply a mathematical way of writing a phrase or sentence.

Ask: **What is the difference between an expression and an equation?** (An expression does not have an equal sign while an equation does.)

Tell students that associating key words with the correct operation is critical to being able to make the connection between words and algebra.

Review with students the table of key words. Provide some real life examples. Start with the following two: **(1)If your age is 10 years more than your sister's, and your sister is 12, how do you find your age?** (Add 12 plus 10.) **If you receive $10 per week allowance for 8 weeks, how do you find the total amount you received?** (Multiply 10 times 8.) Have students provide additional examples.

Review the lawn cutting example with students and then have them complete the exercises.

PRACTICE ON YOUR OWN

In exercises 1–6, students write algebraic expressions and equations.

CHECK

Determine that students know how to write algebraic expressions and equations.

Students who successfully complete the **Practice on Your Own** and **Check** are ready to move on to the next skill.

COMMON ERRORS

Students may not know the key words associated with operations, and as a result may use the wrong operation.

Students who made more than 1 error in the **Practice on Your Own,** or who were not successful in the **Check** section, may benefit from the **Alternative Teaching Strategy.**

Alternative Teaching Strategy

Objective Connect words and algebra.

Materials needed: multiple copies of the flashcards shown below (index cards work nicely), blank index cards

Have students work in pairs. Distribute copies of the flashcards and have students shuffle the cards and divide them in half so that each student has six cards.

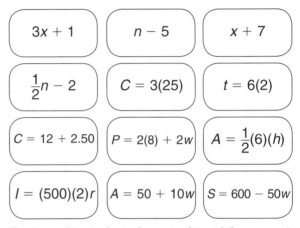

$3x + 1$ $n - 5$ $x + 7$

$\frac{1}{2}n - 2$ $C = 3(25)$ $t = 6(2)$

$C = 12 + 2.50$ $P = 2(8) + 2w$ $A = \frac{1}{2}(6)(h)$

$I = (500)(2)r$ $A = 50 + 10w$ $S = 600 - 50w$

Review with students key words and the operations with which the words are associated.

Tell students they are going to make up phrases or situations that match the algebraic expressions and equations on the cards. Give the following example: $5n + 3$. Ask: **How would you verbalize $5n$?** (5 times a number) **And + 3?** (increased by 3) Write the phrase on the board: "5 times a number increased by 3." Point out that variations of this phrase are also correct, such as 3 more than 5 times a number.

Next, write the equation $C = 40 - 5(d)$ on the board. Remind students that variables typically represent something that makes sense. For example, C might represent cost and d number of days. Or, provide the following scenario: There are 40 cookies in a bag and Tom eats 5 cookies per day. $C = 40 - 5(d)$ could be the number of cookies remaining at the end of any given day.

Instruct students to take turns making up situations to match the cards they have. As an extension of the exercise, have students make flashcards and continue.

Saxon Algebra 1

Prerequisite Skills Intervention
Connect Words and Algebra

To connect words and algebra, you must understand the operations involved and how to represent them. Key words are helpful in determining the operations.

Key Words	Operation or Representation
a number; an unknown quantity	any variable, such as x or n
Twice, three times, etc.	multiplication ($2n$, $3n$, etc.)
sum; more than; increased by	addition ($+$)
difference; less than; decreased by	subtraction ($-$)
each; per	multiplication
is; equals	$=$

Example: Jared must cut 6 lawns over the weekend. Each of the lawns takes 2 hours to cut. Write an equation representing the total time t to cut all 6 lawns.

Answer: Since <u>each</u> lawn takes 2 hours, multiply 2 times the number of lawns to get the total time: $t = 6(2)$.

Practice on Your Own

1. Write an expression that represents the quantity 5 more than a number. _____

2. Write a phrase that could be modeled by the expression $x - 15$. _____

3. John bought 3 CDs and 2 DVDs. Each CD costs $9.95, and each DVD costs $14.98. Write an equation representing the total cost C. _____

4. A triangle has sides of length 7, 10, and s. Write an equation representing the perimeter P of the triangle. _____

5. The value of a painting begins at $12,000 and increases by $500 per year. Write an equation representing the value V of the painting at the end of any given year y. _____

6. David has 56 baseball cards of which he sells 3 cards per week. Write an equation representing the number of cards n he has left at the end of any given week w. _____

Check

7. Write an expression that represents a number decreased by 6. _____

8. Tina bought 6 plates and 2 glasses. Each plate costs $6.99, and each glass costs $22.98. Write an equation representing the total cost C. _____

9. Joseph opens a checking account with $400. Each month he adds $150 to the account. Write an equation representing the total amount A in the account at the end of any given month m. _____

Saxon Algebra 1

Prerequisite Skills Intervention

Properties of Exponents

SKILL 59

Teaching Skill 59

Objective Simplify expressions using properties of exponents.

Review with students the vocabulary at the top of the student page and then the rule for multiplying variables with the same base.

Ask: **Do the expressions x^2 and y^2 have the same base?** (No) **What is the product of x^2 and y^2?** (x^2y^2) **Do you add the exponents?** (No) **Why not?** (The bases are not the same.)

Review with students how to multiply expressions that have numbers and variables. Ask: **In the expression $7x^5$, what is the number 7 called?** (the coefficient)

Emphasize that to find the product of two expressions, <u>multiply</u> the coefficients but <u>add</u> the exponents of those variables that have the same base.

Also point out that when a variable does not have a coefficient, it is understood to be 1. Likewise, when a variable does not have an exponent, it is understood to be 1.

Work through each of the examples and then have students complete the practice exercises.

PRACTICE ON YOUR OWN

In exercises 1–12, students use properties of exponents to simplify expressions.

CHECK

Determine that students understand properties of exponents.

Students who successfully complete the **Practice on Your Own** and **Check** are ready to move on to the next skill.

COMMON ERRORS

When multiplying variables with exponents, students may multiply the exponents rather than adding them.

Students who made more than 2 errors in the **Practice on Your Own,** or who were not successful in the **Check** section, may benefit from the **Alternative Teaching Strategy.**

Alternative Teaching Strategy

Objective Simplify expressions using properties of exponents.

Some students may benefit from seeing numbers and variables raised to exponents written in expanded form.

Write the following on the board: 3^4. Ask: **How would you write this expression without an exponent?** ($3 \cdot 3 \cdot 3 \cdot 3$).

Next, write the following on the board: $3^4 \cdot 3^2$. Ask a volunteer to come to the board and rewrite the product without using any exponents. ($3 \cdot 3 \cdot 3 \cdot 3 \cdot 3 \cdot 3$) Ask: **How would you write this in exponential form?** (3^6) Write $3^4 \cdot 3^2 = 3^{4+2} = 3^6$ and point out that the result is the same.

Move on to variables. Write: x^7. Ask: **How would you write this expression without an exponent?** ($x \cdot x \cdot x \cdot x \cdot x \cdot x \cdot x$) Have the students write the following problem on their paper: $x^4 \cdot x^6$. Instruct them to rewrite the problem without using exponents and to simplify their final answer.
($x \cdot x \cdot x \cdot x \cdot x \cdot x \cdot x \cdot x \cdot x \cdot x = x^{10}$)

Finally, present an example with variables and coefficients. Write on the board: $3n^4 \cdot 7n^2$. Ask: **What are the coefficients in this problem?** (3 and 7) **What do you do with them?** (multiply them)

Instruct students to rewrite the problem without using exponents and simplify.
($3 \cdot 7 \cdot n \cdot n \cdot n \cdot n \cdot n \cdot n = 21n^6$)

Have students use this technique to simplify the expressions below. Remind students that if a variable does not have a coefficient or an exponent, they are understood to be 1.

$2x \cdot 12x^5$ ($24x^6$); $5n^3 \cdot 8n^7$ ($40n^{10}$); $6p^2 \cdot p^4$ ($6p^6$); $7h^5 \cdot 7h^5$ ($49h^{10}$)

When students are comfortable writing out and simplifying expressions, have them redo the problems using properties of exponents; $x^a \cdot x^b = x^{a+b}$. Remind students that you multiply coefficients and add exponents.

© Saxon. All rights reserved.   117   **Saxon** Algebra 1

Name _____ Date _____ Class _____

Prerequisite Skills Intervention
Properties of Exponents

Vocabulary: $x^3 \rightarrow$ exponent
$\searrow$ base

To multiply variables with the same base, <u>add</u> the exponents. | Rule: $x^a \cdot x^b = x^{a+b}$

To multiply expressions that include numbers and variables:

• Multiply the coefficients. If a variable does not have a coefficient, it is understood to be 1.

• <u>Add</u> the exponents of those variables that are the same. If a variable does not have an expressed exponent, it is understood to be 1.

Example 1: $5n \cdot 6n$	Example 2: $-4x^3 \cdot 7x$	Example 3: $h^3 k \cdot 3h^5 k^2$
$(5 \cdot 6)(n^{1+1}) = 30n^2$	$(-4 \cdot 7)(x^{3+1}) = -28x^4$	$(1 \cdot 3)(h^{3+5})(k^{1+2}) = 3h^8 k^3$

Practice on Your Own
Simplify each expression.

1. $2x \cdot 5x$

2. $-3a \cdot 7a^3$

3. $-2 \cdot 8mn$

4. $15p^2 \cdot 3pq$

_____ _____ _____ _____

5. $5b^2 c \cdot 5b^3 c^3$

6. $-2xy \cdot (-3xy)$

7. $-16z^4 \cdot (-z)$

8. $d^2 e \cdot 8de$

_____ _____ _____ _____

9. $6t \cdot (-3t)$

10. $w^2 \cdot w \cdot w^5$

11. $-2r \cdot 11r^2 \cdot (-r^4)$

12. $5x \cdot 10y \cdot xy$

_____ _____ _____ _____

Check
Simplify each expression.

13. $15f \cdot 2f$

14. $-9 \cdot 3x^2 y$

15. $-20h \cdot (-3h^3)$

16. $7ab \cdot 7ab$

_____ _____ _____ _____

17. $p^3 q \cdot 4pq$

18. $-3u \cdot 7u^2 v$

19. $g^3 \cdot g^4 \cdot g$

20. $-2y \cdot 8z \cdot yz$

_____ _____ _____ _____

Saxon Algebra 1

Teaching Skill 60

Objective Evaluate expressions.

Explain to students that evaluating an expression simply means replacing the variable with a given value and simplifying.

Review with students the order of operations and point out that they will need to follow them to correctly simplify expressions. Also review integer operations as some expressions, and some given values, may involve negative numbers.

Have students consider Example 1. Ask: **What two operations will be used to simplify this expression?** (multiplication then addition) **What number replaces *y*?** (6) Work through the example.

Next have students consider Example 2. Ask: **What two operations will be used to simplify this expression?** (multiplication then subtraction) **What number replaces *p*?** (−4) Stress that students must be careful when working with negatives since it is easy to overlook them when simplifying. Work through the example.

Have students complete the practice exercises.

PRACTICE ON YOUR OWN

In exercises 1–9, students evaluate expressions.

CHECK

Determine that students know how to evaluate expressions.

Students who successfully complete the **Practice on Your Own** and **Check** are ready to move on to the next skill.

COMMON ERRORS

Students may not follow the correct order of operations and may arrive at an incorrect result.

Students who made more than 2 errors in the **Practice on Your Own,** or who were not successful in the **Check** section, may benefit from the **Alternative Teaching Strategy.**

Alternative Teaching Strategy

Objective Evaluate expressions.

Explain to students that most expressions can be evaluated for any given number. Create the table below on the board and have students duplicate it. Tell students they are going to evaluate an expression for several different values.

Value	Substitution	Simplification
−2	6( ) + 3	___ + 3 = ___
−1	6( ) + 3	___ + 3 = ___
0	6( ) + 3	___ + 3 = ___
1	6( ) + 3	___ + 3 = ___
2	6( ) + 3	___ + 3 = ___

Ask: **Based on the center column, what expression are you evaluating?** $(6y + 3)$ **For what values are you evaluating the expression?** (−2, −1, 0, 1, and 2)

Have students complete the table and check their answers. (−2, −1, 0, 1, 2; −12, −6, 0, 6, 12; −9, −3, 3, 9, 15)

Have students duplicate the two tables below, identify the expression, and complete the last two columns.

Value	Substitution	Simplification
−3	4( ) − 5	___ − 5 = ___
−1	4( ) − 5	___ − 5 = ___
2	4( ) − 5	___ − 5 = ___
4	4( ) − 5	___ − 5 = ___

Value	Substitution	Simplification
−3	−3( ) + 2	___ + 2 = ___
−2	−3( ) + 2	___ + 2 = ___
1	−3( ) + 2	___ + 2 = ___
2	−3( ) + 2	___ + 2 = ___

When students are comfortable completing tables, give them several expressions and have them create their own tables using the given values −3, −2, −1, 0, 1, 2, and 3.

 Saxon Algebra 1

Prerequisite Skills Intervention
Evaluate Expressions

To evaluate a variable expression, replace the variable(s) with the given value(s) and use the order of operations to simplify.

Example 1: Evaluate $10y + 3$ for $y = 6$.	
$10y + 3 = 10(6) + 3$	Replace y with 6 since 6 is the given value.
$= 60 + 3$	Order of operations says to multiply first.
$= 63$	Add.

Example 2: Evaluate $-6p - 15$ for $p = -4$.	
$-6p - 15 = -6(-4) - 15$	Replace p with -4 since -4 is the given value.
$= 24 - 15$	Order of operations says to multiply first.
$= 9$	Subtract.

Practice on Your Own
Evaluate each expression for the given value of the variable.

1. $7x + 1$ for $x = 5$

2. $8m - 12$ for $m = 5$

3. $2y + 9$ for $y = -6$

_____

_____

_____

4. $6p - 3$ for $p = -4$

5. $27 - 9x$ for $x = 2$

6. $10 + 4q$ for $q = -3$

_____

_____

_____

7. $-7c + 11$ for $c = 3$

8. $\frac{1}{3}t + 5$ for $t = 9$

9. $\frac{1}{2}m - 16$ for $m = 20$

_____

_____

_____

Check
Evaluate each expression for the given value of the variable.

10. $2n - 3$ for $n = 9$

11. $x + 7$ for $x = -5$

12. $15 - 3h$ for $h = 5$

_____

_____

_____

13. $15 - 7m$ for $m = 3$

14. $-5a - 9$ for $a = -1$

15. $\frac{1}{2}y + (-4)$ for $y = 12$

_____

_____

_____

Saxon Algebra 1

Prerequisite Skills Intervention
Multiply and Divide Monomials

Teaching Skill 61

Objective Multiply and divide monomials.

Remind students that a monomial is a number, a variable, or a product of a number and one or more variables.

Review with students the steps for multiplying monomials. Have students consider Example 1. Ask: **What are the coefficients of the two monomials?** (6 and 7) **What do you do with them?** (Find their product by multiplying.) **How many variables are present?** (2; *a* and *b*) **How do you find their products?** (You add the exponents of the corresponding variables.) Work through the example with students.

Next, review the steps for dividing monomials. Point out that the coefficients of the numerator and the denominator may not always reduce to a whole number.

Emphasize that if the exponent in the numerator is larger, then the difference between the exponents stays in the numerator. Likewise, if the exponent in the denominator is larger, then the difference stays in the denominator.

Work through Example 2 and then have students complete the practice exercises.

PRACTICE ON YOUR OWN

In exercises 1–12, students multiply and divide monomials.

CHECK

Determine that students know how to multiply and divide monomials.

Students who successfully complete the **Practice on Your Own** and **Check** are ready to move on to the next skill.

COMMON ERRORS

Students may multiply the exponents of the variables rather than adding them.

Students who made more than 3 errors in the **Practice on Your Own,** or who were not successful in the **Check** section, may benefit from the **Alternative Teaching Strategy.**

Alternative Teaching Strategy

Objective Multiply and divide monomials.

Materials needed: multiple copies of the cards below.

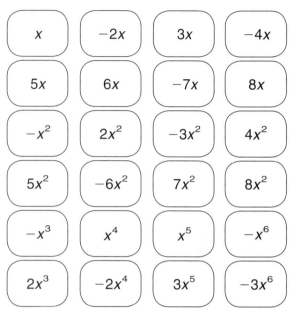

Review with students the rules for multiplying and dividing monomials.

Have students work in pairs. Give each pair of students a well shuffled set of cards. Instruct students to create a table on a piece of paper that has 11 rows and 4 columns with headings as shown below.

First Card	Second Card	Product	Quotient

Tell students they are going to select two cards at a time. They should fill in the first and second column of the table based on what is written on the first and second card.

Then they should find the product of the two monomials and the quotient of the first monomial divided by the second monomial.

Demonstrate using the following example:

You draw a $-6x^2$, then a $3x^5$. Fill in those terms in the first two columns. The third column should be $-18x^7$ and the last column should be $-\dfrac{2}{x^3}$. Have students repeat the exercise 10 times to complete the table and then check each other's answers.

Saxon Algebra 1

Name _____ Date _____ Class _____

Prerequisite Skills Intervention
Multiply and Divide Monomials

Multiplying Monomials	Dividing Monomials
Step 1: Multiply the coefficients. If a variable does not have a coefficient, it is understood to be 1.	**Step 1:** If the expression contains numbers in the numerator and the denominator, simplify the numbers by reducing if possible.
Step 2: Add the exponents of those variables that are the same. If a variable does not have an expressed exponent, it is understood to be 1.	**Step 2:** Subtract the exponents of those variables that are the same. If the exponent in the numerator is larger, then the difference between the exponents stays in the numerator. Likewise, if the exponent in the denominator is larger, then the difference between the exponents stays in the denominator.
Exponents Rule: $x^a \cdot x^b = x^{a+b}$	Exponents Rule: $\dfrac{x^a}{x^b} = x^{a-b}$
Example 1: $6a^3b \cdot 7a^2b^2$ $= (6)(7)a^{3+2}b^{1+2} = 42a^5b^3$	Example 2: $\dfrac{15m^4n^2}{9m^2n^3} = \dfrac{5m^{4-2}}{3n^{3-2}} = \dfrac{5m^2}{3n}$

Practice on Your Own
Multiply or divide.

1. $5mn^2 \cdot 2m^3$

2. $\dfrac{36x^4y}{9x^2}$

3. $-40a^3 \cdot \dfrac{1}{2}ab$

4. $\dfrac{20t^2}{8t^5}$

5. $\dfrac{-2f^4g^3}{6f^2g^3}$

6. $p^2qr^3 \cdot (-3pq)$

7. $-uv \cdot (-u^3)$

8. $\dfrac{-12c^5d^2}{-3c^3d^7}$

9. $12hk \cdot 12hk$

10. $\dfrac{-5tuv^2}{5tuv^2}$

11. $-10xyz \cdot (-y^2z)$

12. $\dfrac{-2w^5z}{18w^4}$

Check
Multiply or divide.

13. $7s \cdot 5s^3t$

14. $\dfrac{-3x^2y^4}{15xy^5}$

15. $8bc \cdot (-b^3c^3)$

16. $\dfrac{45p^3q^4r}{9p^2qr}$

17. $\dfrac{-100m^3n^3}{60m^2n^2}$

18. $-9uw \cdot (-4u^2w^3)$

19. $-\dfrac{1}{3}x^6y \cdot 30x^2y$

20. $\dfrac{56f^4g^2}{8f^5g^2}$

Saxon Algebra 1

Prerequisite Skills Intervention

Multiply Monomials and Polynomials

SKILL **62**

Teaching Skill 62

Objective Multiply monomials and polynomials.

Review with students the definitions at the top of the page. Ask: **How many terms does a monomial have?** (1) **How many terms does a polynomial have?** (any number)

Review with students how to use the Distributive Property. Emphasize that students need to be especially careful when working with negatives.

Direct students' attention to Example 1. Ask: **What are the numbers 15 and 2?** (constants) **What is the number 3?** (the coefficient of *x*) **What do you do with these numbers?** (You multiply them.) Work through the example.

Direct students' attention to Example 2. Point out that the monomial includes a variable, so students will need to pay careful attention to the exponents. Ask: **What do you do with exponents when you multiply variables?** (You add them.)

Work through the example and then have students complete the practice exercises.

PRACTICE ON YOUR OWN

In exercises 1–12, students multiply a polynomial by a monomial.

CHECK

Determine that students know how to multiply monomials and polynomials.

Students who successfully complete the **Practice on Your Own** and **Check** are ready to move on to the next skill.

COMMON ERRORS

Students may incorrectly distribute a negative sign.

Students who made more than 3 errors in the **Practice on Your Own,** or who were not successful in the **Check** section, may benefit from the **Alternative Teaching Strategy.**

Alternative Teaching Strategy

Objective Multiply monomials and polynomials using algebra tiles.

Materials needed: algebra tiles.

Tell students that they are going to model the product of a monomial and a polynomial using algebra tiles.

Ask: **How do you find the area of a rectangle given its length and width?** (You multiply the length times the width.)

Explain that you are going to use algebra tiles to find the area of a rectangle that is $3x$ units long and $(x + 5)$ units wide by counting tiles. Write the equation $A = 3x(x + 5)$ on the board.

Arrange the algebra tiles as shown below. Have students draw a similar arrangement on their paper and label as shown.

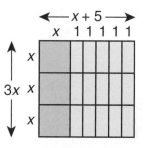

Ask: **What is the area of each of the larger squares?** ($x \cdot x = x^2$) **How many are there?** (3) **What is the area of each of the smaller rectangles?** ($x \cdot 1 = x$) **How many are there?** (15) **What is the total area of the figure?** ($3x^2 + 15x$)

Demonstrate how to find the same product using the Distributive Property to confirm the answer.

Repeat this exercise to find the products of the following monomials and polynomials:

$2x(x + 3)$; $x(3x + 4)$; and $2x(3x + 1)$

Have students confirm their answers each time using the Distributive Property.

Answers: $2x^2 + 6x$; $3x^2 + 4x$; and $6x^2 + 2x$

         Saxon Algebra 1

Name _____ Date _____ Class _____

Prerequisite Skills Intervention

Multiply Monomials and Polynomials

Definition 1: A monomial is a number, a variable, or a product of a number and one or more variables with whole number exponents.

Definition 2: A polynomial is a monomial or a sum or difference of monomials.

<u>To multiply a polynomial by a monomial:</u>
Use the Distributive Property to multiply each term in the polynomial by the monomial. To do this, find the product of the coefficients (or constants) and the product of the variables. Remember, multiply the numbers, but add the exponents of the variables.

Example 1: $15 (3x + 2)$ Distribute.
$= 15(3x) + 15(2)$ Multiply.
$= (15)(3)x + (15)(2)$
$= 45x + 30$

Example 2: $5y(3y^2 - 6y + 5)$ Distribute.
$= 5y(3y^2) - 5y(6y) + 5y(5)$ Multiply.
$= (5)(3)y^{1+2} - (5)(6)y^{1+1} + (5)(5)y$
$= 15y^3 - 30y^2 + 25y$

Practice on Your Own
Multiply.

1. $8(2d + 5)$

2. $m(m - 1)$

3. $3b(3b + 3)$

4. $4(12 - 15q)$

5. $5p(p + 6)$

6. $10w(5 - 3w)$

7. $2r(-5 - r^3)$

8. $n^2(n^2 + 1)$

9. $3g(3g + 1)$

10. $2e^2(e^2 - e)$

11. $2h(h^2 - 5h + 15)$

12. $xy(x^3 + xy^5)$

Check
Multiply.

13. $3(20x - 10)$

14. $4y(y - 9)$

15. $11(5 - 2k)$

16. $7t(7 - 7t)$

17. $w^3(1 - w)$

18. $3g(g^2 - 5g)$

19. $p(p^2 - 2p + 5)$

20. $u^2v^2(3uv + v^2)$

Saxon Algebra 1

Teaching Skill 63

Objective Simplify polynomial expressions.

Point out to students that simplifying polynomials works much the same way as combining like terms. The goal is to "put together" any terms that are similar.

Review with students the steps for simplifying a polynomial expression. Explain that terms inside parentheses may not be similar to other terms in the polynomial before they are multiplied. However, after the Distributive Property has been used, there may be more similar terms in the polynomial. Point out that this is the reason for using the Distributive Property first.

Direct students' attention to the example. Ask: **Before you use the Distributive Property, can you tell what the like terms are?** (No) **Once the Distributive Property has been used, what are the like terms?** ($2x^2$ and x^2; $12x$ and $-10x$) Remind students to be careful of negatives.

Work through the last step of the example and then have students complete the practice exercises.

PRACTICE ON YOUR OWN

In exercises 1–10, students simplify polynomial expressions.

CHECK

Determine that students know how to simplify polynomial expressions.

Students who successfully complete the **Practice on Your Own** and **Check** are ready to move on to the next skill.

COMMON ERRORS

Students may not recognize like terms, particularly when there are multiple variables with different exponents.

Students who made more than 3 errors in the **Practice on Your Own,** or who were not successful in the **Check** section, may benefit from the **Alternative Teaching Strategy.**

Alternative Teaching Strategy

Objective Simplify polynomial expressions.

Some students may benefit from physically matching like terms using circles, squares, triangles, etc.

Remind students that like terms must have identical variable factors, regardless of how many different variables are part of the term.

Write the following problem on the board:

$$12xy + y^2 + 13 + 7x^2 - 9 + 2xy - 3x^2$$

Ask a volunteer to identify the four different types of terms in this expression. (xy, y^2, x^2, and constants) Ask: **How many terms have *xy* in them?** (2) Instruct students to place a circle around those two terms. Ask: **How many terms have a y^2 in them?** (1) Instruct students to place a triangle around that term. Ask: **How many terms have an x^2 in them?** (2) Instruct students to place a square around those terms. Finally, ask: **How many terms are constants?** (2) Instruct students to underline the constants.

Students' expressions should now look like the following:

$$\left(12xy\right) + \triangle{y^2} + \underline{13} + \boxed{7x^2} - \underline{9} + \left(2xy\right) - \boxed{3x^2}$$

Instruct students to simplify the expression by combining like terms. Point out that they should be careful with negatives; if a negative (or a subtraction sign) precedes a term, it goes with that term.

$$(14xy + y^2 + 4x^2 + 4)$$

Have students work the following problems using this technique:

$9t^2 + 3t - 2 + 8t - 4 + 2t^2$
(Answer: $11t^2 + 11t - 6$)

$5x^2y + 14xy - 2xy^2 + 8xy^2 - 9xy + x^2y$
(Answer: $6x^2y + 5xy + 6xy^2$)

Explain to students that if an expression contains any parentheses, they must first distribute before they can match up like terms. Work a few examples.

     Saxon Algebra 1

Name _____ Date _____ Class _____

Prerequisite Skills Intervention

Simplify Polynomial Expressions

To simplify a polynomials expression:

- Step 1: Remove all parentheses by using the Distributive Property (if needed).
- Step 2: Identify and combine like terms.

Example: Simplify $2x(x + 6) + x^2 - 10x$.

$$= 2x(x + 6) + x^2 - 10x$$
$$= 2x(x) + 2x(6) + x^2 - 10x \qquad \text{Use the Distributive Property.}$$
$$= 2x^2 + 12x + x^2 - 10x \qquad \text{Multiply using properties of exponents.}$$
$$= 3x^2 + 2x \qquad \text{Combine like terms.}$$

Practice on Your Own
Simplify each expression.

1. $12m + 7n - 9n$

2. $4x - y - 6x + 9y$

3. $7p - 3q + 4(2p + q)$

4. $5(d - 2e) + 3(5d + 4e)$

5. $24t^2 + 5t - 15t + t$

6. $2r^2s - rs + 5rs^2 - r^2s + 7rs$

7. $5(7f^2 - 3f + 1) - 20f^2 + 10f$

8. $p^2(3p - 5) + p(7p + 8)$

9. $18g^2(1 - 2g) - 5g^2 + 10g^3$

10. $jk(3j^2 + 5k) + j^2(2jk + 4)$

Check
Simplify each expression.

11. $2x - 7x + 5y$

12. $9a + 14b + b - 7a$

13. $20g - 14h + 6(g + 2h)$

14. $9u^3 - 4u^2 + 5u - u^3 - 10u - 3u^2$

15. $10(2p^2 - p - 1) + 7p^2 - 3$

16. $2c(9 - 5c) + 6(c^2 - c)$

Saxon Algebra 1

Prerequisite Skills Intervention

Teaching Skill 64

Objective Multiply binomials.

Review with students the definition of a binomial. Ask: **Will a binomial always have two terms?** (Yes)

Point out that multiplying binomials is much like multiplying a polynomial by a monomial. The only difference is that you must use the Distributive Property twice.

Direct students' attention to the example. Explain that you will be distributing the x to both terms in the second set of parentheses and also the $+6$ to both terms in the second set of parentheses. Ask: **If you are multiplying two terms by two other terms, how many terms should you end up with before combining like terms?** (4) Work through the example.

If time permits, present and explain the FOIL method. Explain that FOIL reminds you to multiply all four sets of terms–the first terms, the outer terms, the inner terms, and the last terms. Remind students that they will still need to combine like terms.

Have students complete the practice exercises using either the Distributive Property or the FOIL method.

PRACTICE ON YOUR OWN

In exercises 1–10, students multiply binomials.

CHECK

Determine that students know how to multiply binomials.

Students who successfully complete the **Practice on Your Own** and **Check** are ready to move on to the next skill.

COMMON ERRORS

Students may multiply only the first terms and the last terms, rather than distributing.

Students who made more than 2 errors in the **Practice on Your Own,** or who were not successful in the **Check** section, may benefit from the **Alternative Teaching Strategy.**

Alternative Teaching Strategy

Objective Multiply binomials.

Materials needed: algebra tiles

Tell students that they are going to model the product of two binomials using algebra tiles.

Ask: **How do you find the area of a rectangle given its length and width?** (You multiply the length times the width.)

Explain that you are going to use algebra tiles to find the area of a rectangle that is $(2x + 3)$ units long and $(3x + 1)$ units wide by counting tiles. Write the equation $A = (2x + 3)(3x + 1)$ on the board.

Arrange the algebra tiles as shown below. Have the students draw a similar arrangement on their paper and label as shown.

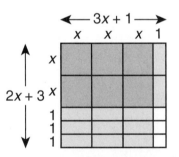

Ask: **What is the area of each of the larger squares?** $(x \cdot x = x^2)$ **How many are there?** (6) **What is the area of each of the smaller rectangles?** $(x \cdot 1 = x)$ **How many are there?** (11) **What is the area of the smaller squares?** $(1 \cdot 1 = 1)$ **How many are there?** (3) **What is the total area of the figure?** $(6x^2 + 11x + 3)$

Demonstrate how to find the same product using the Distributive Property (or FOIL) to confirm the answer.

Repeat this exercise to find the products of the following pairs of binomials:

$(2x + 2)(x + 3)$ and $(3x + 2)(2x + 1)$

Have students confirm their answers each time using the Distributive Property or FOIL.

Answers: $2x^2 + 8x + 6$ and $6x^2 + 7x + 2$

Saxon Algebra 1

Prerequisite Skills Intervention

Multiply Binomials

Definition: A binomial is the sum or difference of two monomials.

To multiply a binomial by another binomial, use the Distributive Property twice.

Example: Multiply $(x + 6)(3x - 5)$.

$$= x(3x - 5) + 6(3x - 5)$$ First use of the Distributive Property.
$$= x(3x) - x(5) + 6(3x) + 6(-5)$$ Second use of the Distributive Property.
$$= 3x^2 - 5x + 18x - 30$$ Multiply using properties of exponents.
$$= 3x^2 + 13x - 30$$ Combine like terms ($-5x + 18x = 13x$).

Practice on Your Own
Find each product.

1. $(n + 6)(n + 3)$

2. $(c + 12)(c - 5)$

3. $(10q + 3)(q + 4)$

4. $(k + 7)(3k - 1)$

5. $(u - 1)(u + 1)$

6. $(r + 6)(r + 6)$

7. $(5a - 4)(5a + 4)$

8. $(3g + 1)(8g + 12)$

9. $(5z + 8)(4z - 2)$

10. $(4p - 9)(2p - 1)$

Check
Find each product.

11. $(x + 4)(x + 7)$

12. $(2w + 6)(w - 9)$

13. $(p + 5)(p + 5)$

14. $(2t + 7)(2t - 7)$

15. $(7y - 3)(y - 1)$

16. $(3m + 4)(9m + 2)$

Saxon Algebra 1

Teaching Skill 65

Objective Find special products of binomials.

Explain to students that there are some special products of binomials for which they can use shortcuts. These are called the squares of sums and differences and difference of two squares.

Remind students that squaring a term means multiplying it by itself. Point out that not only does the variable get squared, but also the coefficient, if applicable.

Review the formulas for finding the special products. Explain that a is always the first term and b is always the second term. The formula applies regardless of whether there is a variable in the first term or the second term, or both.

Review each of the examples with students, point out each time what a is and what b is. Make sure students are comfortable squaring these terms.

Have students complete the practice exercises.

PRACTICE ON YOUR OWN

In exercises 1–10, students find special products of binomials.

CHECK

Determine that students know how to recognize and find special products of binomials.

Students who successfully complete the **Practice on Your Own** and **Check** are ready to move on to the next skill.

COMMON ERRORS

Students may forget to include the middle term in the squares of sums and differences.

Students who made more than 2 errors in the **Practice on Your Own,** or who were not successful in the **Check** section, may benefit from the **Alternative Teaching Strategy.**

Alternative Teaching Strategy

Objective Verify the special products of binomials using the FOIL method.

Tell students they are going to verify the formulas for finding special products of binomials using FOIL. Remind students that FOIL is an acronym for multiplying binomials. It stands for :

First   (Multiply the first term of each binomial together.)

Outer (Multiply the two outside terms together.)

Inner (Multiply the two inside terms together.)

Last   (Multiply the last term of each binomial together.)

Write the problem $(x + 3)^2$ on the board. Ask: **How do you rewrite this problem without using an exponent?**
$[(x + 3)(x + 3)]$ Work through the FOIL method.

$F = x \cdot x = x^2$
$O = x \cdot 3 = 3x$
$I = 3 \cdot x = 3x$
$L = 3 \cdot 3 = 9$

$$(x + 3)(x + 3) = x^2 + 3x + 3x + 9$$
$$= x^2 + 6x + 9$$

Now have students use the formula for finding the square of a sum to confirm that the results are the same.

Have students work the following examples using FOIL: $(2x + 3)^2$ and $(4x + 5)^2$. Then have them confirm the results using the equation. Answers: $4x^2 + 12x + 9$ and $16x^2 + 40x + 25$.

Have students repeat this exercise for a square of a difference using the following examples: $(x - 6)^2$, $(3x - 2)^2$, and $(5x - 1)^2$. Answers: $x^2 - 12x + 36$, $9x^2 - 12x + 4$, and $25x^2 - 10x + 1$.

Finally, have students repeat the exercise for a difference of squares using the following examples: $(x + 7)(x - 7)$, $(2x + 9)(2x - 9)$, and $(10x + 3)(10x - 3)$. Answers: $x^2 - 49$, $4x^2 - 81$, and $100x^2 - 9$.

Saxon Algebra 1

Name _____ Date _____ Class _____

Prerequisite Skills Intervention
Special Products of Binomials

Reminder: An expression squared means that expression multiplied by itself.
For example, $(7x)^2 = (7x)(7x) = 49x^2$.

Formulas for Finding Special Products of Binomials		
Square of a Sum	**Square of a Difference**	**Difference of Two Squares**
$(a + b)^2 = a^2 + 2ab + b^2$	$(a - b)^2 = a^2 - 2ab + b^2$	$(a + b)(a - b) = a^2 - b^2$
Example 1: $(4x + 3)^2$	**Example 2:** $(5x - 2)^2$	**Example 3:** $(3x + 8)(3x - 8)$
$a = 4x; b = 3; ab = (4x)(3)$ $a^2 = (4x)^2 = 16x^2$ $ab = 12x$ so $2ab = 24x$ $b^2 = 3^2 = 9$ $(4x + 3)^2 = 16x^2 + 24x + 9$	$a = 5x; b = 2; ab = (5x)(2)$ $a^2 = (5x)^2 = 25x^2$ $ab = 10x$ so $2ab = 20x$ $b^2 = 2^2 = 4$ $(5x - 2)^2 = 25x^2 - 20x + 4$	$a = 3x$ and $b = 8$ $a^2 = (3x)^2 = 9x^2$ $b^2 = 8^2 = 64$ $(3x + 8)(3x - 8) = 9x^2 - 64$

Practice on Your Own
Multiply.

1. $(7x + 1)^2$

_____

2. $(w + 6)(w - 6)$

_____

3. $(3p - 5)^2$

_____

4. $(m + 9)^2$

_____

5. $(5y + 1)(5y - 1)$

_____

6. $(d - 2)^2$

_____

7. $(4b - 7)(4b + 7)$

_____

8. $(10 - 3h)(10 + 3h)$

_____

9. $(-a + 8)(-a - 8)$

_____

10. $(-2z + 1)(-2z - 1)$

_____

Check
Multiply.

11. $(6x + 4)^2$

_____

12. $(2t - 1)^2$

_____

13. $(u + 3)(u - 3)$

_____

14. $(3h + 5)(3h - 5)$

_____

15. $(y + 7)^2$

_____

16. $(-q + 6)(-q - 6)$

_____

Saxon Algebra 1

Prerequisite Skills Intervention

Factor GCF from Polynomials

Teaching Skill 66

Objective Factor the GCF from a polynomial.

Review with students how to find the GCF of two numbers. Then explain that the GCF of two variable expressions is the largest power of each variable present in both terms.

Have students read the steps for factoring the GCF from polynomials.

Work through Example 1. Point out that there are no variables in common, so the GCF is a number in this case. Ask: **After you have rewritten the expression in factored form, how can you check your answer?** (You can use the Distributive Property to multiply the expression back out—you should get the original polynomial.)

Work through the second example with students. Point out that if a term of the polynomial is exactly the same as the GCF, when you divide it by the GCF you are left with 1, NOT 0.

Have students complete the practice exercises.

PRACTICE ON YOUR OWN

In exercises 1–12, students factor the GCF from polynomials.

CHECK

Determine that students know how to factor the GCF from polynomials.

Students who successfully complete the **Practice on Your Own** and **Check** are ready to move on to the next skill.

COMMON ERRORS

Students may forget that when a term of the polynomial is exactly the same as the GCF, the quotient of the term and the GCF is 1.

Students who made more than 3 errors in the **Practice on Your Own,** or who were not successful in the **Check** section, may benefit from the **Alternative Teaching Strategy.**

Alternative Teaching Strategy

Objective Find the GCF of two polynomials.

Some students have difficulty identifying the GCF of terms that contain variables.

Tell students they are going to find GCFs of variable expressions using factorization.

Ask: **If you were to factor x^5, what would it look like?** ($x \cdot x \cdot x \cdot x \cdot x$)

Write the expressions $15x^3$ and $24x^2$ on the board, one underneath the other. Factor each term as shown below:

$$15x^3 = 3 \cdot 5 \cdot x \cdot x \cdot x$$

$$24x^2 = 3 \cdot 8 \cdot x \cdot x$$

Next, circle the common factors and write them on the board as a product to get a single term.

$$15x^3 = \boxed{3} \cdot 5 \cdot \boxed{x} \cdot \boxed{x} \cdot x$$
$$24x^2 = \boxed{3} \cdot 8 \cdot \boxed{x} \cdot \boxed{x} \longrightarrow 3 \cdot x \cdot x = 3x^2$$

Explain to students that $3x^2$ is the GCF of the two terms.

Next, write the expressions $14x^2$ and $42x^4$ on the board. Instruct students to use factorization to find the GCF. Emphasize that each number should be factored into primes. Encourage students to line up the numbers that are alike and do the same for the variables. Ask a volunteer to present his or her answer, including their factorization and what they circled. The answer should look like:

$$14x^2 = \boxed{2} \cdot \qquad \boxed{7} \cdot \boxed{x} \cdot \boxed{x}$$
$$42x^4 = \boxed{2} \cdot 3 \cdot \boxed{7} \cdot \boxed{x} \cdot \boxed{x} \cdot x \cdot x \quad = 14x^2$$

Have students use this method to find the GCF of the following pairs of expressions:

$22x^2$ and $4x$; $36x$ and $27x^3$; $56x^6$ and $14x^4$
Answers: $2x$; $9x$; $14x^4$

When you are comfortable that students can correctly identify the GCF, write the expressions as polynomials and have them factor the GCF from the polynomials.

Prerequisite Skills Intervention
Factor GCF from Polynomials

To factor the greatest common factor (GCF) from a polynomial:

Step 1: Identify the GCF. Consider the coefficients and the variable terms.
Step 2: Divide the GCF out of every term of the polynomial.
Step 3: Rewrite the expression in factored form.

Example 1: Factor $2a - 18b$.
Step 1: The GCF of 2 and 18 is 2. There are no variables in common so 2 is the GCF.
Step 2: Divide 2 out of each term: $2a$ divided by 2 is a and $-18b$ divided by 2 is $-9b$.
Step 3: $2a - 18b = 2(a - 9b)$

Example 2: Factor $18x^3 + 6x^2$.
Step 1: The largest integer that will divide evenly into 18 and 6 is 6. The largest power of x present in both terms is x^2. So, the GCF is $6x^2$.
Step 2: Divide $6x^2$ out of each term: $18x^3$ divided by $6x^2$ is $3x$ and $6x^2$ divided by $6x^2$ is 1.
Step 3: $18x^3 + 6x^2 = 6x^2(3x + 1)$

Practice on Your Own
Factor each polynomial.

1. $x^2 + 6x$ 　　　 **2.** $3x - 12$ 　　　 **3.** $15x^2 + 5x$ 　　　 **4.** $7x^2 - 14$

_____　　　_____　　　_____　　　_____

5. $6x^2 + 5x$ 　　　 **6.** $4x^2 - 8$ 　　　 **7.** $12x^2 - 9x$ 　　　 **8.** $3x^3 - 3x$

_____　　　_____　　　_____　　　_____

9. $5x^3 + x^2$ 　　　 **10.** $3x^3 - 6x^2$ 　　　 **11.** $x^4 + x^3$ 　　　 **12.** $2x^4 - 2x^2$

_____　　　_____　　　_____　　　_____

Check
Factor each polynomial.

13. $x^2 - 5x$ 　　　 **14.** $20x + 5$ 　　　 **15.** $8x^2 - 16x$ 　　　 **16.** $12x^2 + 9$

_____　　　_____　　　_____　　　_____

17. $10x^3 - x^2$ 　　　 **18.** $27x^3 + 18x$ 　　　 **19.** $x^3 + x^2$ 　　　 **20.** $2x^4 - 6x^2$

_____　　　_____　　　_____　　　_____

Saxon Algebra 1

Teaching Skill 67

Objective Factor trinomials.

Review with students the definition of a trinomial. Explain that most trinomials of the form $ax^2 + bx + c$ can be factored into two binomials.

Instruct students to read Steps 1 and 2. Point out that if the coefficient of x^2 is 1, then both factors will always be x since $x \cdot x = x^2$.

Instruct students to read Step 3. Explain that if the last term in the expression is positive, you use the same signs (either both + or both − depending on the sign of the middle term). If the last term is negative, use opposite signs.

Instruct students to read Step 4. Explain that the factors that go in the last position have to be two numbers such that their product equals c (the constant) and their sum equals b (the coefficient of the middle term).

Work through the example. When you get to Step 4, remind students that they are looking for the factors of -12 that add up to $+4$. Have students verify that the factors are correct using FOIL to multiply the binomials.

Have students complete the practice exercises.

PRACTICE ON YOUR OWN

In exercises 1–9, students factor trinomials.

CHECK

Determine that students know how to factor trinomials.

Students who successfully complete the **Practice on Your Own** and **Check** are ready to move on to the next skill.

COMMON ERRORS

Students may choose the wrong factors of c or may use the wrong signs in one or both of the binomial factors.

Students who made more than 2 errors in the **Practice on Your Own,** or who were not successful in the **Check** section, may benefit from the **Alternative Teaching Strategy.**

Alternative Teaching Strategy

Objective Factor trinomials.

Some students may benefit from discovering patterns on their own when learning to factor trinomials.

Present the following statements:

$(x + 5)(x + 2) = x^2 + 7x + 10$

$(x + 4)(x + 3) = x^2 + 7x + 12$

$(x + 3)(x + 9) = x^2 + 12x + 27$

$(x + 6)(x + 4) = x^2 + 10x + 24$

Ask: **On the left side of the first statement, what is the sum of the two constants?** (7) **Where is the 7 on the right side?** (the coefficient of the middle term) **What is the product of the two constants?** (10) **Where is the 10 on the right side?** (the last term)

Repeat these questions for each of the statements, then ask students to make a general statement about what the sum of the two constants should be and what the product of the two constants should be. (The sum should be equal to the coefficient of the middle term and the product should be equal to the last term.)

Repeat the exercise using the following statements:

$(x + 5)(x - 3) = x^2 + 2x - 15$

$(x - 7)(x + 2) = x^2 - 5x - 14$

$(x - 6)(x - 3) = x^2 - 9x + 18$

Guide students to realize that the general statement they made works regardless of the signs.

Present the following problem:
Factor $x^2 - 7x - 18$. Ask: **What are the factors of 18?** (1, 18 and 2, 9 and 3, 6) Explain that since the product of the factors must equal -18, one of them should be negative. Ask: **Which set of factors has a sum of −7 if one of them is negative?** (2, −9)

Write the factored form on the board and then have students work more problems.

Saxon Algebra 1

Name _____ Date _____ Class _____

Prerequisite Skills Intervention

Factor Trinomials

SKILL
67

Definition: A trinomial is a polynomial that has three terms. For example, $x^2 + 5x + 4$ is a trinomial. The factored form of $x^2 + 5x + 4$ is $(x + 4)(x + 1)$.

To factor a trinomial:
Step 1: Set up a product of two ( ) where each will hold two terms. It will look like (   )(   ).
Step 2: Find the factors that go in the first positions of each set of ( ).
Step 3: Decide on the signs that will go in each set of ( ).
Step 4: Find that factors that go in the last positions of each set of ( ).

Example: Factor: $x^2 + 4x - 12$.
Step 1: (   ) (   )
Step 2: $(x$ $) (x$ $)$ The only possible factors of x^2 are x and x.
Step 3: $(x +$ $) (x -$ $)$ The last term is negative, use opposite signs.
Step 4: $(x + 6) (x - 2)$ The factors of -12 are $\pm 1 \cdot \pm 12$ or $\pm 3 \cdot \pm 4$ or $\pm 6 \cdot \pm 2$ and the only pair of these that can have a sum of 4 (the coefficient of the middle term) is 6 and -2.

Practice on Your Own
Factor each polynomial completely.

1. $x^2 + 5x + 4$

2. $x^2 + 3x - 10$

3. $x^2 - 4x + 3$

4. $x^2 - x - 20$

5. $x^2 + 2x - 24$

6. $x^2 + 10x + 21$

7. $x^2 - 10x + 16$

8. $x^2 - 8x - 9$

9. $x^2 - 18x + 45$

Check
Factor each polynomial completely.

10. $x^2 + 7x + 10$

11. $x^2 - 11x + 28$

12. $x^2 + 7x - 30$

13. $x^2 - 3x + 2$

14. $x^2 + 49x + 48$

15. $x^2 - 7x - 60$

Saxon Algebra 1

Teaching Skill 68

Objective Solve one-step equations.

Explain to students that inverse operations are operations that undo each other.

Direction students' attention to the first example. Ask a volunteer to read the addition equation $x + 5 = 15$. Ask: **What operation is being done to the variable?** (5 is being added to it.) **How can you undo this?** (Subtract 5.) **So, what is the inverse operation of addition?** (subtraction)

Work through the next example. Stress that since subtraction is the inverse operation of addition, addition is the inverse operation of subtraction.

Go through a similar process to explain the multiplication and division examples. Remind students that they should be careful when working with negatives.

Ask: **If a multiplication equation contains $-2x$, what do you divide by?** (-2) **Does that mean the answer is negative?** (not necessarily) Give examples if time permits.

Have students complete the practice exercises.

PRACTICE ON YOUR OWN

In exercises 1–12, students solve one-step equations that require addition, subtraction, multiplication, or division.

CHECK

Determine that students know how to solve one-step equations.

Students who successfully complete the **Practice on Your Own** and **Check** are ready to move on to the next skill.

COMMON ERRORS

Students may forget to use an inverse operation when solving equations.

Students who made more than 2 errors in the **Practice on Your Own,** or who were not successful in the **Check** section, may benefit from the **Alternative Teaching Strategy.**

Alternative Teaching Strategy

Objective Solve one-step equations.
Materials needed: multiple copies of the flashcards shown below (index cards work nicely)

$n + 3 = 9$	$n + 12 = 4$	$n + 6 = -2$
$n - 8 = 12$	$n - 1 = -5$	$n - 15 = -11$
$5n = 50$	$-7n = 42$	$-9n = -45$
$\dfrac{n}{6} = 4$	$\dfrac{n}{15} = -2$	$\dfrac{n}{-5} = -100$

Tell students they are going to practice identifying inverse operations and then solving one-step equations. Remind students that inverse operations undo each other.

Have students work in pairs. Give each pair of students one set of equation cards. Instruct students to mix the cards up and leave them face down.

Students should take turns drawing one card at a time. The student who draws the card should face it toward their partner. The partner should read the equation aloud, identify the operation being done to the variable, and then identify how to undo the operation. The partner does not need to solve the equation. The student holding the card should then turn the card around and read it, confirm their partner's answers, and then solve the equation.

Students should repeat the exercise until all the cards have been drawn and all the equations solved.

An extension of this exercise is to have students make their own index cards which should include addition, subtraction, multiplication and division equations.

Saxon Algebra 1

Prerequisite Skills Intervention

Solve One-Step Equations

SKILL
68

To solve a one-step equation, do the inverse of whatever operation is being done to the variable. Remember, because it is an equation, what is done to one side of the equation must also be done to the other side.

Solve an addition equation using subtraction.	Solve a subtraction equation using addition.
$x + 5 = 15$ $\underline{-5 \quad -5}$ $x \quad = 10$	$x - 8 = -3$ $\underline{+8 \quad +8}$ $x \quad = 5$
Solve a multiplication equation using division.	**Solve a division equation using multiplication.**
$7x = 42$ $\dfrac{7x}{7} = \dfrac{42}{7}$ $x = 6$	$\dfrac{x}{12} = -3$ $12 \cdot \dfrac{x}{12} = -3 \cdot 12$ $x = -36$

Practice on Your Own
Solve.

1. $m - 5 = 9$

2. $\dfrac{h}{6} = -3$

3. $6x = 54$

4. $b + 15 = 25$

_____   _____   _____   _____

5. $4y = -12$

6. $k + 9 = -3$

7. $p - 7 = -2$

8. $\dfrac{t}{3} = 7$

_____   _____   _____   _____

9. $\dfrac{x}{4} = -1$

10. $5 + h = 16$

11. $-12x = -24$

12. $r - 2 = -9$

_____   _____   _____   _____

Check
Solve.

13. $3x = 15$

14. $c - 11 = 1$

15. $d + 9 = 5$

16. $\dfrac{s}{6} = -5$

_____   _____   _____   _____

17. $z - 2 = -17$

18. $\dfrac{w}{4} = 12$

19. $-10b = 120$

20. $x + 99 = 100$

_____   _____   _____   _____

     Saxon Algebra 1

Prerequisite Skills Intervention

SKILL **69**

Solve Multi-Step Equations

Teaching Skill 69

Objective Solve multi-step equations.

Explain that multi-step equations are equations that involve more than one step.

Ask: **When you "do" operations on numbers, which comes first, addition and subtraction or multiplication and division?** (The order of operations tells you to multiply and divide before you add and subtract.) **Since you are "undoing" operations when you solve an equation, what order should you follow?** (the reverse order) Explain that this is not required, but that it makes the process easier.

Review the example with students. Point out that if students divide each term by 9 in the first step, they will be working with fractions for the rest of the problem. If you add 6 first, only the last step may produce a fraction.

Have students complete the practice exercises. Point out that exercises 7, 8, and 9 have parentheses and that students will need to use the Distributive Property before they use inverse operations.

PRACTICE ON YOUR OWN

In exercises 1–9, students solve multi-step equations.

CHECK

Determine that students know how to solve multi-step equations.

Students who successfully complete the **Practice on Your Own** and **Check** are ready to move on to the next skill.

COMMON ERRORS

Students may perform an inverse operation on only one side of the equation.

Students who made more than 2 errors in the **Practice on Your Own,** or who were not successful in the **Check** section, may benefit from the **Alternative Teaching Strategy.**

Alternative Teaching Strategy

Objective Solve multi-step equations.

Tell students they are going to solve multi-step equations to answer the following question: What are two-step equations?

Review with students how to solve multi-step equations. Instruct students to solve each problem and then write the letter corresponding to the correct answer above the problem numbers at the bottom of the page.

1. $5x - 6 = 54$		A	-15
2. $6x + 2 = 1$		C	-8
3. $24 = 2x + 2$		D	25
4. $15 + \frac{x}{5} = 10$		E	12
5. $-20 - 4x = 40$		I	-25
6. $27 = \frac{x}{2} + 15$		K	-12
7. $2(1 - x) = -48$		L	-13
8. $4(2x + 3) - 7x = -1$		N	11
9. $5x - 2 = 9x + 30$		O	$-\frac{1}{6}$
10. $5(x + 6) - 3x = x + 18$		T	24

Two-step equations are equations that:

$\overline{8}\ \overline{4}\ \overline{10}\ \overline{1}\quad \overline{6}\ \overline{2}\quad \overline{7}\ \overline{5}\ \overline{3}\ \overline{9}\ \overline{1}$

Answer: Two-step equations are equations that like to dance.

Saxon Algebra 1

Name _____ Date _____ Class _____

Prerequisite Skills Intervention

Solve Multi-Step Equations

SKILL
69

To solve an equation, you need to isolate the variable on one side of the equals sign. Follow the order of operations in reverse to solve a multi-step equation. That is, add and subtract before you multiply or divide. Sometimes, you need to use the Distributive Property before you use inverse operations.

Example: Solve $9x - 6 = 21$.

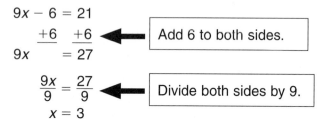

$9x - 6 = 21$
$\underline{+6 \quad +6}$ ← Add 6 to both sides.
$9x \quad = 27$

$\dfrac{9x}{9} = \dfrac{27}{9}$ ← Divide both sides by 9.
$x = 3$

Practice on Your Own
Solve.

1. $3x - 2 = 10$

2. $7m + 3 = 45$

3. $12 + \dfrac{t}{3} = 17$

4. $\dfrac{p}{4} - 3 = -5$

5. $-12 - 9y = -20$

6. $26 = 5c - 4$

7. $3\left(\dfrac{x}{3} + 2\right) = -9$

8. $5(2n - 1) = -5$

9. $2(h + 3) + 5h = -3$

Check
Solve.

10. $8x + 1 = 17$

11. $-3 + \dfrac{d}{5} = -7$

12. $-12 + 6g = 14$

13. $18 = \dfrac{t}{2} + 15$

14. $-3(x + 4) = -5$

15. $5(z - 2) + 3z = 14$

 Saxon Algebra 1

Prerequisite Skills Intervention

SKILL **70**

Solve Equations with Variables on Both Sides

Teaching Skill 70

Objective Solve equations with variables on both sides.

Review with students how to solve multi-step equations. Point out that when there are variables on both sides of an equation, one of the steps will be to move one of the variable terms to the other side. Ask: **Is $x = 3$ equivalent to $3 = x$?** (Yes) **Then, does it matter on which side the variable ends up?** (No) Encourage students to always move the smaller variable expression, rather than the larger one, to avoid having extra negatives.

Have students look at the example. Ask: **To which side do you want to move the variables and why?** (To the left side so that the result will be positive.) Point out that it is not incorrect to move the variable to the other side, but avoiding negative results also avoids possible errors.

Work through the example with students, noting each inverse operation as you perform it.

Have students complete the practice exercises.

PRACTICE ON YOUR OWN

In exercises 1–9, students solve equations with variables on both sides.

CHECK

Determine that students know how to solve equations with variables on both sides.

Students who successfully complete the **Practice on Your Own** and **Check** are ready to move on to the next skill.

COMMON ERRORS

Students may perform an operation on only one side of the equation, particularly when there are several operations involved.

Students who made more than 2 errors in the **Practice on Your Own,** or who were not successful in the **Check** section, may benefit from the **Alternative Teaching Strategy.**

Alternative Teaching Strategy

Objective Solve equations with variables on both sides to complete a magic square.

Explain to students that a magic square is a square in which all the rows, columns, and diagonals have the same sum. Give the following example.

2	7	6
9	5	1
4	3	8

Point out that the sum of the entries in each row, column, and diagonal is 15.

Tell students they are going to complete another magic square by solving equations with variables on both sides.

Have students draw the following magic square on a piece of paper.

1.	2.	3.
4.	0	5.
−1	6.	3

Instruct students to solve each of the equations below and place the answer in the corresponding box.

When complete, students should find the sum of each of the rows, columns and diagonals and confirm that they have created a magic square.

1. $4x + 5 = 6x + 11$
2. $10x - 3 = 15 + x$
3. $-5 + 5x = 4x - 4$
4. $-x + 3 = -3x + 11$
5. $2x - 10 = 6x + 6$
6. $-15 - 3x = -5x - 19$

Answers: 1) −3; 2) 2; 3) 1; 4) 4; 5) −4; 6) −2

The sum of each row, column, and diagonal should be 0.

Saxon Algebra 1

Prerequisite Skills Intervention

Solve Equations with Variables on Both Sides

To solve an equation with variables on both sides:

Step 1: Move all the variable expressions to one side of the equals sign by adding or subtracting.

Step 2: Isolate the variable by adding or subtracting any constants and then multiplying or dividing by any coefficients.

Example: Solve $7x - 12 = 3x + 8$.

Step 1: Subtract $3x$ from both sides.

$$7x - 12 = 3x + 8$$
$$\underline{-3x \qquad\quad -3x}$$
$$4x - 12 = \qquad 8$$

Step 2: Add 12 to both sides, then divide both sides by 4.

$$4x - 12 = \quad 8$$
$$\underline{+12 \quad +12}$$
$$\frac{4x}{4} = \frac{20}{4}$$
$$x = \quad 5$$

Practice on Your Own
Solve.

1. $3y + 5 = 9y - 13$

2. $4 + 11m = 7m - 1$

3. $9x + 15 = 7 + x$

_____

_____

_____

4. $-1 - 3t = 9 - 8t$

5. $x - 11 = 7x - 8$

6. $3b + 5 = -2b + 5$

_____

_____

_____

7. $-k - 7 = -5k - 6$

8. $16 - 3x = 5x - 8$

9. $-6a - 4 = -7a - 5$

_____

_____

_____

Check
Solve.

10. $15x + 1 = 13x + 17$

11. $9 - 4t = 2t - 1$

12. $6y - 5 = 7y + 1$

_____

_____

_____

13. $p + 13 = 5p + 5$

14. $-5b + 11 = 7 - 6b$

15. $-x - 8 = -5x - 10$

_____

_____

_____

Saxon Algebra 1

Prerequisite Skills Intervention

Teaching Skill 71

Objective Solve equations with fractions.

Point out to students that solving equations with fractions is no different than solving equations with integers.

Remind students that the reciprocal of a fraction is the inverted form of the fraction. Ask: **What is the reciprocal of $\frac{2}{3}$?** $\left(\frac{3}{2}\right)$ **What is the reciprocal of 8?** (Since 8 can be written as $\frac{8}{1}$, the reciprocal is $\frac{1}{8}$.)

Review with students the steps for solving equations with fractions. Remind students that when you add fractions that have the same denominators, only the numerators are added—the denominator remains the same.

Work through the example with students following the steps provided. It may be beneficial to review how to simplify the products of fractions.

Have students complete the practice exercises.

PRACTICE ON YOUR OWN

In exercises 1–9, students solve equations that contain fractions.

CHECK

Determine that students know how to solve equations with fractions.

Students who successfully complete the **Practice on Your Own** and **Check** are ready to move on to the next skill.

COMMON ERRORS

Students may add the denominators of the fractions and arrive at an incorrect answer.

Students who made more than 2 errors in the **Practice on Your Own,** or who were not successful in the **Check** section, may benefit from the **Alternative Teaching Strategy.**

Alternative Teaching Strategy

Objective Solve equations with fractions.

Some students are not comfortable working with fractions. Tell students that you are going to show them how to do away with, or clear, the fractions before they begin solving an equation.

Remind students that it is okay to multiply an equation by a constant as long as you multiply each piece of the equation by the same constant. Explain that this will result in an equivalent equation.

Write the equation $3x + \frac{2}{3} = \frac{11}{3}$ on the board. Ask: **What do you need to multiply $\frac{2}{3}$ by to get rid of the denominator?** (3) **Will that take care of the $\frac{11}{3}$ as well?** (Yes) **What happens to the 3x?** (It also gets multiplied by 3.) **Why?** (Anything you do to one piece of the equation, you must do to all the pieces in order to have an equivalent equation.)

Now write the following on the board: $3(3x) + 3\left(\frac{2}{3}\right) = 3\left(\frac{11}{3}\right)$. Instruct students to simplify the equation. ($9x + 2 = 11$) Point out that since this is an equivalent equation to the original equation, the solution will be the same. Have students solve the problem. ($x = 1$)

Tell students that if there is more than one fraction and the denominators of the fractions are not the same, they should multiply by either the LCD of the two fractions or the product of the two denominators. Work the example $\frac{1}{4} + \frac{x}{2} = 5$ first by multiplying the equation by 4 and then by multiplying the equation by 8 to demonstrate that you get the same answer. Then work additional problems.

 Saxon Algebra 1

Prerequisite Skills Intervention

Solve Equations with Fractions

You solve multi-step equations with fractions just like you solve multi-step equations with integers.

Step 1: Use inverse operations to undo any addition or subtraction.

Step 2: When the coefficient of the variable is a fraction, multiply each side of the equation by the reciprocal of the fraction and then simplify. If the coefficient is not a fraction, but there are other fractions in the equation, multiply by the reciprocal of the coefficient rather than dividing.

Example: Solve $\frac{4}{5}x - 12 = 8$.

$$\frac{4}{5}x - 12 + 12 = 8 + 12 \qquad \text{Add 12 to both sides.}$$

$$\frac{4}{5}x = 20$$

$$\frac{5}{4} \cdot \frac{4}{5}x = 20 \cdot \frac{5}{4} \qquad \text{Multiply by the reciprocal.}$$

$$\frac{\cancel{5}}{\cancel{4}} \cdot \frac{\cancel{4}}{\cancel{5}}x = \cancel{20} \cdot \frac{5}{\cancel{4}} \qquad \text{Simplify.}$$

$$x = 25$$

Practice on Your Own
Solve.

1. $\frac{2}{3}x + 5 = 17$

2. $\frac{1}{7}x - 3 = -9$

3. $4y - \frac{5}{3} = \frac{7}{3}$

_____

_____

_____

4. $2x + \frac{1}{6} = -\frac{11}{6}$

5. $x - \frac{1}{8} = -\frac{3}{8}$

6. $\frac{9}{4}x + \frac{1}{5} = \frac{11}{5}$

_____

_____

_____

7. $-\frac{1}{2}y + \frac{3}{7} = \frac{5}{7}$

8. $6x = 3x + \frac{9}{25}$

9. $4y = 9y - \frac{5}{2}$

_____

_____

_____

Check
Solve.

10. $\frac{5}{2}x + 11 = 21$

11. $\frac{3}{4}y - 8 = -7$

12. $5x - \frac{4}{7} = \frac{10}{7}$

_____

_____

_____

13. $y + \frac{10}{11} = \frac{5}{11}$

14. $\frac{7}{5}x - \frac{1}{2} = \frac{3}{2}$

15. $8x = 5x - \frac{3}{8}$

_____

_____

_____

Saxon Algebra 1

Teaching Skill 72
Objective Solve an equation for a given variable.

Explain that there are equations that involve multiple variables and it is helpful to write the equation in terms of a particular variable. To do this, you solve for that variable.

Point out that solving for a variable works exactly the same as solving any equation. Once you have identified the variable that you are solving for, you isolate that variable using inverse operations.

Write the example provided on the board. Ask: **If you are solving for y, what should your final answer look like on one side of the equation?** ($y =$ something) **If you were solving for x instead, what should one side of your equation look like?** ($x =$ something)

Work through the solution. Remind students that they should be following the order of operations in reverse when solving equations. Emphasize that the coefficient of the variable they are solving for should be 1 when they are done.

Have students complete the practice exercises.

PRACTICE ON YOUR OWN
In exercises 1–9, students solve an equation for a given variable.

CHECK
Determine that students know how to solve an equation for a given variable.

Students who successfully complete the **Practice on Your Own** and **Check** are ready to move on to the next skill.

COMMON ERRORS
Students may try to multiply or divide before they add and subtract.

Students who made more than 2 errors in the **Practice on Your Own,** or who were not successful in the **Check** section, may benefit from the **Alternative Teaching Strategy.**

Alternative Teaching Strategy
Objective Solve an equation for a given variable.

Some students may have difficulty determining in which order to take certain steps.

Write the equation $4x - 5 = 2y - 11$ on the board and tell students you are going to guide them in choosing the correct steps to solve this equation for the variable y. Write the following on the board:

$$4x - 5 + \square = 2y - 11 + \square$$
$$4x + \square = 2y$$
$$\frac{4x}{\square} + \frac{6}{\square} = \frac{2y}{\square}$$
$$\square x + \square = y$$

Have students fill in each box based on the operation that is being undone. Ask: **In the first step, if you want to isolate y, should you add 5 to both sides or 11?** (11) Point out that the second step is merely simplifying the addition from the first step. Ask: **In the third step, if you are solving for y, should you divide by 4 or by 2?** (2) Again, point out that the final step is merely simplifying the division from the third step.

When you get to the final step, ask: Have you solved for y? (Yes) **How do you know?** (because y is completely by itself)

Set up and have students solve the additional problems provided below for the variable y in the first problem and for x in the second problem.

$3x + 4y = 7y - 12$ and $\frac{3x}{2} - 12 = y + 3$

Answers: $y = x + 4$ and $x = \frac{2}{3}y + 10$

When you are comfortable that students know in which order the inverse operations should be performed, have them solve other equations without providing the steps.

Name _____ Date _____ Class _____

Prerequisite Skills Intervention

Solve for a Variable

Solving for a variable is the same thing as transforming an equation to represent one quantity in terms of another.

To solve for a variable, identify the variable in the equation that you wish to isolate and then use inverse operations on each side of the equation to isolate the desired variable.

Example: Solve the equation $8x + 3 = 2y + 15$ for y.

You want to isolate y, so you need to move everything else to the other side of the equation.

$$8x + 3 = 2y + 15$$

$8x + 3 - 15 = 2y + 15 - 15$ Subtract 15 from both sides.

$\qquad 8x - 12 = 2y$ Simplify.

$\qquad \dfrac{8x}{2} - \dfrac{12}{2} = \dfrac{2y}{2}$ Divide both sides by 2.

$\qquad 4x - 6 = y$ Simplify.

Practice on Your Own
Solve each equation for the indicated variable.

1. $3x + y = 15$; y

2. $y - 5 = 3x$; y

3. $I = prt$; t

_____

_____

_____

4. $3x + 3y = 12$; y

5. $V = \pi r^2 h$; h

6. $7y - 21x = 14$; y

_____

_____

_____

7. $A = \dfrac{1}{2}bh$; h

8. $2x + 4 = 9 - y$; y

9. $2x + 5 = 6y - 9$; x

_____

_____

_____

Check
Solve each equation for the indicated variable.

10. $y - 6x = 11$; y

11. $V = \ell wh$; h

12. $7x + 7y = 42$; x

_____

_____

_____

13. $8x + 2y = 22$; y

14. $3x - 4 = y + 8$; y

15. $5 - 2y = 8x - 1$; y

_____

_____

_____

Saxon Algebra 1

Teaching Skill 73

Objective Find the length and midpoint of a segment with given endpoints.

Present the distance formula. Explain that the subscripts in the expressions x_1, y_1, x_2, and y_2, are simply a way of labeling the two points, first point and second point.

Encourage students to always assign one of the points as (x_1, y_1) and the other as (x_2, y_2). This will make things less complicated when they are substituting the values into the formula.

Work through the distance example with students. Remind them to be careful when working with negatives.

Next, present the midpoint formula. Explain to students that they are simply finding the average of the x-values and the average of the y-values. Some students find this easier to remember than the formula.

Again, encourage students to always assign one of the points as (x_1, y_1) and the other as (x_2, y_2). Work through the midpoint example with students.

Have students complete the practice exercises.

PRACTICE ON YOUR OWN

In exercises 1–6 students find the length and the midpoint of a segment with given endpoints.

CHECK

Determine that students know how to use the distance and midpoint formulas.

Students who successfully complete the **Practice on Your Own** and **Check** are ready to move on to the next skill.

COMMON ERRORS

Students may not understand how to correctly substitute values into the formulas.

Students who made more than 2 errors in the **Practice on Your Own,** or who were not successful in the **Check** section, may benefit from the **Alternative Teaching Strategy.**

Alternative Teaching Strategy

Objective Find the length of a segment with given endpoints using the Pythagorean Theorem.

Explain to students that the distance formula is actually the Pythagorean Theorem written in a different form.

Remind students that the Pythagorean Theorem states that when a and b are the two legs of a right triangle and c is the hypotenuse, then $c^2 = a^2 + b^2$. Point out that if you solve this equation for c, then $c = \sqrt{a^2 + b^2}$.

Plot the points $(1, 2)$ and $(6, 7)$ on a coordinate plane. Connect the two points and then draw the two legs of a right triangle using dotted lines as shown below.

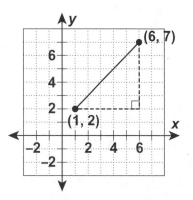

Ask: **How can you find the length of the vertical leg of the right triangle?** (Subtract the y-coordinates of the two points.) Label the two y-coordinates y_1 and y_2 so students will see the connection to the distance formula. Follow a similar process for the horizontal leg.

Rewrite the distance formula using the Pythagorean Theorem and the example above and solve for the length of the hypotenuse. ($\sqrt{25 + 25} = \sqrt{50} = 5\sqrt{2}$)

Have students use this technique to find the length of the segments with the following endpoints: $(2, 3)$ and $(5, 7)$ [5]; and $(-2, 4)$ and $(3, -3)$ [$\sqrt{74}$].

Saxon Algebra 1

Name _____ Date _____ Class _____

Prerequisite Skills Intervention

Distance and Midpoint Formulas

Distance Formula	Midpoint Formula
$d = \sqrt{(x_2 - x_1)^2 + (y_2 - y_1)^2}$	$M = \left(\dfrac{x_1 + x_2}{2}, \dfrac{y_1 + y_2}{2}\right)$
Example: Find the length of the segment with endpoints (4, 3) and (−1, 1). Let (4, 3) be (x_1, y_1) and (−1, 1) be (x_2, y_2). $d = \sqrt{(-1 - 4)^2 + (1 - 3)^2} = \sqrt{(-5)^2 + (-2)^2}$ $= \sqrt{25 + 4} = \sqrt{29}$	Example: Find the midpoint of the segment with endpoints (4, 3) and (−1, 1). Let (4, 3) be (x_1, y_1) and (−1, 1) be (x_2, y_2). $M = \left(\dfrac{4 + -1}{2}, \dfrac{3 + 1}{2}\right) = \left(\dfrac{3}{2}, \dfrac{4}{2}\right) = \left(\dfrac{3}{2}, 2\right)$

Practice on Your Own

Find the length and the midpoint of the segment with the given endpoints.

1. $A(2, 3)$ and $B(5, 7)$

$M = ($, $), d = $ _____

2. $C(1, -1)$ and $D(3, 2)$

$M = ($, $), d = $ _____

3. $E(-5, 7)$ and $F(0, 2)$

$M = ($, $), d = $ _____

4. $G(2, -3)$ and $H(-2, 5)$

$M = ($, $), d = $ _____

5. $J(-4, -4)$ and $K(-2, 1)$

$M = ($, $), d = $ _____

6. $L(-4, -3)$ and $M(0, 0)$

$M = ($, $), d = $ _____

Check

Find the length and the midpoint of the segment with the given endpoints.

7. $A(2, -1)$ and $B(8, 7)$

$M = ($, $), d = $ _____

8. $C(0, 2)$ and $D(5, -1)$

$M = ($, $), d = $ _____

9. $E(-2, -5)$ and $F(1, -2)$

$M = ($, $), d = $ _____

10. $G(3, -6)$ and $H(1, -2)$

$M = ($, $), d = $ _____

                                       Saxon Algebra 1

Teaching Skill 74

Objective Solve an inequality and graph its solution on a number line.

Review with students how to read and interpret the four inequality symbols.

Explain that solving an inequality means finding all the numbers that makes the inequality a true statement. Ask: **If x is less than 3, can x equal 6?** (No) Write the inequality $x < 3$ on the board and draw a number line. Point to 4, 5, and 6 and tell students that these numbers result in a false statement. Ask: **What is the first integer that makes the statement true?** (2) Draw an open circle on 3 and explain that you use an open circle because the inequality is $<$, not $\leq$. Shade the number line from the open circle at 3 to the left. Explain that you include numbers between 2 and 3 because fractions and decimals (less than 3) will also result in a true statement.

Point out that the steps for solving an inequality are the same as those used when solving an equation. Review each example with students. When you review Example 2, stress that you must reverse the inequality symbol.

PRACTICE ON YOUR OWN

In exercises 1–9, students solve and graph inequalities.

CHECK

Determine that students know how to solve an inequality and graph its solution on a number line.

Students who successfully complete the **Practice on Your Own** and **Check** are ready to move on to the next skill.

COMMON ERRORS

Students may forget to reverse the inequality symbol when multiplying or dividing by a negative number.

Students who made more than 2 errors in the **Practice on Your Own,** or who were not successful in the **Check** section, may benefit from the **Alternative Teaching Strategy.**

Alternative Teaching Strategy

Objective Graph an inequality on a number line.

Some students may need additional help with graphing solutions on number lines.

Prepare multiple copies of the cards shown below. Give each student one set of well-shuffled cards and instruct them to leave the cards face down.

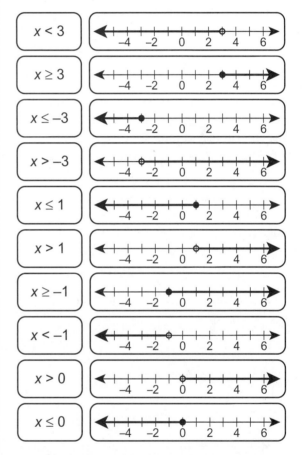

Review with students what each inequality symbol means.

Tell students they are going to play "Speed." When you say "Go," students should flip all their cards over and try to match the correct graph to each inequality. The first student to correctly match all ten sets of cards wins. (Cards are matched in the order presented above.)

An extension of this activity is to prepare cards that have unsolved inequalities and matching graphs.

Saxon Algebra 1

Name _____ Date _____ Class _____

Prerequisite Skills Intervention
Solve and Graph Inequalities

To solve an inequality, you need to find the numbers that make the inequality a true statement.

You use the same process to solve an inequality that you do to solve an equation. The only difference is that when you multiply or divide by a negative number, you must reverse the inequality symbol.

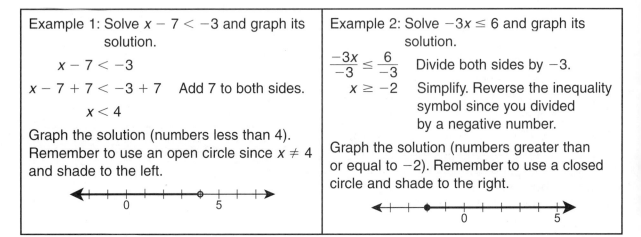

Example 1: Solve $x - 7 < -3$ and graph its solution.

$x - 7 < -3$

$x - 7 + 7 < -3 + 7$ Add 7 to both sides.

$x < 4$

Graph the solution (numbers less than 4). Remember to use an open circle since $x \neq 4$ and shade to the left.

Example 2: Solve $-3x \leq 6$ and graph its solution.

$\dfrac{-3x}{-3} \leq \dfrac{6}{-3}$ Divide both sides by -3.

$x \geq -2$ Simplify. Reverse the inequality symbol since you divided by a negative number.

Graph the solution (numbers greater than or equal to -2). Remember to use a closed circle and shade to the right.

Practice on Your Own
Solve and graph each inequality.

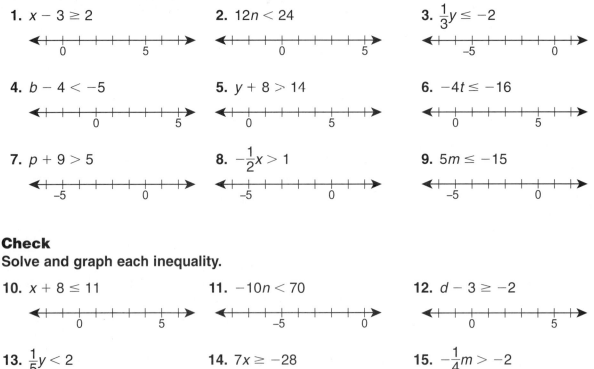

1. $x - 3 \geq 2$

2. $12n < 24$

3. $\frac{1}{3}y \leq -2$

4. $b - 4 < -5$

5. $y + 8 > 14$

6. $-4t \leq -16$

7. $p + 9 > 5$

8. $-\frac{1}{2}x > 1$

9. $5m \leq -15$

Check
Solve and graph each inequality.

10. $x + 8 \leq 11$

11. $-10n < 70$

12. $d - 3 \geq -2$

13. $\frac{1}{5}y < 2$

14. $7x \geq -28$

15. $-\frac{1}{4}m > -2$

Saxon Algebra 1

Teaching Skill 75

Objective Graph a linear function.

Remind students that every linear function can be written in slope-intercept form, $y = mx + b$. Point out that when written in this form, it is possible to graph the linear function using the slope and the y-intercept.

Discuss the concept of slope with students. Remind students that the slope of a line indicates how steep the line is and can be interpreted as the amount of rise (change in vertical position) over the amount of run (change in horizontal position).

Next remind students that the y-intercept is the point where the line crosses the y-axis. Ask: **Which axis is the y-axis?** (the vertical axis)

Direct students' attention to the example. Ask: **What is the slope of the line?** $\left(-\frac{7}{6}\right)$

What is the y-intercept? (0, 5) Work through the example with students.

Ask: **Since you need rise over run for the slope, what do you do if the slope is an integer?** (Put a 1 in the denominator.)

Have students complete the practice exercises.

PRACTICE ON YOUR OWN

In exercises 1–6, students graph linear functions.

CHECK

Determine that students know how to graph linear functions.

Students who successfully complete the **Practice on Your Own** and **Check** are ready to move on to the next skill.

COMMON ERRORS

Students may plot the y-intercept on the wrong axis.

Students who made more than 1 error in the **Practice on Your Own,** or who were not successful in the **Check** section, may benefit from the **Alternative Teaching Strategy.**

Alternative Teaching Strategy

Objective Graph a linear function by finding the x- and y-intercepts.

Remind students that all they need to graph a line is two points. Explain that they can use the x-intercept and the y-intercept as the two points.

Draw and label the following on the board:

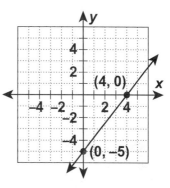

Point to the point (4, 0). Ask: **What is this point called?** (the x-intercept) **Why?** (because it is the point where the line crosses the x-axis) **What is the value of y at this point?** (0) Explain to the students that they can find an x-intercept from an equation by substituting 0 for y and then solving for x.

Follow a similar process to establish that the y-intercept can be determined by substituting 0 for x and then solving for y.

Present the following example: $y = 3x - 9$. Show students how to find the x-intercept by substituting 0 for y ($x = 3$). Then draw a coordinate plane and plot the x-intercept. Remind students that the x-coordinate is always the horizontal position and that the y-coordinate is the vertical position.

Next, have students find the y-intercept by substituting 0 for x and solving for y ($y = -9$). Then plot the point on the coordinate plane. Draw a line through the two points.

Have students use x- and y-intercepts to graph the following equations:

$y = 2x + 4$; $y = \frac{1}{2}x - 3$; and $y = -5x - 5$.

     Saxon Algebra 1

Name _____ Date _____ Class _____

Prerequisite Skills Intervention

Graph Linear Functions

When a linear function is written in slope-intercept form ($y = mx + b$), you have two pieces of information that help you graph the function–the slope and the y-intercept.

> **slope (m)** = rise over run (how much the line rises vertically from left to right compared to how much it runs horizontally). If the slope is negative, the line will fall from left to right, rather than rising.

> **y-intercept (b)** = where the function crosses the vertical (y) axis. The point is (0, b).

Example: Graph the function $y = -\frac{7}{6}x + 5$

Step 1: Place a dot on the y-intercept (0, 5).

Step 2: Fall 7 units vertically and then run 6 units to the right. Place a second dot at the new location.

Step 3: Draw a line through the two dots.

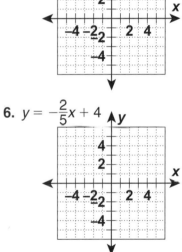

Practice on Your Own

Graph each function.

1. $y = \frac{3}{2}x + 1$

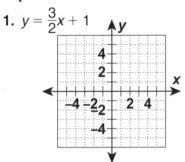

2. $y = \frac{5}{6}x - 4$

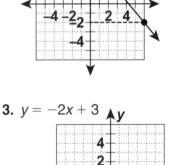

3. $y = -2x + 3$

4. $y = x - 5$

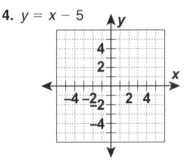

5. $y = -2$

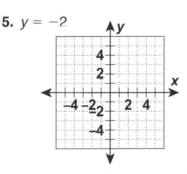

6. $y = -\frac{2}{5}x + 4$

Check

Graph each function.

7. $y = \frac{7}{4}x - 5$

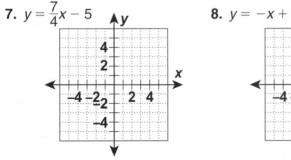

8. $y = -x + 3$

9. $y = 2x - 1$

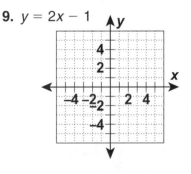

Saxon Algebra 1

Prerequisite Skills Intervention

Slopes of Parallel and Perpendicular Lines

SKILL 76

Teaching Skill 76

Objective Determine when a pair of lines is parallel or perpendicular.

Remind students that the slope of a line determines how steep or how flat the line is. Draw a pair of parallel lines on the board. Ask: **What would you say is true about the steepness of the two lines?** (The steepness is the same.) Explain that this is true for every pair of parallel lines; the steepness is the same so the slopes are equal.

Work through the first example with students.

Next, draw a pair of perpendicular lines on the board and explain that the slopes are negative reciprocals. Give several examples of negative reciprocals. Tell students that it is easy to find the slope of a line written in slope-intercept form, so if the line is written in any other form, rewrite it in slope-intercept form. Then work through the second example with students.

PRACTICE ON YOUR OWN

In exercises 1–9, students determine whether a pair of lines is parallel or perpendicular.

CHECK

Determine that students know how to determine whether a pair of lines is parallel or perpendicular.

Students who successfully complete the **Practice on Your Own** and **Check** are ready to move on to the next skill.

COMMON ERRORS

Students may incorrectly identify two lines as being perpendicular when their slopes are reciprocals, rather than negative reciprocals.

Students who made more than 2 errors in the **Practice on Your Own,** or who were not successful in the **Check** section, may benefit from the **Alternative Teaching Strategy.**

Alternative Teaching Strategy

Objective Graph a pair of lines to determine whether they are parallel, perpendicular, or neither.

Some students may benefit from visualizing why equal slopes produce parallel lines.

Present the following equations:
$$y = 3x - 4$$
$$y = 3x + 1$$

Have students graph the two lines on the same coordinate plane using the *y*-intercept and the slope. Remind students that a slope of 3 means "rise 3 and run 1" and that the *y*-intercept indicates where to place the beginning point. Students' graphs should look like the following:

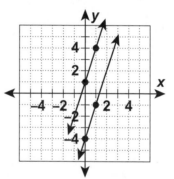

Ask: **What kind of lines are these?** (parallel) Have students repeat the exercise for several sets of parallel lines. When complete, ask: **What is true about every pair of parallel lines?** (They have equal slopes.)

Next, have students graph the following lines on the same coordinate plane:

$y = -\frac{2}{3}x + 4$ and $y = \frac{3}{2}x - 5$. Point out

that the slopes of the two lines are negative reciprocals. Ask: **What kind of lines are these?** (perpendicular lines) Have students graph several sets of perpendicular lines to arrive at the conclusion that lines with negative reciprocal slopes are perpendicular.

Finally, have students graph a pair of lines that is neither parallel nor perpendicular. Explain that these lines are intersecting lines, but not perpendicular.

 Saxon Algebra 1

Prerequisite Skills Intervention

SKILL 76

Slopes of Parallel and Perpendicular Lines

Parallel Lines	Perpendicular Lines
If two lines are parallel, they have equal slopes. So, if two lines have equal slopes, they are parallel.	If two lines are perpendicular, they have slopes that are negative reciprocals. So, if two lines have slopes that are negative reciprocals, they are perpendicular.
Example 1: $y = 7x - 5$ $y = 7x + 9$ Remember, when an equation is written in the form $y = mx + b$, the coefficient of x is the slope. Since the slope of both lines is 7, the lines are parallel.	Example 2: $y = 3x - 5$ $x + 3y = 8$ First, rewrite the second equation in slope-intercept form: $y = -\frac{1}{3}x + \frac{8}{3}$. The slope of the first line is 3 and the slope of the second line is $-\frac{1}{3}$. Since 3 and $-\frac{1}{3}$ are negative reciprocals, the lines are perpendicular.

Practice on Your Own
State whether the linear equations in each pair are parallel, perpendicular, or neither.

1. $y = 6x - 3$
   $y = -\frac{1}{6}x + 7$

2. $y = 3x + 2$
   $2y = 6x - 6$

3. $8x - 2y = 3$
   $x + 4y = -1$

4. $3x + 2y = 5$
   $3y + 2x = -3$

5. $y - 5 = 6x$
   $y - 6x = -1$

6. $y = 3x + 9$
   $y = \frac{1}{3}x - 4$

7. $y = x + 3$
   $y = -x - 5$

8. $y = 6$
   $x = -2$

9. $3y = -x$
   $3x = y$

Check
State whether the linear equations in each pair are parallel, perpendicular, or neither.

10. $y = 5 + 7x$
    $y = -\frac{1}{7}x - 2$

11. $2x + y = 5$
    $2y = -4x + 3$

12. $x = \frac{1}{3}y - 1$
    $2y = 6x$

13. $y = 2$
    $y - 7 = 0$

14. $y = \frac{1}{4}x + 3$
    $2y - 8x = 1$

15. $x - 2y = 0$
    $y + 1 = -2x$

Saxon Algebra 1

Teaching Skill 77

Objective Solve proportions.

Review with students the definition of a proportion. Point out that you can also think of a proportion as two equivalent fractions.

Ask: **If two fractions are equivalent, what is true about their simplest forms?** (They are equal.) Write two equivalent fractions on the board, such as $\frac{1}{2} = \frac{5}{10}$. Ask: **Is this a true statement and why?** (Yes, because the fractions are equivalent.) Tell students that this is a proportion.

Show students by pointing what the cross products of this proportion are. (1×10 and 2×5) Ask: **What is true about the cross products?** (They are equal.) Explain to students that this is the key to solving proportions.

Review with students the steps for solving a proportion. Then work through the example. Remind students that it does not matter which side the variable is on when solving an equation.

PRACTICE ON YOUR OWN

In exercises 1–12, students solve proportions.

CHECK

Determine that students know how to solve proportions.

Students who successfully complete the **Practice on Your Own** and **Check** are ready to move on to the next skill.

COMMON ERRORS

Students may multiply the numerators together and the denominators together, rather than finding the cross products.

Students who made more than 3 errors in the **Practice on Your Own,** or who were not successful in the **Check** section, may benefit from the **Alternative Teaching Strategy.**

Alternative Teaching Strategy

Objective Solve proportions.

Tell students that it is possible in many proportions to follow a pattern to solve the proportion.

Write the following proportion on the board: $\frac{12}{16} = \frac{36}{48}$. Ask: **If you look at the numerators, what are you multiplying by to get from 12 to 36?** (3) **What are you multiplying by in the denominators to get from 16 to 48?** (3)

Write the following on the board:

Explain that because you are multiplying both the numerator and the denominator by the same number, you still have equivalent ratios since $\frac{3}{3} = 1$.

Write the following on the board: $\overset{\times 2}{\overbrace{\frac{9}{16} = \frac{18}{x}}}_{\times 2}$

Have students find the value of x by multiplying 16 times 2. (32)

Tell students that this process also works if you are dividing the numerator and denominator by the same number. Write the following on the board: $\frac{72}{45} = \frac{8}{x}$. Have students draw a diagram of the division, like the multiplication diagrams above. ($\div$ 9 on each piece; answer: $x = 5$)

Have students use this technique to solve the following proportions: $\frac{2}{5} = \frac{8}{x}$; $\frac{9}{12} = \frac{3}{x}$; $\frac{15}{17} = \frac{30}{x}$; $\frac{11}{8} = \frac{77}{x}$; $\frac{18}{33} = \frac{6}{x}$; and $\frac{88}{48} = \frac{11}{x}$.

($x = 20$; $x = 4$; $x = 34$; $x = 56$; $x = 11$; $x = 6$)

Then have students solve problems with x in the numerator.

Saxon Algebra 1

Name _____ Date _____ Class _____

Prerequisite Skills Intervention

Solve Proportions

Definition: A proportion is an equation that shows two equivalent ratios.

Key property: The cross products of a proportion are equal.

To solve a proportion, follow these two steps:

- Step 1: Find the cross products.

- Step 2: Simplify if necessary and solve the equation for the variable.

Example: Solve $\frac{4}{6} = \frac{x}{12}$

Step 1: Find the cross products.	Step 2: Simplify and solve.
$\frac{4}{6} = \frac{x}{12}$ ➡ $6 \cdot x = 4 \cdot 12$	$6 \cdot x = 4 \cdot 12$ Multiply. $6x = 48$ Divide both sides by 6. $x = 8$

Practice on Your Own
Solve each proportion.

1. $\frac{2}{5} = \frac{x}{25}$

2. $\frac{11}{4} = \frac{22}{x}$

3. $\frac{8}{16} = \frac{x}{160}$

4. $\frac{100}{500} = \frac{x}{100}$

_____ _____ _____ _____

5. $\frac{9}{10} = \frac{45}{x}$

6. $\frac{90}{12} = \frac{x}{4}$

7. $\frac{15}{7} = \frac{5}{x}$

8. $\frac{30}{21} = \frac{x}{7}$

_____ _____ _____ _____

9. $\frac{45}{8} = \frac{5}{x}$

10. $\frac{1}{99} = \frac{x}{33}$

11. $\frac{2}{9} = \frac{8}{x}$

12. $\frac{8}{3} = \frac{32}{x}$

_____ _____ _____ _____

Check
Solve each proportion.

13. $\frac{3}{7} = \frac{x}{49}$

14. $\frac{15}{30} = \frac{5}{x}$

15. $\frac{13}{2} = \frac{x}{4}$

16. $\frac{66}{12} = \frac{6}{x}$

_____ _____ _____ _____

17. $\frac{11}{4} = \frac{22}{x}$

18. $\frac{6}{4} = \frac{x}{5}$

19. $\frac{1}{55} = \frac{x}{44}$

20. $\frac{12}{5} = \frac{24}{x}$

_____ _____ _____ _____

Saxon Algebra 1

Teaching Skill 78

Objective Generate ordered pairs for given values of a function.

Explain to students that function tables are used to generate ordered pairs in the form (x, y). These ordered pairs can be used to graph a function.

Review with students how to evaluate a function for a given value of x. Remind students that they should be particularly careful when substituting negative values into a function.

Direct students' attention to the example. Point out that the x-values are called inputs. Ask: **In this example, what are the inputs?** (-2, -1, 0, 1 and 2) Explain that the inputs are substituted into the function, and the y-values that result are called the outputs. The ordered pairs are the points (x, y).

Work through the example, making sure students understand how the function is being applied to the input values to generate the outputs. Then have students complete the practice exercises.

PRACTICE ON YOUR OWN

In exercises 1–8, students generate ordered pairs by completing function tables for given inputs.

CHECK

Determine that students know how to complete function tables.

Students who successfully complete the **Practice on Your Own** and **Check** are ready to move on to the next skill.

COMMON ERRORS

Students may not perform the operations of a function's rule correctly and may arrive at an incorrect output for a given input.

Students who made more than 2 errors in the **Practice on Your Own,** or who were not successful in the **Check** section, may benefit from the **Alternative Teaching Strategy.**

Alternative Teaching Strategy

Objective Generate ordered pairs for given values of a function.

Some students may need additional practice evaluating functions.

Remind students that when you evaluate a function, you apply a rule to an input value to generate an output. Understanding the rule that is being applied is critical to completing a function table.

Write the following function table on the board and have students copy it on their paper.

x	$y = $ _____	y
-2	$y = 3(\boxed{}) - 1 = \boxed{} - 1 = \boxed{}$	$\boxed{}$
-1	$y = 3(\boxed{}) - 1 = \boxed{} - 1 = \boxed{}$	$\boxed{}$
0	$y = 3(\boxed{}) - 1 = \boxed{} - 1 = \boxed{}$	$\boxed{}$
1	$y = 3(\boxed{}) - 1 = \boxed{} - 1 = \boxed{}$	$\boxed{}$
2	$y = 3(\boxed{}) - 1 = \boxed{} - 1 = \boxed{}$	$\boxed{}$

Have students consider the "rule" that is being applied to the input values, -2, -1, 0, 1, and 2. Have a volunteer try to write an algebraic expression that represents the rule. Guide the volunteer if needed. ($y = 3x - 1$) Then have students write the function in the center column of the table and complete the function table.

Have students work in pairs for the next part of the exercise. Instruct each student to write down a function (rule) in the form of an algebraic expression (e.g. $y = 2x + 6$), but not show their partner. Each student should then create a function table similar to the one above for their function. They should use boxes, rather than variables, as above. When they have created their tables, they should exchange papers, try to figure out their partner's rule, and then complete the table. Repeat the exercise until you feel comfortable that students understand how to complete function tables.

Saxon Algebra 1

Name _____ Date _____ Class _____

Prerequisite Skills Intervention

Function Tables

SKILL
78

A function table is a set of solutions to an equation. When given a set of *x*-values, substitute the values into the equation to find the corresponding *y*-values. Use the *x*- and *y*-values to generate ordered pairs.

Example: Generate ordered pairs for the function $y = 5x + 2$ for $x = -2, -1, 0, 1, 2$.

x	$y = 5x + 2$	y
-2	$y = 5(-2) + 2 = -10 + 2 = -8$	-8
-1	$y = 5(-1) + 2 = -5 + 2 = -3$	-3
0	$y = 5(0) + 2 = 0 + 2 = 2$	2
1	$y = 5(1) + 2 = 5 + 2 = 7$	7
2	$y = 5(2) + 2 = 10 + 2 = 12$	12

x	y
-2	-8
-1	-3
0	2
1	7
2	12

Practice on Your Own
Generate ordered pairs for each function for $x = -2, -1, 0, 1, 2$.

1. $y = 3x + 1$

x	y
-2	
-1	
0	
1	
2	

2. $y = -4x + 5$

x	y
-2	
-1	
0	
1	
2	

3. $y = x^2$

x	y
-2	
-1	
0	
1	
2	

4. $y = x^2 - 3$

x	y
-2	
-1	
0	
1	
2	

5. $y = \frac{1}{2}x + \frac{3}{2}$

x	y
-2	
-1	
0	
1	
2	

6. $y = -\frac{1}{2}x + 4$

x	y
-2	
-1	
0	
1	
2	

7. $y = (x + 2)^2$

x	y
-2	
-1	
0	
1	
2	

8. $y = (x - 2)^2$

x	y
-2	
-1	
0	
1	
2	

Check
Generate ordered pairs for each function for $x = -2, -1, 0, 1, 2$.

9. $y = 4x + 3$

x	y
-2	
-1	
0	
1	
2	

10. $y = -3x - 10$

x	y
-2	
-1	
0	
1	
2	

11. $y = \frac{1}{2}x - \frac{1}{2}$

x	y
-2	
-1	
0	
1	
2	

12. $y = (x - 3)^2$

x	y
-2	
-1	
0	
1	
2	

Saxon Algebra 1

Prerequisite Skills Intervention

Ordered Pairs

SKILL
79

Teaching Skill 79

Objective Plot ordered pairs on a coordinate plane.

Remind students that all points in the coordinate plane have two coordinates, an *x*-coordinate and a *y*-coordinate.

Sketch a coordinate plane on the board. Point to the origin and explain that the intersection of the *x*- and *y*-axes is called the origin and has coordinates (0, 0).

Explain that the *x*-coordinate of a point tells how many units to move to the left or right of the origin. The *y*-coordinate tells how many units to move above or below the origin.

Tell students you are going to plot the point (3, 4). Place your marker at the origin and draw 3 small hops to the right and then 4 small hops up. Draw a dot at (3, 4). Point out that you always move horizontally before you move vertically.

Label the four quadrants on the coordinate plane and review with students where the *x*-coordinates are positive (to the right of the *y*-axis), and where they are negative (to the left of the *y*-axis.) Do the same for the *y*-coordinates and then work the examples.

PRACTICE ON YOUR OWN

In exercises 1–12 students plot ordered pairs on a coordinate plane.

CHECK

Determine that students know how to plot ordered pairs on a coordinate plane.

Students who successfully complete the **Practice on Your Own** and **Check** are ready to move on to the next skill.

COMMON ERRORS

Students may use the *x*-coordinate to move vertically and the *y*-coordinate to move horizontally.

Students who made more than 2 errors in the **Practice on Your Own,** or who were not successful in the **Check** section, may benefit from the **Alternative Teaching Strategy.**

Alternative Teaching Strategy

Objective Plot ordered pairs on a coordinate plane to determine what kind of quadrilateral a four-sided polygon is.

Materials needed: multiple copies of the grid below with points already plotted

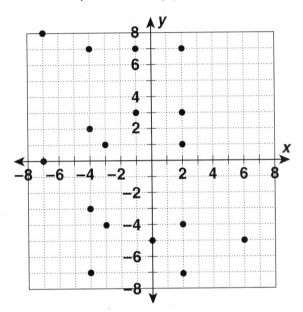

Tell students they are going to locate points on a coordinate plane to identify four special quadrilaterals.

Review with students how to plot ordered pairs on the coordinate plane. Emphasize when to move to the left and/or down.

Next, write the four ordered pairs on the board: $A(-3, 1)$; $B(2, 1)$; $C(2, -4)$; and $D(-3, -4)$. Instruct students to locate, label, and connect the four points and to name quadrilateral $ABCD$. (square)

Repeat the exercise for points $E(-7, 8)$; $F(-7, 0)$; $G(-4, 2)$; and $H(-4, 7)$. (trapezoid)

Repeat the exercise for points $J(0, -5)$; $K(-4, -7)$; $L(6, -5)$; and $M(2, -7)$. (parallelogram)

Repeat the exercise for points $N(-1, 3)$; $P(-1, 7)$; $Q(2, 7)$; and $R(2, 3)$. (rectangle)

As an extension of this exercise, have students locate and plot points that form a scalene triangle, an isosceles triangle, an equilateral triangle, and a right triangle.

     Saxon Algebra 1

Name _____ Date _____ Class _____

Prerequisite Skills Intervention
Ordered Pairs

Ordered pairs are *x*- and *y*-coordinates of points in a coordinate plane. Points look like (*x*, *y*).

The *x*-coordinate is the horizontal coordinate of the point. It tells how many units to move to the left or right of the origin. The *y*-coordinate is the vertical coordinate. It tells us how many units to move above or below the origin. Positive coordinates indicate movement to the right and up. Negative coordinates indicate movement to the left and down.

The table shows in which quadrant points lie.

Example: Plot the points $A(2, 5)$ and $B(-3, -1)$ on the coordinate plane given.

Q1	(+, +)
Q2	(−, +)
Q3	(−, −)
Q4	(+, −)

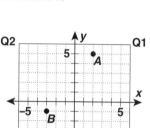

Point *A* lies in Quadrant 1 and point *B* lies in Quadrant 3.

Practice on Your Own
Graph each point on the coordinate plane provided.

1. $A(2, 5)$

2. $B(-3, 1)$

3. $C(0, -6)$

4. $D(-7, -4)$

5. $E(-9, 6)$

6. $F(8, 0)$

7. $G(5, -5)$

8. $H(-8, 1)$

9. $J(0, 2)$

10. $K(-2, -2)$

11. $L(1, 9)$

12. $M(4, -1)$

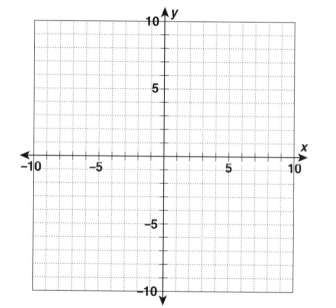

Check
Graph each point on the coordinate plane provided.

13. $A(0, 4)$

14. $B(2, -3)$

15. $C(-5, 3)$

16. $D(4, 2)$

17. $E(-3, 0)$

18. $F(-5, -4)$

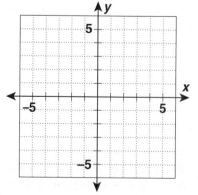

158   **Saxon** Algebra 1

Teaching Skill 80
Objective Graph functions on a coordinate plane.

Remind students that all points in a coordinate plane have two coordinates, an *x*-coordinate and a *y*-coordinate. Point out that function tables are one way to generate ordered pairs. With enough ordered pairs, it is possible to sketch the graph of most functions.

Review with students the steps for graphing functions. Stress that if a specific domain is given, only the ordered pairs generated from that domain should be plotted. The points should not be connected since there are no other points in the domain of the function.

Work through the example with students. Remind students that when plotting points on a coordinate plane, you always move horizontally first, then vertically. Also remind students that first degree polynomials should have graphs that are lines, and second degree polynomials should have graphs that are parabolas. Have students complete the practice exercises.

PRACTICE ON YOUR OWN
In exercises 1–3, students graph functions for a given domain. In exercises 4–6, students graph continuous functions.

CHECK
Determine that students know how to graph functions.

Students who successfully complete the **Practice on Your Own** and **Check** are ready to move on to the next skill.

COMMON ERRORS
Students may not perform the operations of a function's rule correctly and may arrive at an ordered pair that is not on the graph of the function.

Students who made more than 2 errors in the **Practice on Your Own,** or who were not successful in the **Check** section, may benefit from the **Alternative Teaching Strategy.**

Alternative Teaching Strategy
Objective Graph quadratic functions.

Remind students that quadratic functions are functions with degree 2. Ask: **Is $y = x^2$ a quadratic function?** (Yes) **How about $y = x^2 + 6$?** (Yes)

Tell students they are going to graph the standard quadratic function, $y = x^2$.

Have students complete a function table for the *x*-values $-2, -1, 0, 1,$ and 2. Check student answers.

x	$y = x^2$	Ordered Pair
-2	$(-2)^2 = 4$	$(-2, 4)$
-1	$(-1)^2 = 1$	$(-1, 1)$
0	$(0)^2 = 0$	$(0, 0)$
1	$(1)^2 = 1$	$(1, 1)$
2	$(2)^2 = 4$	$(2, 4)$

Next have students plot the points and connect them. (The graph should be a parabola with vertex at (0, 0).) Tells students they have just graphed the standard parabola.

Next, have students complete a function table for $y = x^2 + 2$ and graph the function on the same coordinate plane as their first graph. (The graph should be a parabola with vertex at (0, 2).) Ask: **What happened to the standard parabola?** (All the points were shifted up 2 units.)

Repeat the exercise for the function $y = x^2 - 5$. (The graph should be a parabola with vertex at (0, −5) since all the points were shifted down 5 units.) Ask: **What do you think will happen to the standard parabola if you graph the function $y = x^2 + 7$?** (All the points will be shifted up 7 units.) **What if you graph $y = x^2 - 15$?** (All the points will be shifted down 15 units.)

Repeat the process to demonstrate horizontal shifts. On a new set of axes, graph $y = (x - 3)^2$; $y = (x + 4)^2$; $y = (x - 7)^2$. Point out that a horizontal shift is backwards of what you might think.

Prerequisite Skills Intervention

Graph Functions

SKILL
80

To graph a function, follow these steps:

Step 1: Make a table of values. If the domain is given, use those *x*-values. If a
domain is not given, choose several values such as $-2, -1, 0, 1,$ and 2.
Step 2: Plot the ordered pairs.
Step 3: If a specific domain is not given, draw a line or curve through the points.

Example: Graph $y = x^2 - 3$ for
the domain, D: $\{-2, -1, 0, 1, 2\}$.

Note: Since a specific domain is given,
do <u>not</u> draw a line through the points.

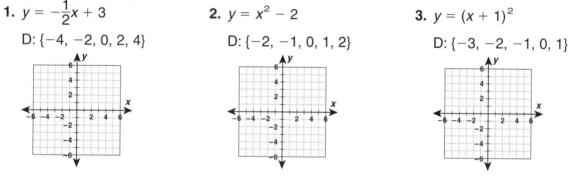

x	$y = x^2 - 3$	(x, y)
-2	$(-2)^2 - 3 = 4 - 3 = 1$	$(-2, 1)$
-1	$(-1)^2 - 3 = 1 - 3 = -2$	$(-1, -2)$
0	$(0)^2 - 3 = 0 - 3 = -3$	$(0, -3)$
1	$(1)^2 - 3 = 1 - 3 = -2$	$(1, -2)$
2	$(2)^2 - 3 = 4 - 3 = 1$	$(2, 1)$

Practice on Your Own

Graph each function for the given domain.

1. $y = -\frac{1}{2}x + 3$

D: $\{-4, -2, 0, 2, 4\}$

2. $y = x^2 - 2$

D: $\{-2, -1, 0, 1, 2\}$

3. $y = (x + 1)^2$

D: $\{-3, -2, -1, 0, 1\}$

Graph each function.

4. $y = x^2 - 5$

5. $y = 2x - 3$

6. $y = (x - 2)^2$

Check

Graph each function. If the domain is given, graph the function for only that domain.

7. $y = \frac{2}{3}x + 1$

D: $\{-6, -3, 0, 3, 6\}$

8. $y = x^2 + 1$

9. $y = (x + 2)^2$

Saxon Algebra 1

Teaching Skill 81

Objective Solve quadratic equations by taking the square root.

Remind students that there are a number of ways to solve quadratic equations: factoring; grouping; using the quadratic formula; and taking square roots. Point out that when the equation to be solved has only an x^2 term and a constant, the quickest way to solve the equation is to find the square root.

Remind students that when you solve the equation $x^2 = 9$, you get two answers, $+3$ and -3. To illustrate this, ask: **Is 3^2 equal to 9?** (Yes) **Is $(-3)^2$ also equal to 9?** (Yes)

Review with students the steps for solving a quadratic equation by taking square roots. Emphasize that the x^2 term must be on one side of the equal sign and the constant must be on the other side. Also point out that the coefficient of the x^2 term should be 1 before finding the square root.

Work through the example with students. Remind students to use inverse operations when moving terms from one side of the equation to the other.

PRACTICE ON YOUR OWN

In exercises 1–9, students solve quadratic equations by finding the square root.

CHECK

Determine that students know how to solve quadratic equations by isolating the variable and taking square roots.

Students who successfully complete the **Practice on Your Own** and **Check** are ready to move on to the next skill.

COMMON ERRORS

Students may forget that finding the square root of a number results in both a positive answer and a negative answer.

Students who made more than 2 errors in the **Practice on Your Own,** or who were not successful in the **Check** section, may benefit from the **Alternative Teaching Strategy.**

Alternative Teaching Strategy

Objective Solve quadratic equations by factoring a difference of squares.

Some students are more comfortable solving quadratics by factoring. Explain to students that they can factor any quadratic equation that can be solved by the square root method.

Remind students that there are special quadratics called differences of squares. Write the following equation on the board: $x^2 - 36 = 0$. Then remind students that the factored form of this equation is $(x - 6)(x + 6)$. Ask: **What happens to the middle terms when this product is multiplied out?** (They are opposites, $6x$ and $-6x$, and have a sum of zero.) Have students practice factoring simple differences of squares.

Next, remind students that when solving quadratic equations, if either factor is equal to zero, then the whole product is equal to zero. This explains why you are allowed to set each factor equal to zero and solve. Write $(x + 6)(x - 6) = 0$ on the board and demonstrate how to solve the equation to get $x = 6$ and $x = -6$.

Next, write the equation $x^2 = 49$ on the board. Ask: **How can you make this look like a difference of squares?** (Subtract 49 from both sides of the equation). **Then how can you solve the equation?** (Factor and solve.) Have students practice several of these types of problems.

Next, write the problem $7x^2 = 28$ on the board, and then subtract 28 from both sides to get the equation $7x^2 - 28 = 0$. Ask: **Is this a difference of squares?** (No) **Why not?** (7 is not a perfect square, nor is 28.) Remind students that they can factor out the GCF. Demonstrate using the problem above. $[7(x^2 - 4) = 0]$ Point out that there is now a difference of squares and the problem can be solved by factoring. Work several problems similar to the example.

Saxon Algebra 1

Name _____ Date _____ Class _____

Prerequisite Skills Intervention
Solve Quadratic Equations

One method of solving quadratic equations is to find the square root of both sides of the equation. This method only works when the equation is limited to an x^2 term and a constant.

To solve a quadratic equation by the square root method, follow these steps:

• Step 1: Simplify the expression by combining like terms and then isolate the x^2 term.

• Step 2: Divide both sides of the equation by the coefficient of x^2.

• Step 3: Find the square root of both sides of the equation. Remember, you will get a positive and a negative value as your answers.

Example: Solve $5x^2 = 3x^2 + 32$.

$$2x^2 = 32$$
$$x^2 = 16$$
$$x = 4 \text{ or } -4$$

Step 1: Subtract $3x^2$ from both sides.
Step 2: Divide both sides by 2.
Step 3: Find the square root of both sides.

Practice on Your Own
Solve each equation.

1. $7x^2 = 28$

$x =$ _____ or _____

2. $3x^2 = x^2 + 32$

$x =$ _____ or _____

3. $4x^2 - 4 = 60$

$x =$ _____ or _____

4. $2x^2 + x^2 = 3$

$x =$ _____ or _____

5. $200 = 2x^2$

$x =$ _____ or _____

6. $10x^2 - 27 = 7x^2$

$x =$ _____ or _____

7. $-220 = 5 - x^2$

$x =$ _____ or _____

8. $10x^2 = 5x^2 + 125$

$x =$ _____ or _____

9. $2x^2 - 6 = x^2 + 30$

$x =$ _____ or _____

Check
Solve each equation for the indicated variable.

10. $12x^2 = 12$

$x =$ _____ or _____

11. $6x^2 - 10 = 140$

$x =$ _____ or _____

12. $19 = x^2 - 17$

$x =$ _____ or _____

13. $8 + x^2 = 3x^2$

$x =$ _____ or _____

14. $20 - x^2 = -80$

$x =$ _____ or _____

15. $2x^2 - 150 = 650$

$x =$ _____ or _____

Saxon Algebra 1

Teaching Skill 82

Objective Complete the square and write a trinomial as the square of a binomial.

Remind students that some quadratic equations can be solved by finding the square root of both sides. Write the example $(x + 3)^2 = 7$ on the board and point out that since both sides of the equation are squares, the square root method can be used to solve the equation.

Emphasize that before you can take the square root, both sides of the equation must be in the form of a perfect square. Point out that completing the square allows you to rewrite an equation in this form.

Review with students the steps for completing the square and work through the example. Then briefly discuss the limitations of this method: the coefficient of x^2 must be 1 before you begin the process, and when the coefficient of x (b) is an odd number, the answers will contain fractions.

Have students complete the practice exercises.

PRACTICE ON YOUR OWN

In exercises 1–9, students complete the square and write the given trinomial as the square of a binomial.

CHECK

Determine that students know how to complete the square.

Students who successfully complete the **Practice on Your Own** and **Check** are ready to move on to the next skill.

COMMON ERRORS

Students may forget to divide b in half when writing the trinomial in factored form.

Students who made more than 2 errors in the **Practice on Your Own,** or who were not successful in the **Check** section, may benefit from the **Alternative Teaching Strategy.**

Alternative Teaching Strategy

Objective Recognize perfect square trinomials and rewrite them as the square of a binomial.

Remind students that some products are special. Provide the following examples: $(x + 6)^2$ and $(x - 6)^2$. Explain to students that these special products are called respectively the square of a sum and the square of a difference.

Have students FOIL the first product to get $x^2 + 12x + 36$. Ask: **Once you multiply out the product, what is true about the middle term in relation to the original product?** (It is twice 6.) **What is true about the last term in relation to the original product?** (It is the square of 6.) Repeat this exercise for $(x - 6)^2$.

To reinforce this, have students square several sums and several differences.

Next, write the following on the board: $x^2 +$ ____$x + 49$. Ask: **If the last number is the square of the constant in the product, how do you find that constant?** (Find the square root of the last number.) **Then what would you do to find the coefficient of the middle term?** (Double it since it should be twice the constant in the product.) Demonstrate using the problem above. ($\sqrt{49} = 7$ then $2(7) = 14$) **How would you write the trinomial as a square?** $(x + 7)^2$ Have students use this process to find the middle term of several square trinomials and then write them as squares.

Next, write the following on the board: $x^2 + 10x +$ ____. Ask: **Since the middle term is always twice the constant in the product, what can you do to the 10 to find the middle term?** (Divide it by 2 to get 5.) **Then what do you do to find the last term?** (Square the 5 to get 25.) **How do you write the trinomial as a square?** $(x + 5)^2$ Have students work several problems using this process.

Saxon Algebra 1

Prerequisite Skills Intervention

Complete the Square

Completing the square makes it possible to solve a quadratic equation by creating a perfect square trinomial on one side of the equation so that you can find the square root of both sides.

If a quadratic is in the form $x^2 + bx$, follow these steps to complete the square and write the trinomial as the square of a binomial.

Step1: Add the quantity $\left(\frac{b}{2}\right)^2$ to the expression.	**Step 2:** Write the trinomial as $\left(x + \frac{b}{2}\right)^2$.
Example: $x^2 - 18x + \boxed{}$ $b = -18$, so $\frac{b}{2} = -9$ and $\left(\frac{b}{2}\right)^2 = (-9)^2 = 81$ $x^2 - 18x + 81$	Since $\frac{b}{2} = -9$, rewrite the expression as $(x - 9)^2$.

Practice on Your Own

Complete the square for each expression. Write the resulting expression as the square of a binomial.

1. $x^2 + 8x + \boxed{}$ **2.** $x^2 - 12x + \boxed{}$ **3.** $x^2 + x + \boxed{}$

_____   _____   _____

4. $x^2 - 10x + \boxed{}$ **5.** $x^2 - 22x + \boxed{}$ **6.** $x^2 - 3x + \boxed{}$

_____   _____   _____

7. $x^2 + 14x + \boxed{}$ **8.** $x^2 - 24x + \boxed{}$ **9.** $x^2 + 9x + \boxed{}$

_____   _____   _____

Check

Complete the square for each expression. Write the resulting expression as the square of a binomial.

10. $x^2 + 6x + \boxed{}$ **11.** $x^2 - 16x + \boxed{}$ **12.** $x^2 + 5x + \boxed{}$

_____   _____   _____

13. $x^2 - 20x + \boxed{}$ **14.** $x^2 + 2x + \boxed{}$ **15.** $x^2 - 7x + \boxed{}$

_____   _____   _____

Saxon Algebra 1

Prerequisite Skills Intervention

SKILL
83

Tables and Charts

Teaching Skill 83
Objective Determine percentages from a table of data.

Explain to students that tables are often used to organize data into categories. The left column is usually a description of the category, and the right column is usually the number of items that fit into that category.

Have students consider the table in the example. Ask: **What are the categories of data?** (white, silver, red, and black) **How many items are in the white category?** (336) **How many items are in the black category?** (96)

Explain to students how to find the percentage of the data that any given category represents using the formula provided. Then work through the example with students.

Also point out that to determine what percentage multiple categories represent, first find the sum of the items in the categories you are interested in, and then divide by the total number of items.

Have students complete the practice exercises.

PRACTICE ON YOUR OWN
In exercises 1–6, students use tables to determine percentages.

CHECK
Determine that students know how to find percentages based on data in a table.

Students who successfully complete the **Practice on Your Own** and **Check** are ready to move on to the next skill.

COMMON ERRORS
Students may add the total number of items incorrectly.

Students who made more than 2 errors in the **Practice on Your Own,** or who were not successful in the **Check** section, may benefit from the **Alternative Teaching Strategy.**

Alternative Teaching Strategy
Objective Create a table of data and determine percentages for various categories of the data.

Materials needed: coins (18 pennies, 12 nickels, 12 dimes, and 8 quarters); marbles or any other colored counter such as skittles or M&Ms (14 of one color, 16 of another, 20 of another, and 10 of another)

Tell students they are going to create a table of data and then find the percentage that each category of data represents.

Have students divide into two groups. Give one group of students the coins and the other group the colored counters. Have the students discuss what the categories should be for their tables. (types of coins, and colors of counters) Using these categories, have students draw a table and fill in the title row and the four categories in the left column. The tables should look like:

Coin	Number of Coins		Color	Number of Marbles
Pennies				
Nickels				
Dimes				
Quarters				

Next have the students count the total number of items they have. Then, they should divide their items into the categories they have created and count the items in each category. Have the students record their findings in the right column of their tables.

Review with students how to find the percentage that each category represents. Have the students find the percentages for each of their categories. Ask: **What is the sum of all the percentages?** (100%) **Why?** (Because all the items have been accounted for.)

Have the two groups trade items, create new tables, and find new percentages.

© Saxon. All rights reserved.

165

Saxon Algebra 1

Prerequisite Skills Intervention
Tables and Charts

A table can be used to organize data into categories.

To determine what percentage any one category represents, divide the number of items in that category by the total number of items.

Example: The table shows the distribution of colors of cars sold by a certain car dealership in Florida. Find the percentage of cars that are white.

Color	Number of Cars
White	336
Silver	192
Red	176
Black	96

$$\frac{\text{number of white cars}}{\text{total number of cars}} = \frac{336}{336 + 192 + 176 + 96} = \frac{336}{800} = 0.42 = 42\%$$

Find the percentage of cars that are red or silver.

$$\frac{\text{number of red cars or silver cars}}{\text{total number of cars}} = \frac{176 + 192}{336 + 192 + 176 + 96} = \frac{368}{800} = 0.46 = 46\%$$

Practice on Your Own

The table shows the number of students at a local high school who prefer certain types of sports activities. Find each of the following:

Sports Activity	Number of Students
Hiking	90
In-line skating	114
Bicycling	168
Canoeing	180
Weight-lifting	48

1. the percentage of students who prefer bicycling _____

2. the percentage of students who prefer canoeing _____

3. the percentage of students who prefer hiking or weight-lifting _____

The table shows the number of baseball players in the Major League, including pitchers, who have achieved certain batting averages throughout the regular season. Find each of the following:

Batting Average	Number of Players
0 to 99	209
100 to 199	165
200 to 299	638
300 to 399	88

4. the percentage of players whose batting average is under 100 _____

5. the percentage of players whose average is between 200 and 299 _____

6. the percentage of players whose average is between 100 and 399 _____

Check

The table shows the number of people in each age group who attended a middle school concert. Find each of the following:

Age Group	Number of People
Under 20	96
20 – 29	30
30 – 39	123
40 – 49	36
50 and over	15

7. the percentage of people whose age is between 20 and 29 _____

8. the percentage of people whose age is 50 or older _____

9. the percentage of people whose age is under 30 _____

Saxon Algebra 1

Teaching Skill 84

Objective Find the mean, median, and mode of data.

Explain to students that there are three common measures of central tendency used to represent a set of data: the mean, the median, and the mode.

Explain that the mean is the arithmetic average. Ask: **How do you calculate an average?** (Find the sum of the values and divide by the number of values.) Have students review the mean example.

Next, explain that the median is the middle number when the data values are written in order from least to greatest, if there is an odd number of data values. Ask: **If there is an even number of data values, is there a middle number?** (No) Explain that the median is the average of the two middle numbers. Have students review the median example.

Finally, explain that the mode is the data value that appears the most often. Point out that there can be two modes (called bi-modal) if two values appear the most often. Have students review the mode example and then complete the practice exercises.

PRACTICE ON YOUR OWN

In exercises 1–9, students find the mean, median, and mode of sets of data.

CHECK

Determine that students know how to find measures of central tendency.

Students who successfully complete the **Practice on Your Own** and **Check** are ready to move on to the next skill.

COMMON ERRORS

When finding the median, students may forget to order the data values before they select the middle term.

Students who made more than 2 errors in the **Practice on Your Own,** or who were not successful in the **Check** section, may benefit from the **Alternative Teaching Strategy.**

Alternative Teaching Strategy

Objective Find the mean, median, and mode of a set of data collected by the student.

Tell the students they are going to collect data from their class mates and then find the mean, median, and mode of the data.

Ask: **Can you find the average of data such as favorite kind of car, favorite color, type of pet, etc?** (No) **What about the median of such data?** (No) **Why not?** (There are no numerical values.) Explain that this type of data is called qualitative data, while numerical data is called quantitative. Point out that only quantitative data has measures of central tendency.

Have the students select the data they would like to collect from their classmates. Discuss their choices to make sure the data is quantitative (and appropriate). Provide examples if needed (e.g. average number of math homework problems they do every night, how many miles they live from school, number of movies they watch per month, etc.)

Once each student has selected an appropriate data topic, have them write a specific question to collect their data. Then have the students ask each of the other students in the class their question. They should record the answers on a sheet of paper.

When everyone's data has been collected and recorded, review with students how to find the mean, median, and mode of sets of data.

Instruct each student to count the number of data values they collected (Everyone's should be the same if they asked each student their question.) Then have students find the mean, median, and mode of the data they collected.

Write all the data topics on the board and have students select a new set of data to collect. Repeat the exercise.

167 **Saxon** Algebra 1

Name _____ Date _____ Class _____

Prerequisite Skills Intervention
Find Measures of Central Tendency

Example: Find the mean, median, and mode of the data set: 10, 12, 13, 15, 10.

Mean	Median	Mode
The mean is the average of the data values: $\dfrac{\text{sum of all the values}}{\text{number of values}}$	The median is the middle number when the values are in order from least to greatest.	The mode is the data value that appears the most often.
$\dfrac{10 + 12 + 13 + 15 + 10}{5} = \dfrac{60}{5} = 12$	10, 10, (12,) 13, 15	10 is the only data value that appears more than one time.

Practice on Your Own
Find the mean, median, and mode of each data set.

1. 7, 6, 11, 9, 7

Mean = _____

Median = _____

Mode = _____

2. 2, 2, 3, 3, 4, 4, 4

Mean = _____

Median = _____

Mode = _____

3. 4, 5, 6, 7, 8, 9

Mean = _____

Median = _____

Mode = _____

4. 5, 4, 4, 4, 7, 6, 6, 6

Mean = _____

Median = _____

Mode = _____

5. 3, 1, 7, 10, 4

Mean = _____

Median = _____

Mode = _____

6. 22, 16, 24, 18

Mean = _____

Median = _____

Mode = _____

7. 5, 13, 1, 9, 5, 10, 6

Mean = _____

Median = _____

Mode = _____

8. 7, 7, 7, 9, 9, 9

Mean = _____

Median = _____

Mode = _____

9. 42, 35, 15, 18, 25

Mean = _____

Median = _____

Mode = _____

Check
Find the mean, median, and mode of each data set.

10. 4, 12, 7, 10, 7

Mean = _____

Median = _____

Mode = _____

11. 15, 10, 15, 25, 10, 15

Mean = _____

Median = _____

Mode = _____

12. 8, 8, 8, 9, 9, 9

Mean = _____

Median = _____

Mode = _____

13. 2, 10, 5, 9, 4, 6

Mean = _____

Median = _____

Mode = _____

14. 9, 9, 4, 4, 5, 5, 5

Mean = _____

Median = _____

Mode = _____

15. 12, 23, 18, 36, 11

Mean = _____

Median = _____

Mode = _____

Saxon Algebra 1

Teaching Skill 85

Objective Read and understand information presented in a circle graph.

Remind students that there are a number of different types of graphs used to organize data: bar charts, line graphs, circle graphs, etc. Tell students that circle graphs are also sometimes called pie graphs.

Point out that each type of graph has some special feature. The circle graph is used when you want to present data as a fraction or percentage of a whole. Ask: **What does the whole circle represent as a percentage?** (100%) **What determines how big a "slice" any one category of data gets?** (what percentage of the data it represents)

Have students look at the circle graph in the example. Ask: **Why does Brand E have the biggest slice?** (Because it represents the biggest percentage of the data.)

Explain to students how to calculate the number of items in any one category using the given percentages. Then work through the examples.

PRACTICE ON YOUR OWN

In exercises 1–4, students use circle graphs to answer questions.

CHECK

Determine that students know how to read and understand information presented in a circle graph.

Students who successfully complete the **Practice on Your Own** and **Check** are ready to move on to the next skill.

COMMON ERRORS

Students may forget to add the percentages before multiplying when answering an "or" question.

Students who made more than 1 error in the **Practice on Your Own,** or who were not successful in the **Check** section, may benefit from the **Alternative Teaching Strategy.**

Alternative Teaching Strategy

Objective Create a circle graph to understand what the percentages represent.

Materials needed: protractors and a compass

Have students work in groups of 2 or 3. Give each group a compass and a protractor. Then assign each group one of the questions below. It is okay to have multiple groups working on the same question.

- How many pets does your family have? (0, 1, 2, 3, or more than 3)

- How far do you live from school? (less than 1 mile; 1 to 5 miles; 6 to 10 miles; 11 to 15 miles; or more than 15 miles)

- What is your favorite subject? (math, English, history, science, or foreign language)

Tell the students they are going to create their own circle graphs by following the steps below:

1) Ask each student in the room and the teacher the question you were assigned. Record the answers and then count the total number of answers you have.

2) Find the percentage of your data in each of the categories by dividing the number of answers in that category by the total number of answers you recorded. The titles of the categories and the percentages will be the labels on your circle graph.

3) To determine how big a slice (central angle) of the circle graph each category should get, express your percents as decimals and multiply by 360°. (You may need to remind students why this works.)

4) Use your compass to draw a large circle. Then use a protractor to draw each central angle.

5) Label your circle graph with the appropriate category titles and percentages.

Name _____ Date _____ Class _____

Prerequisite Skills Intervention

Circle Graphs

Circle graphs are used to present data as a fraction or percentage of a total. When you know the percentage of the data that a certain category represents, you can find the number of items by multiplying the percentage (converted to a decimal) times the total number.

Example: The circle graph shows the distribution of cars manufactured by certain makers found in a high school parking lot one day. The total number of cars is 350.

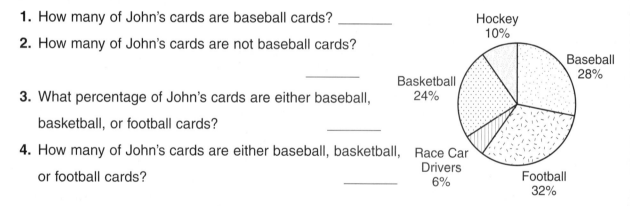

How many of the cars are made by Brand C?
   Multiply: $0.12 \times 350 = 42$

How many of the cars are made by Brand E or Brand A?
   First add the two percentages $(32 + 18 = 50\%)$,
   then multiply by the total.

   $0.50 \times 350 = 175$

Practice on Your Own
John has a collection of 600 sports cards. The circle graph shows the distribution by sport of the cards John owns.

1. How many of John's cards are baseball cards? _____

2. How many of John's cards are not baseball cards?

   _____

3. What percentage of John's cards are either baseball, basketball, or football cards? _____

4. How many of John's cards are either baseball, basketball, or football cards? _____

Check
The circle graph shows the grade distribution of students who attended a high school football game. The total number of students who attended is 250.

5. How many juniors attended the game? _____

6. How many middle school students attended the game?

   _____

7. What percentage of the students who attended the game were either freshmen or sophomores? _____

8. How many of the students who attended the game were either freshmen or sophomores? _____

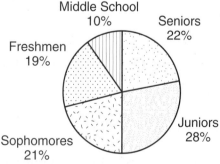

Saxon Algebra 1

Teaching Skill 86

Objective Read and understand information presented in a line graph.

Remind students that line graphs are created by plotting points on a coordinate plane and then connecting the points.

Point out that when written as x and $f(x)$, $f(x)$ represents the y-value of the point. Explain that it is possible to locate the y-value for any given x-value, and visa versa.

Have students look at the line graph in the example. Ask: **Which axis is the x-axis?** (the horizontal axis) **Which is the y-axis?** (the vertical axis) **In a coordinate pair, which value is written first?** (the x-value)

Next, direct students' attention to the questions in the example. Ask: **In the first and second questions, which value is given, x or y?** (x) Work through the first two questions. Ask: **In the third and fourth questions, which value is given?** (y) Work through the last two questions.

Have students complete the practice exercises.

PRACTICE ON YOUR OWN

In exercises 1–6, students find values on a line graph.

CHECK

Determine that students know how to read and understand information presented in a line graph.

Students who successfully complete the **Practice on Your Own** and **Check** are ready to move on to the next skill.

COMMON ERRORS

Students may not understand whether they should be looking for the x-value or the y-value on the graph.

Students who made more than 1 error in the **Practice on Your Own,** or who were not successful in the **Check** section, may benefit from the **Alternative Teaching Strategy.**

Alternative Teaching Strategy

Objective Create a line graph by plotting given points and connecting line segments.

Materials needed: rulers; multiple copies of a grid with values −2 to 22 on the x-axis and −2 to 22 on the y-axis. Grid should be labeled in increments of 2.

Some students may better understand how to read a line graph if they practice making one.

Tell students they are going to create a line graph using a few critical points and then locate other points on the graph.

Write the following points on the board: (0, 0); (10, 6); (14, 16); and (20, 22).

Instruct the students to plot these points on their grids. Be sure students understand which coordinate represents horizontal movement and which represents vertical movement. Before moving on, check students' points to make sure they are plotted correctly.

Next, instruct students to use a ruler to connect the points they plotted and then label the graph as $f(x)$. Explain that the point (14, 16) means the following: when x is 14, $f(x)$ is 16.

Then instruct students to use their graph to answer the following questions:

1) When x is 5, what is $f(5)$? (Answer: 3)
2) When x is 12, what is $f(12)$? (Answer: 11)
3) When $f(x)$ is 19, what is x? (Answer: 17)
4) When $f(x)$ is 6, what is x? (Answer: 10)

Repeat the exercise using the following points and questions.

(0, 2); (4, 6); (6, 14); and (20, 20)

1) When x is 2, what is $f(2)$? (Answer: 4)
2) When x is 13, what is $f(13)$? (Answer: 17)
3) When $f(x)$ is 19, what is x? (Answer: 17)
4) When $f(x)$ is 10, what is x? (Answer: 5)

Saxon Algebra 1

Name _____ Date _____ Class _____

Prerequisite Skills Intervention
Line Graphs

SKILL
86

To read a line graph, remember that a function table generates coordinate pairs.
So, $(x, f(x))$ is also a coordinate point (x, y).

To find $f(x)$ at a particular x, look for the y-value of the point with that x-coordinate.
To find an x such that $f(x)$ is a specific value, look for the value on the y-axis, and
then find the corresponding x-coordinate.

Example: Find each value for the graph of $f(x)$ shown.

What is $f(8)$?
Answer: 16 since $y = 16$ when $x = 8$

What is $f(4)$?
Answer: 6 since $y = 6$ when $x = 4$

What is x such that $f(x) = 8$?
Look for the x value where $y = 8$.
Answer: $x = 6$

What is x such that $f(x) = 17$
Look for the x value where $y = 17$.
Answer: $x = 13$

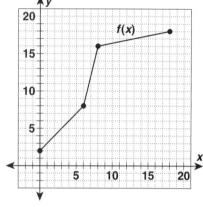

Practice on Your Own
Find each value for the graph of $f(x)$ shown.

1. $f(4) =$ _____

2. $f(0) =$ _____

3. $f(15) =$ _____

4. What is x such that $f(x) = 10$? _____

5. What is x such that $f(x) = 4$? _____

6. What is x such that $f(x) = 18$? _____

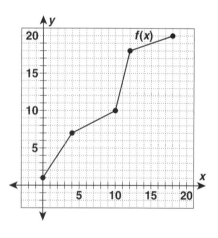

Check
Find each value for the graph of $f(x)$ shown.

7. $f(11) =$ _____

8. $f(7) =$ _____

9. What is x such that $f(x) = 16$? _____

10. What is x such that $f(x) = 4$? _____

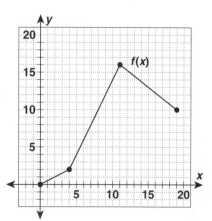

172   **Saxon** Algebra 1

Teaching Skill 87

Objective Draw conclusions from given statements.

Remind students that a conditional statement consists of a hypothesis and a conclusion and that it provides information about relationships between facts or events.

Point out that sometimes, when the conditional statement is true, additional conclusions can be drawn from the statement. However, sometimes no additional conclusion can be drawn without more information.

Make the following statement: If it rains today, I am going to read a book. Ask: **Do you know what I am going to do if it does not rain today?** (No). **Can you draw any conclusions if it does not rain?** (No)

Next have students consider the example provided. Here, two statements have been given and both are assumed to be true. Point out that between the two statements, there is enough information to draw a valid conclusion. Work through the example.

Have students complete the practice exercises.

PRACTICE ON YOUR OWN

In exercises 1–5, students draw conclusions based on a set of true statements.

CHECK

Determine that students know how to draw conclusions from true statements.

Students who successfully complete the **Practice on Your Own** and **Check** are ready to move on to the next skill.

COMMON ERRORS

Students may try to draw a conclusion even when there is not enough information.

Students who made more than 1 error in the **Practice on Your Own,** or who were not successful in the **Check** section, may benefit from the **Alternative Teaching Strategy.**

Alternative Teaching Strategy

Objective Determine when a conclusion drawn is an incorrect conclusion.

Tell students they are going to determine which conclusions you read are incorrect.

Instruct students to write the numbers 1 through 3 on a piece of paper. If the conclusion you provide is true, students should place a *T* beside that number. If the conclusion is false, they should place an *F* beside the number.

Write the following statements on the board and tell students the statements are true.

- If an angle is acute, then the measure of the angle is less than 90 degrees.

- The measure of $\angle ABC$ is not less than 90 degrees.

Read the first conclusion: $\angle ABC$ is an obtuse angle. (False)

Read the second conclusion: $\angle ABC$ is a right angle. (False)

Read the third conclusion: $\angle ABC$ is not an acute angle. (True)

Discuss the correct answers with students.

Repeat the exercise using the following statements and conclusions.

- An isosceles triangle has exactly two sides with equal lengths.

- $\triangle DEF$ has two sides of length 8.

Conclusion 1: $\triangle DEF$ is an isosceles triangle. (False)

Conclusion 2: $\triangle DEF$ could be an isosceles triangle. (True)

Conclusion 3: $\triangle DEF$ could be an equilateral triangle. (True)

Discuss the correct answers with students.

Saxon Algebra 1

Prerequisite Skills Intervention
Logical Reasoning

Certain types of statements, called conditionals, provide information about relationships between facts or events. You can often draw conclusions based on conditional statements.

Example: Draw a conclusion from the two true statements below.

> If two lines are parallel, then they have equal slopes.
> Line *m* is parallel to line *n* and the slope of line *m* is −2.

> Conclusion: Since the two lines are parallel, they must have equal slopes.
> So, the slope of line *n* is also −2.

Practice on Your Own
Draw a conclusion from each set of true statements.

1. If a polygon is a quadrilateral, then it has 4 sides.
   Figure *ABCD* is a quadrilateral.

   _____

2. If two angles are adjacent, then they share a common vertex.
   Angle *ABC* and angle *CBD* are adjacent angles.

   _____

3. If the sum of two angles is 180 degrees, then the angles are supplementary.
   ∠*A* has a measure of 70° and ∠*B* has a measure of 110°.

   _____

4. If a triangle is an isosceles triangle, then it has exactly two sides of equal length.
   △*DEF* is an isosceles triangle with one side of length 8 and the other side of length 13.

   _____

5. If the coordinates of a point are both negative, then the point lies in the third quadrant.
   The coordinates of point *P* are (−1, −9).

   _____

Check
Draw a conclusion from each set of true statements.

6. If a triangle is equilateral, then it is equiangular.
   Triangle *MNP* has sides of length 8, 8, and 8 and an angle with measure 60°.

   _____

7. If an angle is obtuse, then its measure is greater than 90 degrees.
   ∠*HJK* is an obtuse angle.

   _____

8. If the product of the slopes of two lines is −1, then the lines are perpendicular.
   Line *p* has a slope of $\frac{2}{3}$ and line *q* has a slope of $-\frac{3}{2}$.

   _____

Prerequisite Skills Intervention
Conditional Statements

Teaching Skill 88
Objective Determine whether a conditional statement is true, write its converse, and determine whether the converse is true.

Review with students the different parts of a conditional statement.

Point out that all conditional statements are not necessarily true. Provide the following example: If a polygon has 4 sides, then it is a rectangle. Ask: **Is this always a true statement?** (No) **Why not?** (There are other types of quadrilaterals that have 4 sides.)

Review with students how to find the converse of a statement. Ask: **What is the converse of the previous statement?** (If a polygon is a rectangle, then it has 4 sides.) **Is the converse true?** (Yes) Stress that the truth value of a statement and its converse may be the same, or may be different.

Review the example with students and then have them complete the practice exercises.

PRACTICE ON YOUR OWN
In exercises 1–4, students examine conditional statements, write converses, and determine truth values of both.

CHECK
Determine that students understand conditional statements, converses, and truth values.

Students who successfully complete the **Practice on Your Own** and **Check** are ready to move on to the next skill.

COMMON ERRORS
Students may incorrectly determine truth values, particularly when the conditional statement and its converse have different results.

Students who made more than 1 error in the **Practice on Your Own,** or who were not successful in the **Check** section, may benefit from the **Alternative Teaching Strategy.**

Alternative Teaching Strategy
Objective Complete conditional statements based on well known geometric properties.

Tell students they are going to match several hypotheses with a conclusion that makes the conditional a true statement.

Remind students that the hypothesis is the "if" part of a conditional statement, and the conclusion is the "then" part.

Provide students with copies of the following conclusions.

1) then it is equidistant from the sides of the angle.
2) then they are complementary angles.
3) then the intersect in exactly one point.
4) then it is a rectangle.
5) then corresponding angles are congruent.
6) then the triangles are similar.
7) then it is a right triangle.
8) then they are congruent.
9) then it is an octagon.
10) then the lines are parallel.

Next, read one hypothesis at a time (with its corresponding letter) and have students write that letter beside the correct conclusion. When you have read all the hypotheses, read the answers aloud and discuss any errors students made.

A) If a triangle has one right angle, (7)
B) If a quadrilateral has diagonals of equal length, (4)
C) If the slopes of two lines are equal, (10)
D) If two lines intersect, (3)
E) If two angles are vertical, (8)
F) If the sum of the measures of two angles is 90 degrees, (2)
G) If a point is on the bisector of an angle, (1)
H) If two parallel lines are cut by a transversal, (5)
I) If the corresponding sides of two triangles are proportional, (6)
J) If a polygon has eight sides, (9)

Name _____ Date _____ Class _____

Prerequisite Skills Intervention
Conditional Statements

Conditional Statements		
Hypothesis—the *if* part of a conditional statement	Conclusion—the *then* part of a conditional statement	Converse—a statement formed by interchanging the hypothesis and the conclusion
Example: Conditional statement: If a polygon is a pentagon, then it has 5 sides. (True)		
Hypothesis: A polygon is a pentagon.	Conclusion: It has 5 sides.	Converse: If a polygon has 5 sides, then it is a pentagon. (True)

Practice on Your Own
Identify the hypothesis and conclusion of each conditional.

1. If a triangle is a right triangle, then the sum of its acute angles is 90 degrees.

   Hypothesis: _____   Conclusion: _____

2. If two lines are parallel to a third line, then they are parallel to each other.

   Hypothesis: _____   Conclusion: _____

Tell whether the given statement is true or false. Write the converse.
Tell whether the converse is true or false.

_____ 3. If a polygon is a triangle, then the sum of the measures of its angles is 180 degrees.

   Converse: _____

_____ 4. If two angles are right angles, then they are congruent.

   Converse: _____

Check
Identify the hypothesis and conclusion of each conditional.

5. If two planes intersect, then they intersect in a line.

   Hypothesis: _____   Conclusion: _____

Tell whether the given statement is true or false. Write the converse.
Tell whether the converse is true or false.

_____ 6. If two angles are vertical, then they are congruent.

   Converse: _____

_____ 7. If the diagonals of a parallelogram are perpendicular, then the parallelogram is a rhombus.

   Converse: _____

176   **Saxon** Algebra 1

Prerequisite Skills Intervention
Counterexamples

Teaching Skill 89
Objective Find counterexamples to prove that a given statement is false.

Explain to students that when you determine whether a mathematical statement is true or false, you determines its truth value.

In order to determine that a mathematical statement is true, the statement must be true for all real numbers. However, to determine that a statement is false, you need to find only one counterexample.

Review with students the definition of a counterexample. Emphasize that if you can find a single number for which a statement is not true, then the statement is false.

Have students consider the example. Remind students that real numbers consist of whole numbers, integers (positive and negative), fractions, decimals, and irrational numbers.

Work through the example with students, reviewing the strategy as you go. Then, have students complete the practice exercises.

PRACTICE ON YOUR OWN
In exercises 1–6, students find counterexamples to prove that given statements are false.

CHECK
Determine that students know how to find counterexamples.

Students who successfully complete the **Practice on Your Own** and **Check** are ready to move on to the next skill.

COMMON ERRORS
Students may forget to try fractions or negative numbers when searching for counterexamples.

Students who made more than 2 errors in the **Practice on Your Own,** or who were not successful in the **Check** section, may benefit from the **Alternative Teaching Strategy.**

Alternative Teaching Strategy
Objective Determine which given values are counterexamples for false statements.

Some students may benefit from working problems where there are several types of counterexamples.

Write the following numbers on the board:

$5, 1, \frac{1}{2}, 0, -\frac{1}{2}, -1$, and -5.

Remind students that a counterexample to a statement is a particular example or instance of the statement that is NOT true. If you can find a single counterexample, then the given statement is false.

Tell students they are going to test several statements to try to determine if they are false.

Work through the first statement with students. Write the following on the board: $n \geq -n$. Instruct students to try each of the numbers you wrote on the board and identify each number that is a counterexample.

$5 \geq -5$ True $-5 \geq -(-5) \rightarrow -5 \geq 5$ False

$1 \geq -1$ True $-1 \geq -(-1) \rightarrow -1 \geq 1$ False

$\frac{1}{2} \geq -\frac{1}{2}$ True $-\frac{1}{2} \geq -(-\frac{1}{2}) \rightarrow -\frac{1}{2} \geq \frac{1}{2}$ False

$0 \geq 0$ True

Review students' findings with them. Based on the results of the test, all negative numbers are counterexamples for the given statement.

Have students repeat this exercise for the statement below.

$\frac{1}{n} \geq \frac{1}{n^2}$ (counterexamples: $\frac{1}{2}, -\frac{1}{2}, -1, -5$)

$5n \neq -5n$ (only 0 is a counterexample)

$\frac{1}{n} < n$ (counterexamples: $1, \frac{1}{2}, -1, -5$)

Name _____ Date _____ Class _____

Prerequisite Skills Intervention
Counterexamples

Definition: A counterexample to a statement is a particular example or instance of the statement that is NOT true.

Example: Find a counterexample to show that the statement below is false.

Statement: $1 + n \geq 1 - n$, where n is a real number.

Strategy to find a counterexample:

Step 1: Always try $n = 0$ first. $1 + 0 \geq 1 - 0$ → $1 \geq 1$ **True**

Step 2: Try $n = 1$ next. $1 + 1 \geq 1 - 1$ → $2 \geq 0$ **True**

Step 3: Try $n = -1$ next. $1 + (-1) \geq 1 - (-1)$ → $0 \geq 2$ **False**

STOP: $n = -1$ is your counterexample.

If $n = -1$ had produced another true statement, then you would try a positive and negative fraction, such as $\frac{1}{2}$ and $-\frac{1}{2}$. Then larger numbers, both positive and negative, until you found a number that produced a false statement.

Practice on Your Own
Find a counterexample to show that each statement is false.

1. $n^3 + 2n = 3n^2$, where n is a real number

$n =$

2. $-\frac{1}{n} \leq \frac{1}{n}$, where n is a real number

$n =$

3. $\frac{n}{3} \neq \frac{3}{n}$, where n is a real number

$n =$

4. $\frac{n}{2} < 2n$, where n is a real number

$n =$

5. $-(n + 1) \neq n + 1$, where n is a real number

$n =$

6. $n^2 \geq n$, where n is a real number

$n =$

Check
Find a counterexample to show that each statement is false.

7. $\frac{1}{n} \neq \frac{1}{n^2}$, where n is a real number $\neq 0$

$n =$

8. $n^3 \geq n^2$, where n is a real number

$n =$

9. $\frac{n}{5} < 5n$, where n is a real number

$n =$

10. $-3n \neq 3n$, where n is a real number

$n =$

Saxon Algebra 1

Teaching Skill 90
Objective Draw a tree diagram.

Explain to students that a tree diagram can be used to organize all the possible outcomes in a sample space, particularly when an experiment involves more than one event.

Point out that a tree diagram looks like the branches of a tree. As you move from left to right on the diagram, each smaller branch represents a new type of possible outcome.

Have students read the example. Ask: **When Marie spins the first spinner, how many possible outcomes are there?** (4) **What are they?** (1, 2, 3, or 4) Point out that these will be the first branches of the tree. Ask: **When Marie spins the second spinner, how many outcomes are there?** (3) **What are they?** (red, blue, or yellow) Explain that each number branch should have three smaller branches that list each of the colors.

Work through the example with students and then have them complete the practice exercise.

PRACTICE ON YOUR OWN
In Practice on Your Own, students draw a tree diagram.

CHECK
Determine that students know how to create a tree diagram showing all possible outcomes for a given experiment.

Students who successfully complete the **Practice on Your Own** and **Check** are ready to move on to the next skill.

COMMON ERRORS
Students may forget to connect each of the first sets of outcomes with each of the second set.

Students who made more than 1 error in the **Practice on Your Own,** or who were not successful in the **Check** section, may benefit from the **Alternative Teaching Strategy.**

Alternative Teaching Strategy
Objective Draw a tree diagram as part of an experiment.

Materials needed: several coins and several sets of 4 cards (Ace, King, Queen, and Jack)

Tell students they are going to flip a coin and then draw a card. While doing so, they will be making a tree diagram showing all the outcomes that did occur and all those that did not occur. When they put them together, the tree diagram will show all possible outcomes of the experiment.

Give each student a coin and a set of four cards. Instruct students to begin a tree diagram by creating a starting point labeled "Flip and Draw." Next, have each student flip their coin. Then, they should draw one branch from their starting point and label it with the outcome they got (either heads or tails).

Next, instruct students to draw one card from the four they were given. Then, they should draw one branch from their already existing branch and label it with the card they drew.

For example, if a student flipped a head and then drew a King, his or her diagram should look like the following:

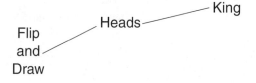

Ask: **When you flipped the coin, how many possible outcomes did you NOT get?** (1) Instruct students to add that outcome to their tree beneath the outcome they did get. Ask: **When you drew the card, how many possible outcomes did you NOT get?** (3) Have students add those outcomes to the branch on the outcomes they did get. Ask: **Should the bottom branch of your tree have the same set of second outcomes as the first?** (Yes) Have students complete their tree using this information.

Saxon Algebra 1

Name _____ Date _____ Class _____

Prerequisite Skills Intervention
Tree Diagrams

Tree diagrams can be used to organize all the possible outcomes in a sample space, particularly when an experiment involves more than one event.

Example: **Marie is playing a game in which she must spin two spinners. The first spinner is divided into four equal sections, each numbered 1, 2, 3, or 4. The second spinner is divided into three equal sections, one that is red, one blue, and one yellow. Draw a tree diagram showing all the possible combinations of numbers and colors that Marie could spin.**

Answer: Since there are two events, there should be two sets of branches. One set will represent the first spin and should include all four numbers as possibilities. The second set will represent the second spin and should include all three colors on each of the number branches.

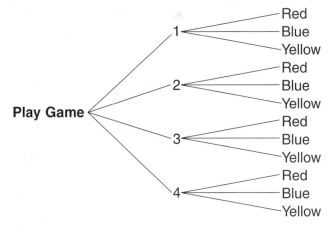

Practice on Your Own

Elizabeth is at a carnival. She is playing a game that asks her to pick a door and then pick a curtain behind the door. There are 3 doors and 4 curtains behind each door. Draw a tree diagram showing all possible ways that Elizabeth could choose a door and a curtain behind the door.

**Play
Game**

Check

Mark gets to choose a snack when he gets home from school. He can have plain or chocolate milk to drink, and either a piece of fruit, popcorn, or peanut butter sticks to eat. Draw a tree diagram showing all possible snacks that Mark could choose if he gets only one drink and one thing to eat.

**Snack
Choices**

 Saxon Algebra 1

ANSWER KEY

SKILL 1 ANSWERS:

Practice on Your Own

1. 3, 6, 9, 12, 15
2. 7, 14, 21, 28, 35
3. 12, 24, 36, 48, 60
4. 16, 32, 48, 64, 80
5. 25, 50, 75, 100, 125
6. 20, 25, 30
7. 24, 30, 36
8. 4, 5, 6
9. 44, 55, 66
10. 32, 40, 48
11. 8, 10, 12
12. 400, 500, 600
13. 2000; 2500; 3000

Check

14. 16, 20, 24, 28
15. 36, 45, 54, 63
16. 40, 50, 60, 70
17. 60, 75, 90, 105
18. 180, 225, 270, 315
19. 1000; 1250; 1500; 1750
20. 8000; 10,000; 12,000; 14,000

SKILL 2 ANSWERS:

Practice on Your Own

1. 24
2. 40
3. 20
4. 60
5. 105
6. 96
7. 60

8. 90
9. 48
10. 120
11. 48
12. 180

Check

13. 18
14. 30
15. 90
16. 150
17. 84
18. 36
19. 192
20. 84

SKILL 3 ANSWERS:

Practice on Your Own

1. No
2. Yes
3. Yes
4. Yes
5. {1, 2, 3, 4, 6, 8, 12, 24}
6. {1, 2, 4, 7, 8, 14, 28, 56}
7. {1, 23}
8. {1, 2, 3, 4, 5, 6, 8, 10, 12, 15, 20, 24, 30, 40, 60, 120}
9. {1, 19}
10. {1, 2, 4, 5, 10, 20}
11. {1, 5, 7, 35}
12. {1, 2, 4, 5, 10, 20, 25, 50, 100}

Check

13. No
14. Yes
15. Yes

Answer Key continued

16. No

17. {1, 17}

18. {1, 3, 5, 9, 15, 45}

19. {1, 2, 4, 5, 8, 10, 16, 20, 32, 40, 80, 160}

20. {1, 2, 4, 7, 14, 28}

SKILL 4 ANSWERS:

Practice on Your Own

1. 4

2. 14

3. $4a$

4. x^2y

5. $6a^2$

6. $2x^2y$

7. $16ef$

8. $14rs$

9. $5xz$

Check

10. 12

11. $12e^2f$

12. $4a^3$

13. gh

14. $6a^3$

15. $10x^3$

SKILL 5 ANSWERS:

Practice on Your Own

1. {1, 3, 11, 33}

2. {1, 23}

3. {1, 2, 3, 5, 6, 9, 10, 15, 18, 30, 45, 90}

4. {1, 2, 4, 5, 10, 20}

5. composite, 5×5 or 1×25

6. composite, 2×23 or 1×46

7. prime

8. composite, 2×6 or 3×4 or 1×12

9. prime

10. prime

11. composite, 11×11 or 1×121

12. prime

Check

13. composite, 3×9 or 1×27

14. prime

15. composite, 9×9 or 1×81

16. composite, 2×14 or 4×7 or 1×28

17. prime

18. composite, 2×9 or 3×6 or 1×18

19. composite, 3×7 or 1×21

20. prime

SKILL 6 ANSWERS:

1. 9

2. 64

3. 256

4. 625

5. 4

6. 12

7. 20

8. 9

9. No

10. Yes, 1

11. Yes, 15

12. No

13. Yes, 13

14. Yes, 14

15. No

16. No

Answer Key continued

Check

17. 49

18. 5

19. 144

20. 10

21. Yes, 6

22. No

23. Yes, 11

24. No

SKILL 7 ANSWERS:

Practice on Your Own

1. $9 \cdot 9 \cdot 9 \cdot 9$

2. $1 \cdot 1 \cdot 1 \cdot 1 \cdot 1$

3. $x \cdot x \cdot x$

4. $8 \cdot 8$

5. $(-2) \cdot (-2) \cdot (-2)$

6. $p \cdot p \cdot p \cdot p \cdot p \cdot p$

7. 10^6

8. 12^4

9. m^5

10. 5^6

11. 9^2

12. p^3

Check

13. $2 \cdot 2 \cdot 2 \cdot 2$

14. $(-4) \cdot (-4)$

15. $h \cdot h \cdot h \cdot h \cdot h$

16. 25^3

17. s^4

18. 8^3

19. 4^1 or 4

SKILL 8 ANSWERS:

1. 32

2. 16

3. 1

4. $15^2 = 225$

5. $(-10)^3 = -1000$

6. $1 + 1 = 2$

7. $16 + 9 = 25$

8. $36 \cdot 4 = 144$

9. $64 \div 16 = 4$

Check

10. 64

11. 1

12. $9^2 = 81$

13. $100 - 1 = 99$

14. $-8 + 27 = 19$

15. $-1 \cdot 32 = -32$

16. $25 \cdot 10 = 250$

17. $1000 \div 125 = 8$

18. $81 \div 1 = 81$

SKILL 9 ANSWERS:

Practice on Your Own

1. 146.39

2. 236

3. 50

4. 15.3

5. 0.005

6. 4.0

7. 230; $(80 + 150)$

8. 180; (9×20)

9. 5; $(10 \div 2)$

10. 1200; $(400 + 700 + 100)$

Saxon Algebra 1

Answer Key continued

11. 14; (7 × 2)

12. 78; (780 ÷ 10)

Check

13. 0.07

14. 1325

15. 19.0

16. 600; (12 × 50)

17. 960; (900 + 60)

18. 3; (9 ÷ 3)

SKILL 10 ANSWERS:

Practice on Your Own

1. {1, 2, 4, 8, 16}; {1, 2, 3, 4, 6, 8, 12, 24}; 8

2. {1, 2, 3, 4, 6, 9, 12, 18, 36};
{1, 3, 7, 9, 21, 63}; 9

3. $\dfrac{6 \div 2}{20 \div 2} = \dfrac{3}{10}$

4. $\dfrac{60 \div 12}{72 \div 12} = \dfrac{5}{6}$

5. $\dfrac{45 \div 9}{54 \div 9} = \dfrac{5}{6}$

6. $1\dfrac{5}{6}$ or $\dfrac{11}{6}$

7. $\dfrac{7}{8}$

8. $\dfrac{12}{13}$

Check

9. 4

10. 1

11. 5

12. 12

13. $\dfrac{15 \div 3}{21 \div 3} = \dfrac{5}{7}$

14. $\dfrac{5 \div 1}{18 \div 1} = \dfrac{5}{18}$

15. $\dfrac{14 \div 7}{49 \div 7} = \dfrac{2}{7}$

16. $\dfrac{4}{5}$

17. $1\dfrac{1}{4}$ or $\dfrac{5}{4}$

18. $\dfrac{8}{9}$

SKILL 11 ANSWERS:

Practice on Your Own

1. 0.6

2. 0.625

3. 2.25

4. 0.8

5. −0.9

6. 1.5

7. 2.3

8. −3.2

Check

9. 0.7

10. −1.375

11. 6.15

12. 0.08

13. 0.875

14. 5.5

15. −0.8

16. 0.24

SKILL 12 ANSWERS:

Practice on Your Own

1. 13 to 12; 13:12; $\dfrac{13}{12}$

2. 12 to 13; 12:13; $\dfrac{12}{13}$

3. 5 to 13; 5:13; $\dfrac{5}{13}$

4. 1 to 1; 1:1; $\dfrac{1}{1}$

5. $\dfrac{20}{43}$

6. $\dfrac{2}{1}$

7. $\dfrac{20}{53}$

8. $\dfrac{20}{73}$

Saxon Algebra 1

Answer Key continued

Check

9. 1 to 1; 1:1; $\frac{1}{1}$

10. 2 to 3; 2:3; $\frac{2}{3}$

11. 2 to 7; 2:7; $\frac{2}{7}$

SKILL 13 ANSWERS:

Practice on Your Own

1. 58 miles per hour

2. 260 calories per serving

3. $2.50 per hour

4. 50 homes per subdivision

5. 10 miles per gallon

6. 75¢ per pen

7. 4.5 grams per ounce

8. 6 francs per dollar

9. 5.75¢ per copy

Check

10. 300 trees per acre

11. $45 per credit hour

12. 0.25 km per minute

13. 80 miles per hour

14. 16 books per shelf

15. 80¢ per ride

SKILL 14 ANSWERS:

Practice on Your Own

1. 0.5

2. 0.28

3. 0.7

4. 0.84

5. 0.85

6. 0.06

7. 0.375

8. 1.5

9. 75%

10. 60%

11. 30%

12. 9%

13. 62.5%

14. 45%

15. 120%

16. 125%

Check

17. 0.97

18. 0.8

19. 0.025

20. 0.11

21. 80%

22. 40%

23. 5.5%

24. 62%

SKILL 15 ANSWERS:

Practice on Your Own

1. 5.4×10^{9}

2. 2.6×10^{-4}

3. 6×10^{6}

4. 8.59×10^{-9}

5. 1.1275×10^{2}

6. 6.1×10^{-4}

7. 4,220,000

8. 0.00071

9. 9000

10. 0.000000001365

11. 684,000,000

12. 0.000000000002

Saxon Algebra 1

Answer Key continued

Check

13. 1.2×10^{-13}

14. 6.25×10^{10}

15. 2.0648×10^{2}

16. 410

17. 0.000000000208

18. 1,001,000

SKILL 16 ANSWERS:

Practice on Your Own

1. $<$

2. $>$

3. $>$

4. $<$

5. $<$

6. $=$

7. $>$

8. $>$

9. $\frac{8}{12}$, 70%, 0.72, $\frac{3}{4}$

10. 140%, $1\frac{3}{7}$, 1.5, $\frac{8}{5}$

11. $\frac{3}{10}$, 0.33, $\frac{1}{3}$, 35%

Check

12. $<$

13. $>$

14. $>$

15. $<$

16. $\frac{3}{20}$, 16%, 0.165, $\frac{1}{6}$, $\frac{1}{5}$, 0.22

SKILL 17 ANSWERS:

Practice on Your Own

1. Rational, Integer, Whole, Natural

2. Rational, Integer

3. Rational, Integer, Whole

4. Rational

5. Rational, Integer, Whole, Natural

6. Rational

7. Rational

8. Rational

9. Rational, Integer, Whole, Natural

Check

10. Rational, Integer

11. Rational, Integer, Whole, Natural

12. Rational

13. Rational

14. Rational

15. Rational, Integer, Whole, Natural

SKILL 18 ANSWERS:

Practice on Your Own

Exercises 1–5

Exercises 6–10

Check

Exercises 11–15

Exercises 16–20

SKILL 19 ANSWERS:

Practice on Your Own

1. 100 yd

2. 6 ft

3. 1.5 ft

4. $\frac{1}{10}$ gram

5. 300 mph

Saxon Algebra 1

Answer Key continued

6. 2.5 ft

7. 15 in.

8. 8 oz

Check

9. 6 in.

10. 6 in.

11. 25 cm

12. 5 ft

13. 2 cm

14. 30 lbs

15. 50,000 gal

16. 26 mi

SKILL 20 ANSWERS:

Practice on Your Own

1. $1\frac{1}{4}$ in.; 3 cm

2. $\frac{5}{8}$ in.; 1.5 cm

3. $\frac{7}{8}$ in.; 2.5 cm

4. $1\frac{7}{8}$ in.; 5 cm

5. 4 in.; 10 cm

6. $2\frac{5}{8}$ in.; 6.5 cm

7. 6 in.; 15 cm

Check

8. $1\frac{1}{2}$ in.; 4 cm

9. $\frac{3}{8}$ in.; 1 cm

10. $\frac{3}{4}$ in.; 2 cm

11. $\frac{5}{8}$ in.; 1.5 cm

12. $5\frac{1}{8}$ in.; 13 cm

SKILL 21 ANSWERS:

Practice on Your Own

1. 2.5 yr

2. 4 ft

3. 48 oz

4. 6.5 m

5. 36 hr

6. 4 gal

7. 3.5 T

8. 2200 ml

9. 21 ft

Check

10. 920 cm

11. 150 min

12. 11 qt

13. 4.5 g

14. 3.5 lb

15. 54 mo

SKILL 22 ANSWERS:

Practice on Your Own

1. M, N, O, P, or Q

2. Sample answer: $\overleftrightarrow{MP}$, $\overleftrightarrow{PM}$, $\overleftrightarrow{NO}$, or $\overleftrightarrow{ON}$

3. $\overline{MN}$, $\overline{NM}$, $\overline{NP}$, $\overline{PN}$, $\overline{NO}$, $\overline{ON}$, $\overline{MP}$, or $\overline{PM}$

4. Sample answer: $\overrightarrow{MP}$, $\overrightarrow{PM}$, $\overrightarrow{NM}$, $\overrightarrow{NP}$, $\overrightarrow{NO}$, or $\overrightarrow{ON}$

5. $\mathcal{T}$ or $\mathcal{W}$

6. $\overrightarrow{ON}$

7. Sample answer: $\overleftrightarrow{MP}$ or $\overleftrightarrow{PM}$

8. $\mathcal{T}$

9. $\overline{NO}$ or $\overline{ON}$

10. N

Check

11. Sample answer: A, B, C, D, or E

12. Sample answer: $\overline{CD}$, $\overline{DC}$, $\overline{CE}$, $\overline{EC}$, $\overline{CB}$, $\overline{BC}$, $\overline{BE}$, or $\overline{EB}$

13. Sample answer: $\overrightarrow{CB}$, $\overrightarrow{CD}$, $\overrightarrow{CE}$, $\overrightarrow{EB}$, or $\overrightarrow{BE}$

14. Sample answer: $\overleftrightarrow{BE}$, $\overleftrightarrow{EB}$, $\overleftrightarrow{CD}$, or $\overleftrightarrow{DC}$

Saxon Algebra 1

Answer Key continued

15. $\mathscr{X}$ or $\mathscr{L}$

16. $\mathscr{X}$

SKILL 23 ANSWERS:

Practice on Your Own

1. $\angle ABC$ or $\angle CBA$; right

2. $\angle XYZ$ or $\angle ZYX$; obtuse

3. $\angle EDF$ or $\angle FDE$; acute

4. $\angle PQR$ or $\angle RQP$; obtuse

5. $\angle ABC$ or $\angle CBA$; straight

6. $\angle PQR$ or $\angle RQP$; acute

7. $\angle XYZ$ or $\angle ZYX$; straight

8. $\angle EDF$ or $\angle FDE$; right

9. $\angle ACB$ or $\angle BCA$; acute

Check

10. $\angle QPR$ or $\angle RPQ$; acute

11. $\angle ABC$ or $\angle CBA$; straight

12. $\angle SQP$ or $\angle PQS$; acute

13. $\angle DEF$ or $\angle FED$; right

14. $\angle YXZ$ or $\angle ZXY$; acute

15. $\angle ABC$ or $\angle CBA$; obtuse

SKILL 24 ANSWERS:

Practice on Your Own

1. $66°$

2. $90°$

3. $130°$

4. $85°$

5. $160°$

6. $28°$

Check

7. $42°$

8. $150°$

9. $90°$

SKILL 25 ANSWERS:

Practice on Your Own

1. supplementary angles

2. vertical angles

3. adjacent angles

4. complementary angles

5. answers will vary; any two angles that share the vertex (C) and one side

6. *GCF* and *FCE* or *ECD* and *DCB*

7. *ACG* and *BCD* or *GCD* and *ACB*

8. *ACB* and *BCD* or *ACB* and *ACG* or *ACG* and *GCD* or *BCD* and *DCG* or *DCE* and *ECA* or *DCF* and *FCA*

Check

9. adjacent angles

10. complementary angles

11. *TPU* & *QPR* or *UPQ* & *TPR*

12. *SPR* & *RPQ*

13. answers will vary; any two angles that share the vertex (P) and a side

14. *UPQ* & *QPR* or *UPT* & *TPR* or *UPS* & *SPR* or *TPU* & *UPQ* or *TPS* & *SPQ* or *TPR* & *RPQ*

SKILL 26 ANSWERS:

Practice on Your Own

1. *h*

2. *a, c*

3. *h*

4. *e*

5. *h*

6. $65°$

7. $115°$

8. $65°$

9. $115°$

Saxon Algebra 1

Answer Key continued

10. 65°

11. 65°

12. 115°

Check

13. k

14. k

15. h

16. g

17. 105°

18. 75°

19. 105°

20. 75°

SKILL 27 ANSWERS:

Practice on Your Own

1. triangle

2. not a polygon

3. regular pentagon (should be circled)

4. not a polygon

5. not a polygon

6. octagon

7. decagon

8. quadrilateral

Check

9. not a polygon

10. quadrilateral

11. not a polygon

12. pentagon

13. regular hexagon (should be circled)

14. dodecagon

15. decagon

16. not a polygon

SKILL 28 ANSWERS:

Practice on Your Own

1. 1080°

2. 135°

3. 360°

4. 45°

5. $\left(128\frac{4}{7}\right)°$

6. $\left(51\frac{3}{7}\right)°$

7. 67.5

Check

8. 720°

9. 120°

10. 360°

11. 60°

SKILL 29 ANSWERS:

Practice on Your Own

1. acute

2. obtuse

3. obtuse

4. right

5. acute

6. right

7. acute

8. obtuse

Check

9. obtuse

10. right

11. acute

12. obtuse

Answer Key continued

SKILL 30 ANSWERS:

Practice on Your Own

1. 27
2. 59
3. 45
4. 20
5. 36
6. 10
7. 37
8. 20

Check

9. 32
10. 33
11. 30
12. 30

SKILL 31 ANSWERS:

Practice on Your Own

1. 10
2. 17
3. $6\sqrt{2}$
4. $2\sqrt{13}$
5. 15
6. $2\sqrt{17}$

Check

7. 13
8. 30
9. $5\sqrt{2}$
10. 41

SKILL 32 ANSWERS:

Practice on Your Own

1. 6
2. $7\sqrt{3}$

3. $8\sqrt{2}$
4. 9
5. $4\sqrt{3}$
6. 4
7. $6\sqrt{2}$
8. $\dfrac{20\sqrt{3}}{3}$

Check

9. 15
10. $9\sqrt{3}$
11. $10\sqrt{2}$
12. 11

SKILL 33 ANSWERS:

Practice on Your Own

1. Yes; ASA
2. No
3. Yes; HL
4. Yes; ASA
5. Yes; SAS
6. No

Check

7. No
8. Yes; HL
9. Yes; SSS

SKILL 34 ANSWERS:

Practice on Your Own

1. A and D
2. B and C
3. Yes; corresponding sides are in proportion (1:2)
4. Yes; corresponding sides are in proportion (7:1)
5. Yes; corresponding sides are in proportion (2:1)
6. No

Saxon Algebra 1

Answer Key continued

Check

7. A and C

8. Yes; corresponding sides are in proportion (1:2.5)

9. Yes; corresponding sides are in proportion (1:3)

SKILL 35 ANSWERS:

Practice on Your Own

1. *ZYX*

2. $\angle TUS$

3. 115°

4. *LM*

5. *MP*

6. 10

7. 72

Check

8. $\angle NLM$

9. 80°

10. *JM*

11. 8

12. 44

SKILL 36 ANSWERS:

Practice on Your Own

1. 11 in.

2. 52 cm

3. 48 in.

4. 22 m

5. 13 ft

6. 12 in.

Check

7. 9 in.

8. 19 ft

9. 34 cm

SKILL 37 ANSWERS:

Practice on Your Own

1. 10 in.^{2}

2. 12 ft^2

3. 144 cm^2

4. 24 m^2

5. 210 ft^2

6. 35 yd^2

7. 9 in.^{2}

8. 22 m^2

Check

9. 102 cm^2

10. 66 m^2

11. 36 ft^2

12. 20 in.^{2}

SKILL 38 ANSWERS:

Practice on Your Own

1. 36 units^2

2. 40 units^2

3. 400π units^2

4. 31.5 units^2

5. 20 units^2

6. 9 units^2

Check

7. 30 units^2

8. 16π units^2

9. 1200 units^2

10. 126 units^2

11. 20 units^2

12. 9π units^2

Saxon Algebra 1

Answer Key continued

SKILL 39 ANSWERS:

Practice on Your Own

1. $C = 6\pi$ cm; $A = 9\pi$ cm^2

2. $C = 12\pi$ in.; $A = 36\pi$ in.^{2}

3. $C = 14\pi$ ft; $A = 49\pi$ ft^2

4. $C = 22\pi$ m; $A = 121\pi$ m^2

5. $C = 16\pi$ in.; $A = 64\pi$ in.^{2}

6. $C = 13\pi$ m; $A = 42.25\pi$ m^2

7. $C = 12$ cm; $A = \dfrac{36}{\pi}$ cm^2

8. $C = 20$ ft; $A = \dfrac{100}{\pi}$ ft^2

Check

9. $C = 18\pi$ cm; $A = 81\pi$ cm^2

10. $C = 2\pi$ ft; $A = 1\pi$ ft^2

11. $C = 24\pi$ m; $A = 144\pi$ m^2

12. $C = 8$ in.; $A = \dfrac{16}{\pi}$ in.^{2}

SKILL 40 ANSWERS:

Practice on Your Own

1.

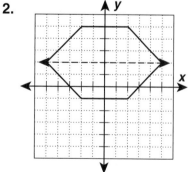

2.

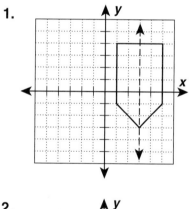

3.

4.

5.

6.

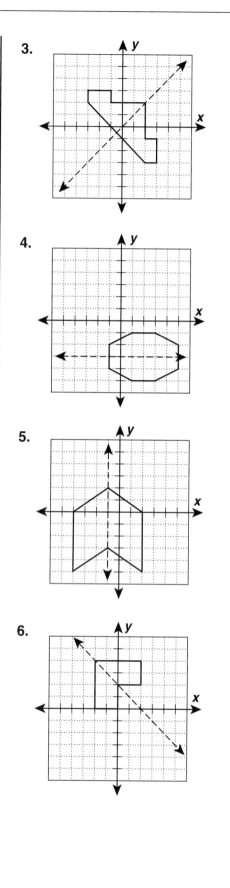

Saxon Algebra 1

Answer Key continued

Check

7.

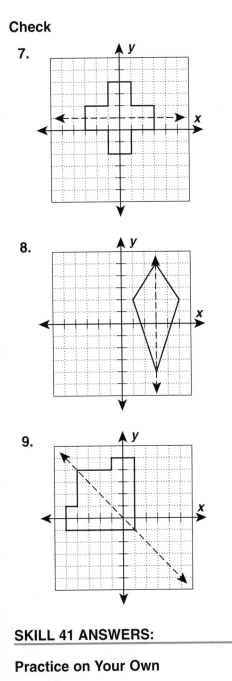

8.

9.

SKILL 41 ANSWERS:

Practice on Your Own

1. 158 ft^2

2. 96 in.^{2}

3. 198 m^2

4. 158 m^2

5. 150 in.^{2}

6. 90 cm^2

Check

7. 390 cm^2

8. 376 ft^2

9. 600 in.^{2}

SKILL 42 ANSWERS:

Practice on Your Own

1. 120 ft^3

2. 64 in.^{3}

3. 108 m^3

4. 63 m^3

5. 125 in.^{3}

6. 54 cm^3

Check

7. 378 cm^3

8. 320 ft^3

9. 1000 in.^{3}

SKILL 43 ANSWERS:

Practice on Your Own

1. 54

2. 207

3. 74

4. 26

5. 28

6. 187

7. 79

8. 1395

9. 11

10. 94

11. 1064

12. 102

Check

13. 36

14. 245

Saxon Algebra 1

Answer Key continued

15. 61

16. 54

17. 150

18. 31

19. 28

20. 1624

SKILL 44 ANSWERS:

Practice on Your Own

1. 7.4

2. 14.03

3. 16.5

4. 0.87

5. 13.63

6. 0.58

7. 109

8. 2.57

Check

9. 10.21

10. 14.5

11. 88.14

12. 0.61

13. 20.93

14. 4.51

15. 0.62

16. 72

SKILL 45 ANSWERS:

Practice on Your Own

1. 0.45

2. 1.26

3. 1.69

4. 1.825

5. 2.248

6. 0.1625

7. 56.2

8. 49.3

Check

9. 0.14

10. 3.95

11. 4.84

12. 2.196

13. 0.2485

14. 9.6

15. 462,200

16. 0.9

SKILL 46 ANSWERS:

Practice on Your Own

1. 1.6

2. 2.03

3. 2.48

4. 0.17

5. 39

6. 7.2

7. 37.5

8. 1.27

Check

9. 2.5

10. 1.66

11. 2.49

12. 0.29

13. 21

14. 5.1

15. 16

16. 0.88

Answer Key continued

SKILL 47 ANSWERS:

Practice on Your Own

1. $\frac{4}{15}$
2. 3
3. $\frac{1}{9}$
4. $1\frac{1}{2}$
5. $\frac{1}{7}$
6. $\frac{1}{11}$
7. $4\frac{1}{2}$
8. 6

Check

9. $\frac{1}{18}$
10. $\frac{2}{3}$
11. $\frac{5}{14}$
12. 9
13. $\frac{1}{12}$
14. $\frac{1}{7}$
15. $1\frac{1}{2}$
16. 15

SKILL 48 ANSWERS:

Practice on Your Own

1. $\frac{3}{5}$
2. $\frac{3}{7}$
3. $\frac{1}{2}$
4. $\frac{1}{9}$
5. $1\frac{1}{3}$
6. $1\frac{5}{8}$
7. $\frac{5}{6}$
8. $1\frac{1}{4}$

Check

9. $\frac{9}{11}$
10. $\frac{2}{3}$
11. $\frac{5}{14}$
12. $\frac{1}{3}$
13. $1\frac{1}{2}$
14. $1\frac{3}{10}$
15. $\frac{3}{8}$
16. $\frac{23}{30}$

SKILL 49 ANSWERS:

Practice on Your Own

1. 18
2. 9
3. 280
4. 30
5. 6
6. 21
7. 33
8. 45
9. 84
10. 2600

Check

11. 20
12. 21
13. 240
14. 360
15. 6
16. 23
17. 81
18. 285

Answer Key continued

SKILL 50 ANSWERS:

Practice on Your Own

1. 75
2. 800
3. 0.02
4. $300
5. $144
6. $2000
7. 3%
8. 4%

Check

9. 200
10. 500
11. 0.015
12. $2400
13. $12,000
14. 5%

SKILL 51 ANSWERS:

Practice on Your Own

1. 5
2. −4
3. 25
4. −17
5. 11
6. −11
7. 19
8. −6
9. −5
10. −17
11. 0
12. 15

Check

13. 6
14. −8
15. −7
16. 10
17. 5
18. −21
19. 0
20. 31

SKILL 52 ANSWERS:

Practice on Your Own

1. −15
2. −4
3. −55
4. −8
5. 63
6. 6
7. −150
8. −15
9. 26
10. 7
11. −32
12. −3

Check

13. −70
14. 6
15. −72
16. −7
17. 64
18. −12
19. 9
20. 12

Saxon Algebra 1

Answer Key continued

SKILL 53 ANSWERS:

Practice on Your Own

1. 5
2. 18
3. $\frac{9}{11}$
4. -9
5. 20
6. 8
7. 13
8. $-\frac{1}{25}$

Check

9. 4
10. 72
11. -7
12. $\frac{2}{5}$
13. 10
14. -12
15. -6
16. $\frac{1}{2}$

SKILL 54 ANSWERS:

Practice on Your Own

1. 15
2. 8
3. 0.4
4. 1.19
5. 10
6. 4
7. 0.75
8. 0.7
9. 6
10. 7

11. 0
12. 12

Check

13. 11
14. 2.3
15. 10
16. 25
17. 13
18. 0
19. 1.1
20. 1

SKILL 55 ANSWERS:

Practice on Your Own

1. 3
2. 4
3. 31
4. 3
5. 6
6. 14
7. 50
8. 9
9. 26
10. 43
11. 0
12. 4

Check

13. 4
14. 0
15. 25
16. 22
17. 2
18. 58

Saxon Algebra 1

Answer Key continued

SKILL 56 ANSWERS:

Practice on Your Own

1. $5x + 30$
2. $5z - 35$
3. $2n - 4$
4. $12 + 4k$
5. $48 - 8y$
6. $6m + 18$
7. $10p + 10$
8. $60 - 3c$
9. $7q - 7$
10. $55 + 11t$
11. $14 + 2b$
12. $36 - 9w$

Check

13. $12c + 24$
14. $15 - 5a$
15. $25 + 25d$
16. $50 - 10j$
17. $4x + 12$
18. $30 + 15y$
19. $3g - 75$
20. $9m - 9$

SKILL 57 ANSWERS:

Practice on Your Own

1. $12x$
2. $4m$
3. $7a^2$
4. $-7t$
5. $-3b$
6. $8d^2$
7. $-x$

8. 0
9. $11h$
10. $-9y - 9$
11. $10 + 10x$
12. $5 - 5u$
13. $13y + 6x$
14. 4

Check

15. $10x$
16. $-3c$
17. $-3a^2$
18. $8.4z$
19. $10m + 11$
20. $8q - 5r$

SKILL 58 ANSWERS:

Practice on Your Own

1. $5 + n$
2. a number decreased by 15; 15 less than a number; the difference between a number and 15; etc.
3. $C = 3(9.95) + 2(14.98)$
4. $P = 7 + 10 + s$
5. $V = 12,000 + 500y$
6. $n = 56 - 3w$

Check

7. $n - 6$
8. $C = 6(6.99) + 2(22.98)$
9. $A = 400 + 150m$

SKILL 59 ANSWERS:

Practice on Your Own

1. $10x^2$
2. $-21a^4$
3. $-16mn$

Saxon Algebra 1

Answer Key continued

4. $45p^3q$

5. $25b^5c^4$

6. $6x^2y^2$

7. $16z^5$

8. $8d^3e^2$

9. $-18t^2$

10. w^8

11. $22r^7$

12. $50x^2y^2$

Check

13. $30f^2$

14. $-27x^2y$

15. $60h^4$

16. $49a^2b^2$

17. $4p^4q^2$

18. $-21u^3v$

19. g^8

20. $-16y^2z^2$

SKILL 60 ANSWERS:

Practice on Your Own

1. 36

2. 28

3. -3

4. -27

5. 9

6. -2

7. -10

8. 8

9. -6

Check

10. 15

11. 2

12. 0

13. -6

14. -4

15. 2

SKILL 61 ANSWERS:

Practice on Your Own

1. $10m^4n^2$

2. $4x^2y$

3. $-20a^4b$

4. $\dfrac{5}{2t^3}$

5. $-\dfrac{f^2}{3}$

6. $-3p^3q^2r^3$

7. u^4v

8. $\dfrac{4c^2}{d^5}$

9. $144h^2k^2$

10. -1

11. $10xy^3z^2$

12. $-\dfrac{wz}{9}$

Check

13. $35s^4t$

14. $-\dfrac{x}{5y}$

15. $-8b^4c^4$

16. $5pq^3$

17. $-\dfrac{5mn}{3}$

18. $36u^3w^4$

19. $-10x^8y^2$

20. $\dfrac{7}{f}$

Saxon Algebra 1

Answer Key continued

SKILL 62 ANSWERS:

Practice on Your Own

1. $16d + 40$

2. $m^2 - m$

3. $9b^2 + 9b$

4. $48 - 60q$

5. $5p^2 + 30p$

6. $50w - 30w^2$

7. $-10r - 2r^4$

8. $n^4 + n^2$

9. $9g^2 + 3g$

10. $2e^4 - 2e^3$

11. $2h^3 - 10h^2 + 30h$

12. $x^4y + x^2y^6$

Check

13. $60x - 30$

14. $4y^2 - 36y$

15. $55 - 22k$

16. $49t \quad 49t^2$

17. $w^3 - w^4$

18. $3g^3 - 15g^2$

19. $p^3 - 2p^2 + 5p$

20. $3u^3v^3 + u^2v^4$

SKILL 63 ANSWERS:

Practice on Your Own

1. $12m - 2n$

2. $-2x + 8y$

3. $15p + q$

4. $20d + 2e$

5. $24t^2 - 9t$

6. $r^2s + 6rs + 5rs^2$

7. $15f^2 - 5f + 5$

8. $3p^3 + 2p^2 + 8p$

9. $13g^2 - 26g^3$

10. $5j^3k + 5jk^2 + 4j^2$

Check

11. $-5x + 5y$

12. $2a + 15b$

13. $26g - 2h$

14. $8u^3 - 7u^2 - 5u$

15. $27p^2 - 10p - 13$

16. $12c - 4c^2$

SKILL 64 ANSWERS:

Practice on Your Own

1. $n^2 + 9n + 18$

2. $c^2 + 7c - 60$

3. $10q^2 + 43q + 12$

4. $3k^2 + 20k - 7$

5. $u^2 - 1$

6. $r^2 + 12r + 36$

7. $25a^2 - 16$

8. $24g^2 + 44g + 12$

9. $20z^2 + 22z - 16$

10. $8p^2 - 22p + 9$

Check

11. $x^2 + 11x + 28$

12. $2w^2 - 12w - 54$

13. $p^2 + 10p + 25$

14. $4t^2 - 49$

15. $7y^2 - 10y + 3$

16. $27m^2 + 42m + 8$

Saxon Algebra 1

Answer Key continued

SKILL 65 ANSWERS:

Practice on Your Own

1. $49x^2 + 14x + 1$

2. $w^2 - 36$

3. $9p^2 - 30p + 25$

4. $m^2 + 18m + 81$

5. $25y^2 - 1$

6. $d^2 - 4d + 4$

7. $16b^2 - 49$

8. $100 - 9h^2$

9. $a^2 - 64$

10. $4z^2 - 1$

Check

11. $36x^2 + 48x + 16$

12. $4t^2 - 4t + 1$

13. $u^2 - 9$

14. $9h^2 - 25$

15. $y^2 + 14y + 49$

16. $q^2 - 36$

SKILL 66 ANSWERS:

Practice on Your Own

1. $x(x + 6)$

2. $3(x - 4)$

3. $5x(3x + 1)$

4. $7(x^2 - 2)$

5. $x(6x + 5)$

6. $4(x^2 - 2)$

7. $3x(4x - 3)$

8. $3x(x^2 - 1)$

9. $x^2(5x + 1)$

10. $3x^2(x - 2)$

11. $x^3(x + 1)$

12. $2x^2(x^2 - 1)$

Check

13. $x(x - 5)$

14. $5(4x + 1)$

15. $8x(x - 2)$

16. $3(4x^2 + 3)$

17. $x^2(10x - 1)$

18. $9x(3x^2 + 2)$

19. $x^2(x + 1)$

20. $2x^2(x^2 - 3)$

SKILL 67 ANSWERS:

Practice on Your Own

1. $(x + 4)(x + 1)$

2. $(x + 5)(x - 2)$

3. $(x - 1)(x - 3)$

4. $(x + 4)(x - 5)$

5. $(x + 6)(x - 4)$

6. $(x + 3)(x + 7)$

7. $(x - 2)(x - 8)$

8. $(x + 1)(x - 9)$

9. $(x - 3)(x - 15)$

Check

10. $(x + 2)(x + 5)$

11. $(x - 4)(x - 7)$

12. $(x + 10)(x - 3)$

13. $(x - 1)(x - 2)$

14. $(x + 1)(x + 48)$

15. $(x + 5)(x - 12)$

Saxon Algebra 1

Answer Key continued

SKILL 68 ANSWERS:

Practice on Your Own

1. $m = 14$
2. $h = -18$
3. $x = 9$
4. $b = 10$
5. $y = -3$
6. $k = -12$
7. $p = 5$
8. $t = 21$
9. $x = -4$
10. $h = 11$
11. $x = 2$
12. $r = -7$

Check

13. $x = 5$
14. $c = 12$
15. $d = -4$
16. $s = -30$
17. $z = -15$
18. $w = 48$
19. $b = -12$
20. $x = 1$

SKILL 69 ANSWERS:

Practice on Your Own

1. $x = 4$
2. $m = 6$
3. $t = 15$
4. $p = -8$
5. $y = \dfrac{8}{9}$
6. $c = 6$
7. $x = -15$

8. $n = 0$
9. $h = -\dfrac{9}{7}$

Check

10. $x = 2$
11. $d = -20$
12. $g = \dfrac{13}{3}$
13. $t = 6$
14. $x = -\dfrac{7}{3}$
15. $z = 3$

SKILL 70 ANSWERS:

Practice on Your Own

1. $y = 3$
2. $m = -\dfrac{5}{4}$
3. $x = -1$
4. $t = 2$
5. $x = -\dfrac{1}{2}$
6. $b = 0$
7. $k = \dfrac{1}{4}$
8. $x = 3$
9. $a = -1$

Check

10. $x = 8$
11. $t = \dfrac{5}{3}$
12. $y = -6$
13. $p = 2$
14. $b = -4$
15. $x = -\dfrac{1}{2}$

SKILL 71 ANSWERS:

Practice on Your Own

1. $x = 18$
2. $x = -42$
3. $y = 1$

Saxon Algebra 1

Answer Key continued

4. $x = -1$

5. $y = -\dfrac{1}{4}$

6. $x = \dfrac{8}{9}$

7. $y = -\dfrac{4}{7}$

8. $x = \dfrac{3}{25}$

9. $y = \dfrac{1}{2}$

Check

10. $x = 4$

11. $y = \dfrac{4}{3}$

12. $x = \dfrac{2}{5}$

13. $y = -\dfrac{5}{11}$

14. $x = \dfrac{10}{7}$

15. $x = -\dfrac{1}{8}$

SKILL 72 ANSWERS:

Practice on Your Own

1. $y = 15 - 3x$

2. $y = 3x + 5$

3. $t = \dfrac{I}{pr}$

4. $y = 4 - x$

5. $h = \dfrac{V}{\pi r^2}$

6. $y = 2 + 3x$

7. $h = \dfrac{2A}{b}$

8. $y = 5 - 2x$

9. $x = 3y - 7$

Check

10. $y = 11 + 6x$

11. $h = \dfrac{V}{\ell w}$

12. $x = 6 - y$

13. $y = 11 - 4x$

14. $y = 3x - 12$

15. $y = -4x + 3$

SKILL 73 ANSWERS:

Practice on Your Own

1. $M = (\frac{7}{2}, 5); \, d = 5$

2. $M = (2, \frac{1}{2}); \, d = \sqrt{13}$

3. $M = (-\frac{5}{2}, \frac{9}{2}); \, d = 5\sqrt{2}$

4. $M = (0, 1); \, d = 4\sqrt{5}$

5. $M = (-3, -\frac{3}{2}); \, d = \sqrt{29}$

6. $M = (-2, -\frac{3}{2}); \, d = 5$

Check

7. $M = (5, 3); \, d = 10$

8. $M = (\frac{5}{2}, \frac{1}{2}); \, d = \sqrt{34}$

9. $M = (-\frac{1}{2}, -\frac{7}{2}); \, d = 3\sqrt{2}$

10. $M = (2, -4); \, d = 2\sqrt{5}$

SKILL 74 ANSWERS:

Practice on Your Own

1. $x \geq 5$

2. $n < 2$

3. $y \leq -6$

4. $b < -1$

5. $y > 6$

6. $t \geq 4$

7. $p > -4$

8. $x < -2$

9. $m \leq -3$

Check

10. $x \leq 3$

11. $n > -7$

12. $d \geq 1$

Answer Key continued

13. $y < 10$

14. $x \geq -4$

15. $m < 8$

SKILL 75 ANSWERS:

Practice on Your Own

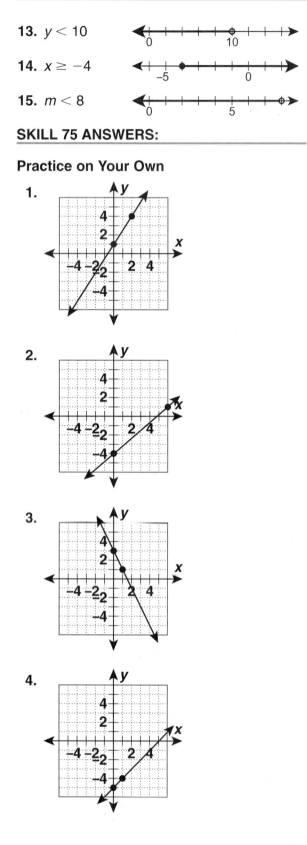

1.

2.

3.

4.

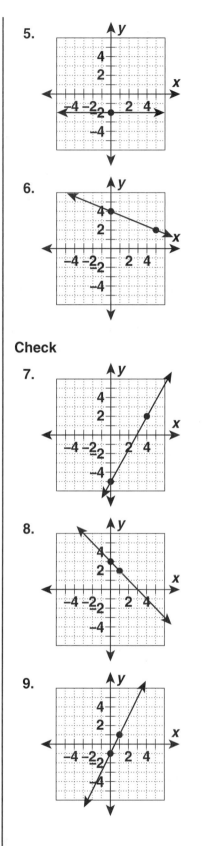

5.

6.

Check

7.

8.

9.

204   **Saxon** Algebra 1

Answer Key continued

SKILL 76 ANSWERS:

Practice on Your Own

1. perpendicular
2. parallel
3. perpendicular
4. neither
5. parallel
6. neither
7. perpendicular
8. perpendicular
9. perpendicular

Check

10. perpendicular
11. parallel
12. parallel
13. parallel
14. neither
15. perpendicular

SKILL 77 ANSWERS:

Practice on Your Own

1. $x = 10$
2. $x = 8$
3. $x = 80$
4. $x = 20$
5. $x = 50$
6. $x = 30$
7. $x = \frac{7}{3}$
8. $x = 10$
9. $x = \frac{8}{9}$
10. $x = \frac{1}{3}$
11. $x = 36$
12. $x = 12$

Check

13. $x = 21$
14. $x = 10$
15. $x = 26$
16. $x = \frac{12}{11}$
17. $x = 8$
18. $x = \frac{15}{2}$
19. $x = \frac{4}{5}$
20. $x = 10$

SKILL 78 ANSWERS:

Practice on Your Own

1.

x	y
−2	−5
−1	−2
0	1
1	4
2	7

2.

x	y
−2	13
−1	9
0	5
1	1
2	−3

3.

x	y
−2	4
−1	1
0	0
1	1
2	4

4.

x	y
−2	1
−1	−2
0	−3
1	−2
2	1

5.

x	y
−2	0.5
−1	1
0	1.5
1	2
2	2.5

6.

x	y
−2	5
−1	4.5
0	4
1	3.5
2	3

7.

x	y
−2	0
−1	1
0	4
1	9
2	16

8.

x	y
−2	16
−1	9
0	4
1	1
2	0

Saxon Algebra 1

Answer Key continued

Check

9.

x	y
−2	−5
−1	−1
0	3
1	7
2	11

10.

x	y
−2	−4
−1	−7
0	−10
1	−13
2	−16

11.

x	y
−2	−1.5
−1	−1
0	−0.5
1	0
2	0.5

12.

x	y
−2	25
−1	16
0	9
1	4
2	1

SKILL 79 ANSWERS:

Practice on Your Own
Numbers 1–12 are plotted by letters.

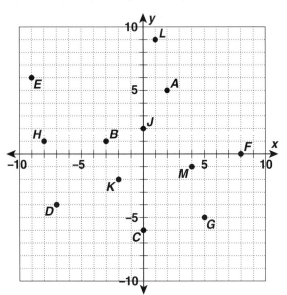

Check
Numbers 13–18 are plotted by letters.

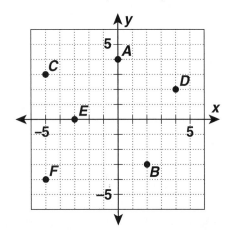

SKILL 80 ANSWERS:

Practice on Your Own

1.

2.

3.

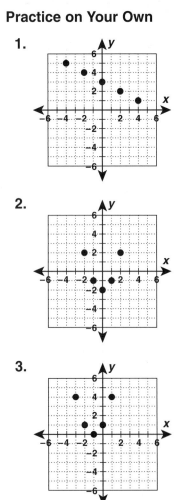

Answer Key continued

4.

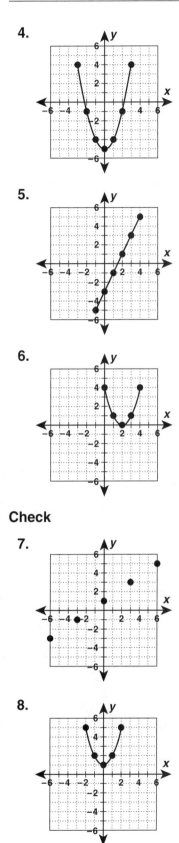

5.

6.

Check

7.

8.

9.

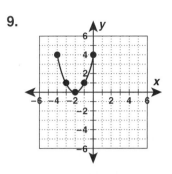

SKILL 81 ANSWERS:

Practice on Your Own

1. $x = 2$ or -2

2. $x = 4$ or -4

3. $x = 4$ or -4

4. $x = 1$ or -1

5. $x = 10$ or -10

6. $x = 3$ or -3

7. $x = 15$ or -15

8. $x = 5$ or -5

9. $x = 6$ or -6

Check

10. $x = 1$ or -1

11. $x = 5$ or -5

12. $x = 6$ or -6

13. $x = 2$ or -2

14. $x = 10$ or -10

15. $x = 20$ or -20

SKILL 82 ANSWERS:

Practice on Your Own

1. $16; (x + 4)^2$

2. $36; (x - 6)^2$

3. $\frac{1}{4}; \left(x + \frac{1}{2}\right)^2$

4. $25; (x - 5)^2$

5. $121; (x - 11)^2$

6. $\frac{9}{4}; \left(x - \frac{3}{2}\right)^2$

Saxon Algebra 1

Answer Key continued

7. $49; (x + 7)^2$

8. $144; (x - 12)^2$

9. $\dfrac{81}{4}; \left(x + \dfrac{9}{2}\right)^2$

Check

10. $9; (x + 3)^2$

11. $64; (x - 8)^2$

12. $\dfrac{25}{4}; \left(x + \dfrac{5}{2}\right)^2$

13. $100; (x - 10)^2$

14. $1; (x + 1)^2$

15. $\dfrac{49}{4}; \left(x - \dfrac{7}{2}\right)^2$

SKILL 83 ANSWERS:

Practice on Your Own

1. 28%

2. 30%

3. 23%

4. 19%

5. 58%

6. 81%

Check

7. 10%

8. 5%

9. 42%

SKILL 84 ANSWERS:

Practice on Your Own

1. mean = 8; median = 7; mode = 7

2. mean = $\dfrac{22}{7} \approx 3.1$; median = 3; mode = 4

3. mean = $\dfrac{39}{6} = 6.5$; median = 6.5; mode = none

4. mean = 5.25; median = 5.5; mode = 4 and 6

5. mean = 5; median = 4; mode = none

6. mean = 20; median = 20; mode = none

7. mean = 7; median = 6; mode = 5

8. mean = 8; median = 8; mode = 7 and 9

9. mean = 27; median = 25; mode = none

Check

10. mean = 8; median = 7; mode = 7

11. mean = 15; median = 15; mode = 15

12. mean = $\dfrac{51}{6} = 8.5$; median = 8.5; mode = 8 and 9

13. mean = 6; median = 5.5; mode = none

14. mean = $\dfrac{41}{7} \approx 5.9$; median = 5; mode = 5

15. mean = 20; median = 18; mode = none

SKILL 85 ANSWERS:

Practice on Your Own

1. 168

2. 432

3. 84%

4. 504

Check

5. 70

6. 25

7. 40%

8. 100

SKILL 86 ANSWERS:

Practice on Your Own

1. 7

2. 1

3. 19

4. 10

Saxon Algebra 1

Answer Key continued

5. 2

6. 12

Check

  7. 16

  8. 8

  9. 11

10. 5

SKILL 87 ANSWERS:

Practice on Your Own

  1. Figure *ABCD* has 4 sides.

  2. Angle *ABC* and angle *CBD* share a common vertex.

  3. $\angle A$ and $\angle B$ are supplementary.

  4. The third side of $\triangle DEF$ has length 8 or 13.

  5. Point *P* lies in the third quadrant.

Check

  6. The other two angles of triangle *MNP* have measures of 60 degrees.

  7. The measure of $\angle HJK$ is greater than 90 degrees.

  8. Lines *p* and *q* are perpendicular.

SKILL 88 ANSWERS:

Practice on Your Own

  1. Hypothesis: a triangle is a right triangle; Conclusion: the sum of its acute angles is 90 degrees.

  2. Hypothesis: two lines are parallel to a third line; Conclusion: the lines are parallel to each other

  3. True
    Converse: If the sum of the measures of a polygon's angles is 180 degrees, then the polygon is a triangle.
    True

  4. True
    Converse: If two angles are congruent, then they are right angles.
    False

Check

  5. Hypothesis: two planes intersect; Conclusion: they intersect in a line.

  6. True
    Converse: If two angles are congruent, then they are vertical.
    False

  7. True
    Converse: If a parallelogram is a rhombus, then the diagonals of the parallelogram are perpendicular.
    True

SKILL 89 ANSWERS:

Practice on Your Own

  1. any real number other than 0, 1, or 2 are all counterexamples

  2. any negative number

  3. $n = 3$

  4. any negative number or 0

  5. $n = -1$

  6. any fraction such that $-1 < n < 1$,
    e.g. $\frac{1}{2}, \frac{1}{3}, \frac{1}{4}, \cdots \frac{2}{3}, \frac{3}{4}, \frac{5}{6}, \cdots$

Check

  7. $n = 1$

  8. any negative number or any positive fraction such that $0 < n < 1$

  9. any negative number or 0

10. $n = 0$

Saxon Algebra 1

Answer Key continued

SKILL 90 ANSWERS:

Practice on Your Own

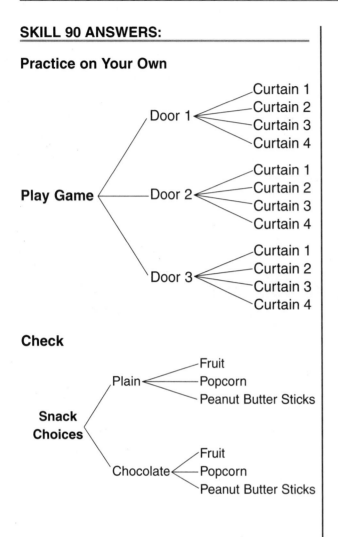

Check

© Saxon. All rights reserved.

Saxon Algebra 1